The Least of These

Fair Taxes and the Moral Duty
of Christians

The Least of These

Fair Taxes and the Moral Duty of Christians

Susan Pace Hamill

SWEET WATER PRESS

Printed in the United States of America
Published by Sweetwater Press by arrangement with Cliff Road Books

ISBN 1-58173-203-1

Library of Congress Cataloging-in-Publication Data
  available

10 9   8   7   6   5   4   3   2   1

Table of Contents

Dedicated in loving memory
of my mother,
Nancy Lee Hiemstra Hamill
(1938-1980),
defender of
"the least of these."

S.P.H.

A portion of the proceeds from the sale
of this book will be donated to the
Alabama Poverty Project,
whose mission is to reduce and eventually
eliminate poverty in Alabama.

ABOUT THIS BOOK

This book started as an article published in the *Alabama Law Review*, titled "An Argument for Tax Reform Based on Judeo-Christian Ethics." Susan Pace Hamill, a law professor at the University of Alabama, wrote it in 2002 as the thesis for completion of her masters degree in theological studies at Samford University's Beeson Divinity School in Birmingham, Alabama.

In the article, Professor Hamill shows how the teachings of the Bible command Christians to care for "the least of these" – those who are least fortunate among us – and how the oppression of the poor for the benefit of the rich is wrong. The article then applies these biblical teachings to Alabama's long outdated, special-interest dominated tax structure which severely oppresses the poorest Alabamians, and calls for Christian support of tax reform.

The law review article set off a firestorm of response, first in Alabama, then in surrounding states, then across the nation. Churches, civic groups, and concerned citizens all over the United States have taken up the hue and cry on behalf of their own states' taxation issues, while others have remained silent or maliciously lashed out.

This book gives you an opportunity to decide for yourself. It contains an introduction by Professor Hamill that summarizes and explains how and why she reached her conclusions, and tells what you should know about taxation in general. The book also contains, in its entirety, the original law review article that started what now appears to be a fast-growing grassroots tax revolution. Unless you are an academician, you'll want to read just the text of the law review article, skipping the lengthy footnotes. In this book you'll also find some of the "op-ed" newspaper columns Professor Hamill wrote that further explore the issues, along with reprints of selected newspaper editorial responses to her work.

Finally, there's a section at the end that will tell you what you can do to help make ethically based tax reform a reality, wherever you live.

"I tell you the truth, whatever you did not do for one of the least of these, you did not do for me."

Matthew 25:45

speech, while fully recognizing the supremacy of the secular state in all matters related to governmental power.[7]

Part I of this Article examines the internal structures and the effectiveness towards collecting revenue behind Alabama's income, sales, and property taxes and compares Alabama to its closest Southeastern neighbors. The evidence shows that Alabama's income and sales taxes are grossly regressive, requiring Alabamians at the lowest income levels to pay a greater percentage of their earnings in taxes than Alabamians at higher income levels. The Alabama income tax, which has been nationally identified as the least fair of the fifty states, starts imposing tax on income tax levels well under the poverty line while at the same time greatly favoring higher income taxpayers by allowing full use of exemptions regardless of income level and a full deduction for federal income taxes paid. The sales tax, imposed at a rate of four percent at the state level, appears deceptively reasonable. A closer look, however, reveals that most of the counties and cities within the state significantly increase this percentage, requiring Alabamians to pay sales taxes among the highest in the nation, often exceeding eight percent. The combination of unreasonably high rates and the lack of exemptions for basic necessities such as food, clothing, and certain medicines causes Alabama's sales taxes to be among the most burdensome in the nation to low-income citizens.

By requiring only a minimum amount of property tax, in contrast—the lowest property tax level of the fifty states—Alabama's property taxes fail to raise adequate revenues and directly favor the wealthiest Alabamians, who tend to own the greatest concentration of property with significant fair market value. Depending on the classification of the particular property, the property tax rates apply to a mere fraction, which for some property equals as little as ten percent, of the property's fair market value. Moreover, the combination of this low percent assessment ratio and a special formula which values certain property according to its current use

---

7. The First Amendment to the United States Constitution provides that "Congress shall make no law respecting an establishment of religion, or prohibiting the free exercise thereof; or abridging the freedom of speech . . . ." U.S. CONST. amend. I. The Establishment Clause forbids the law from imposing religious ideas or conduct on people against their will. The main three categories of actions that would violate the Establishment Clause include the government forcing a person to go to or remain away from religious services, forcing a person to profess a belief or disbelief in any religion, preferring one religion over another, or preferring religion to non-religion because preferential treatment indirectly affects persons in the non-favored group. *See* Everson v. Bd. of Educ., 330 U.S. 1 (1947). Although different views exist concerning whether individual citizens should rely on religious views when adopting political positions, *see* Michael J. Perry, *Why Political Reliance on Religiously Grounded Morality is not Illegitimate in a Liberal Democracy*, 36 WAKE FOREST L. REV. 217 (2001) (arguing that political positions supported by religious reasons are legitimate); Kent Greenawalt, *Religion and American Political Judgments*, 36 WAKE FOREST L. REV. 401 (2001) (arguing that legislators should not publicly use religious justifications as a matter of prudent judgment, even though they have a constitutional right to do so), the Free Exercise and Freedom of Speech clauses guarantee all citizens the right to express and rely on religious views when adopting political positions.

because the overwhelming majority of Alabama's citizens[4] and the elected members of Alabama's Senate and House of Representatives practice Christianity,[5] and many denominations and other religious organizations have urged tax reform to address hardship suffered by low-income Alabamians,[6] the principles of Judeo-Christian ethics offer compelling moral reasons for Alabamians practicing Christianity or Judaism to support tax reform. Moreover, these Judeo-Christian based ethical arguments do not violate the Establishment Clause of the United States Constitution because this Article urges Alabama's citizens to individually support tax reform, using their constitutional rights to free exercise of religion and freedom of

---

4.   *See* ADHERENTS—RELIGION BY LOCATION, *at* http://www.adherents.com/adhloc/Wh_6.html (last visited Sept. 27, 2002) (citing B. KOSMIN & S. LACHMAN, ONE NATION UNDER GOD: RELIGION IN CONTEMPORARY AMERICAN SOCIETY 88-93 (1993)) (indicating that approximately 93% of Alabamians practice Christianity). Only a very small number of Alabama's citizens practice Judaism. *See id.* (citing U.S. DEP'T OF COMMERCE, STATISTICAL ABSTRACT OF THE UNITED STATES 70 (117th ed. 1997)) (citing AMERICAN JEWISH COMMITTEE, AMERICAN JEWISH YEAR BOOK (1995), which shows that less than 1%, 0.20% precisely, of Alabamians practice Judaism). Because the principles of Judeo-Christian ethics, forbidding the oppression of poor people and requiring that the community provide them with a minimum opportunity to meet their basic needs and improve their circumstances, is strongly rooted in the Old Testament, the arguments in this Article equally apply to people of both the Christian and the Jewish faiths. *See, e.g.*, MICHAEL NOVAK, BUSINESS AS A CALLING 146 (1996).

5.   *See infra* app. A, Religious Affiliations of Members of Alabama's Senate and House of Representatives (including Governor and Lieutenant Governor), and underlying compilation of data on file with author. [hereinafter Comp. & app. A] (showing that out of 142 individuals with direct access to the legislative process (the Governor, the Alabama Senate, the Lieutenant Governor, and the Alabama House of Representatives), 136, which is 96% of all elected public officials, clearly identify themselves as practicing Christianity in a variety of denominations). The research team created the compilation by consulting the Web site for each individual or by directly confirming their religious affiliation by letter from the particular person's office. The greatest percentage, sixty-six individuals making up 46% of all elected public officials, belong to a Baptist congregation. The second greatest percentage, thirty-four individuals making up 24% of all elected officials, belong to a Methodist (including AME and CME) congregation. A total of ten elected public officials, 7% of all elected public officials, belong to Presbyterian and Church of Christ congregations, respectively. A total of five individuals, 4% of all elected public officials, are members of the Catholic Church. A total of three individuals, 2% of all elected public officials, are members of the Episcopal Church. A total of eight individuals, 6% of all elected public officials, are members of other Protestant denominations. Only six elected public officials, 4% of all elected public officials, have religious affiliations that are unknown.

6.   Many churches throughout Alabama have commented on the need for tax reform in the state. At the 2000 Annual Alabama Baptist State Convention, the convention stated that because Alabama's tax structure places a disproportionate burden on low-income citizens they called on the governor and state legislature to pass tax reform that, "will bring relief and justice to the poor who are our neighbors." *See* 2000 Annual Alabama Baptist State Convention, Proceedings, 178th Annual session, 98-99. Also, the Methodist Church in Alabama found that the income tax, which taxes very low incomes, causes suffering, as does a sales tax that is imposed on food and medication. As a result of this finding, they resolved to work through local churches to provide relief to low-income Alabamians without depriving public schools of much needed resources. *See* United Methodist Church North Alabama Conference, 200, at 316. The Episcopal Church also resolved at their annual state meeting to encourage the governor and legislature to adopt tax reform measures that would help poor Alabamians. #4 Resolution for Tax Reform in the State of Alabama, Resolutions Adopted by the 170th Convention of the Diocese of Alabama, *at* http://www.diocesanconvention.org/resolutions.htm#4 (last visited Sept. 27, 2002). Also, the Jewish Synagogue has spoken out on the issue of taxes and the poor, with the Central Conference of American Rabbis resolving to oppose tax policy that inequitably benefits the wealthy in society. Cent. Conference of Am. Rabbis, *Resolution on Tax Policy*, *at* http://www.ccarnet.org/cgi-bin/resodisp.pl?file=tax&year=2001 (last visited Sept. 27, 2002).

and have continued to be invoked in political debates.[3] Moreover, when distinguishing ethical from unethical tax structures, Judeo-Christian ethics use broad principles similar to traditional tax policy theory, both indicating that tax burdens should be apportioned according to some measure of the taxpayer's ability to pay and should raise adequate revenues to meet at least the minimum needs of the community subject to the tax. In addition,

---

religiously inspired message of social justice—a message deeply influenced by the Social Gospel Movement, particularly as espoused by Walter Rauschenbusch and the religious philosophy of Reinhold Niebuhr. *See* STROUT, *supra*, at 317-19. At the same time, Protestant and Catholic clergy and Jewish rabbis played a crucial role in the lobbying effort that led to the passage of The Civil Rights Act of 1964. *See* REICHLEY, *supra*, at 246-50; Allen D. Hertzke, *An Assessment of the Mainline Churches Since 1945*, *in* THE ROLE OF RELIGION IN THE MAKING OF PUBLIC POLICY 43, 49-52 (James E. Wood, Jr. & Derek Davis eds., 1991).

3.   One very controversial organization, known as the Christian Coalition, which uses theological arguments to urge Christian voters to support political candidates with conservative positions on a variety of issues, has been criticized as attempting to impose the values of conservative evangelicals on the rest of American society. *See* JUSTIN WATSON, THE CHRISTIAN COALITION: DREAMS OF RESTORATION, DEMANDS FOR RECOGNITION 2 (1997). Those in the organization, however, argue that they are merely demanding recognition to exercise their constitutional rights to engage in political action based on their evangelical beliefs. *See id.* at 2-3. This Article expresses no opinion on whether the Christian Coalition's political positions are properly viewed as biblically mandated. However, one of the goals set forth by the Christian Coalition to "defend the rights of the poor and marginalized" because "[f]ew biblical mandates are as clear as our requirement to care for those in need," RALPH REED, ACTIVE FAITH 274 (1996), is relevant to this Article's argument that Alabama's tax structure violates the moral principles of Judeo-Christian ethics. The Christian Coalition's political positions and actions regarding tax policy urge an overhaul of America's tax system through the implementation of a flat tax. *See id.* at 127 (indicating founder Pat Robertson advocated a flat tax in his unsuccessful campaign for President). The Christian Coalition has also advocated "[e]asing the tax burden on families." Christian   Coalition   of   Am.,   Mission   Statement   of   Christian   Coalition, http://www.cc.org/aboutcca/mission.html (last visited Sept. 27, 2002). At least one state affiliate has proposed, inter alia, "disposing of the current system completely and replacing it with either a uniform tax rate (flat tax), or a sales tax," as a method of easing the tax burden. Texas Christian Coalition, *at* http://www.texascc.org/issues.htm (last visited Sept. 27, 2002). This proposal is arguably inconsistent with their goals and the clear biblical mandates concerning poor and marginalized people. Although some of the Christian Coalition's individual ideas for improving the tax system would modestly benefit lower and middle income families, see CHRISTIAN COALITION, CONTRACT WITH THE AMERICAN FAMILY: A BOLD PLAN BY THE CHRISTIAN COALITION TO STRENGTHEN THE FAMILY AND RESTORE COMMON SENSE VALUES 59-60 (1995) (suggesting additional child tax credits and other allowances extending retirement benefits to homemakers), their major idea which supports "the concept of a flatter tax structure" even with "a generous exemption for children," *id.* at 60, cannot be characterized as pro-family when you consider the negative effect flat tax proposals would have on many families. The Christian Coalition's proposals to replace progressive tax structures with flat or sales tax structures would have the effect of benefiting wealthy families at the expense of middle and low-income families. *See* notes 156-158 and accompanying text (showing that unless structured carefully, proposals to replace progressive tax structures with flat or sales tax structures will disproportionately burden low-income taxpayers, and even if structured carefully, will always favor upper income taxpayers, allowing the most substantial tax cuts to be enjoyed by the highest income taxpayers, while always increasing the tax burden of middle income taxpayers). Because flat and sales tax proposals benefit those families enjoying the best economic circumstances at the expense of all other families within the vast range of the middle class and even those at the lower end of the economic spectrum, such proposals are not consistent with helping poor and marginalized people, therefore, they cannot be represented as required or even affirmatively supported by the ethical principles of the Bible. *See infra* notes 216-235 and accompanying text (illustrating that ethical principles from the teachings of Jesus impose strong moral obligations, especially on those members of society enjoying high levels of material wealth, to value God more than material possessions, which must take the form of helping poor and marginalized people).

INTRODUCTION

This Article applies the moral principles of Judeo-Christian ethics as a basis for urging the citizens of Alabama to insist that Alabama's elected political leaders reform Alabama's state tax structure, a critically important step towards ensuring that Alabama's children, especially children from low-income families, enjoy an opportunity to build a positive future.[1] Although using these principles as a reason to support tax reform may seem unusual, principles of Judeo-Christian ethics offer moral arguments that complement and often strengthen secularly based ethical arguments illustrating the need for social reform. Throughout American history, the moral principles of Judeo-Christian ethics have been used as one of many effective tools to evaluate and reform a wide variety of social structures,[2]

---

1. The need for tax reform in Alabama is not a new idea. *See* Report of the Alabama Commission on Tax and Fiscal Policy Reform (Jan. 1991), *reprinted in* Daniel C. Hardman, *Tax Reformers Must Stress Fairness, Simplicity, Communication*, 43 ALA. L. REV. 727 app. (1992) (providing an extensive report on possible tax reform options after establishment of the commission in 1990); James D. Bryce, *Tax Reform Issues in Alabama*, 43 ALA. L. REV. 541 (1992) (containing extensive discussion of this commission's report, *supra*); Laura D. Chaney, *Alabama's Constitution—A Royal Pain in the Tax: The State's Constitutionally Defective Tax System*, 32 CUMB. L. REV. 233 (2001) (arguing extensively for tax reform). *See also How Alabama's Taxes Compare*, THE PARCA REPORT (Pub. Affairs Research Council of Ala.), Spring 2001, at 1, *available at* http://parca.samford.edu/How%20Alabama's%20Taxes%20Compare%20-%2097.htm [hereinafter PARCA REPORT] (concluding that Alabama's tax system is inequitable for low-income taxpayers, that it does not provide efficient distribution of tax dollars, and that it does not produce adequate revenue to provide sufficient funding for important services); MICHAEL A. CIAMARRA, ALABAMA POLICY INSTITUTE, LEGISLATIVE AGENDA 2002 21-35 (2002) [hereinafter ALABAMA POLICY INSTITUTE] (indicating a need for tax reform in order to mitigate the inequities experienced by low-income Alabamians due to the income and sales tax structures, but arguing that it is unclear whether the state's revenues are insufficient due to inefficient and ineffective spending and earmarking of funds). Also, because the issues of tax reform and constitutional reform cannot be separated, the moral principles of Judeo-Christian ethics urge each Alabamian to support constitutional reform. *See generally* Susan Pace Hamill, *Constitutional Reform in Alabama: A Necessary Step Towards Achieving a Fair and Efficient Tax Structure*, 33 CUMB. L. REV. (forthcoming 2003).

2. Examples of this phenomenon in American history include the push for the abolition of slavery, the development of the Social Gospel Movement around the turn of the last century, and the struggle for civil rights in the 1960s. Abolitionism was driven almost entirely by religious moral thought, specifically Christian evangelicalism associated with the so-called "Second Great Awakening," and was implemented through religious societies, Northern churches, and the actions of religiously motivated individuals like William Lloyd Garrison, Harriet Beecher Stowe, and John Brown. *See* SYDNEY E. AHLSTROM, A RELIGIOUS HISTORY OF THE AMERICAN PEOPLE 387, 648-69 (1972); A. JAMES REICHLEY, RELIGION IN AMERICAN PUBLIC LIFE 189-93 (1985); *see also* CUSHING STROUT, THE NEW HEAVENS AND NEW EARTH: POLITICAL RELIGION IN AMERICA 140-204 (1974) (analyzing in detail the historical and philosophical contributions of American Christianity to the Abolitionist struggle). Beginning in the late nineteenth century, proponents of the Social Gospel Movement, a theological focus on social reform in accordance with Judeo-Christian ideals, played major roles in the development of Populism under William Jennings Bryan and in the growth of the early workers' rights movement. This social project culminated in the passage of national child labor legislation under President Woodrow Wilson, who was himself a member of the Federal Council of Churches in America—an organization dedicated to the advancement of the Social Gospel Movement. *See id.* at 224-45; REICHLEY, *supra*, at 206-15. Finally, and most strikingly, during the Civil Rights Movement of the 1960s, people of all races and faiths marched in support of the Reverend Martin Luther King, Jr.'s

ALABAMA LAW REVIEW

Volume 54	Fall 2002	Number 1

AN ARGUMENT FOR TAX REFORM BASED ON JUDEO-CHRISTIAN ETHICS

*Susan Pace Hamill**

"I tell you the truth, whatever you did not do for one of the least of these, you did not do for me."

Matthew 25:45[**]

With hope that soon Alabama's leaders will find the courage to reform Alabama's tax structure, the author dedicates this Article to Alabama's children, who today are "the least of these," the most vulnerable and powerless segment of Alabama's population, but who tomorrow hold the keys to Alabama's future.—SPH

 * Professor of Law, The University of Alabama School of Law. Professor Hamill gratefully acknowledges the support of The University of Alabama Law School Foundation, the Edward Brett Randolph Fund, and the William H. Sadler Fund, and thanks her faculty colleagues Wythe Holt, Norman Stein, Martha Morgan, and Jamie Leonard for their valuable comments, and especially thanks Howard Walthall, Tom Berg, and Dean John Carroll of the Cumberland Law School for their support. This Article partially fulfilled the requirements for the Masters in Theological Studies degree at the Beeson Divinity School, Samford University, which Professor Hamill pursued during a sabbatical leave of absence and received in May 2002. Without the superb teaching and guidance of Dr. Frank Thielman and Dr. Ken Mathews, the biblical studies scholars of the Beeson Divinity School Faculty, this Article would not have been possible. Professor Hamill also thanks: Dean Timothy George, Dr. Wilton Bunch, Dr. Gerald Bray, Dr. Randy Todd, Dr. Fisher Humphreys, Dr. Wallace Williams, and Dr. Paul House of the Beeson Divinity School faculty for providing an excellent learning experience; Connie Happell, a classmate at the Beeson Divinity School, and Phillis Belcher, who tirelessly works on the Greene County Industrial Board to improve Alabama's economic future, for their unlimited friendship and support; and her secretary Donna Warnack. This Article would not have been possible without the excellent support of the staff of the Bounds Law Library at The University of Alabama including: Paul Pruitt, Penny Gibson, Robert Marshall, and especially Creighton Miller, who went well beyond the call of duty. Finally, Professor Hamill especially recognizes the hard work and tireless efforts of the members of her research assistance team: Kevin McGovern, Leslie Patton, Jessica Westbrook, Brian Warwick, April Williams, and Rachel Johnson. These students toiled in the trenches, conducting the empirical research needed to fully discover the truth concerning the effects of Alabama's tax structure, as public servants seeking to help their state find a better way.

 ** *Matthew* 25:45 (New International Version).

CHAPTER 1

An Argument for Tax Reform Based on Judeo-Christian Ethics

Reprinted in its entirety from *Alabama Law Review*,
Volume 54, Number 1, Fall 2002

that many approach the degree of unfairness found in Alabama. So I urge readers who live in states outside of Alabama to think about the state and local taxes where you live as you read the rest of this book. Does your state impose unfair taxes on those least able to pay? Does your state raise adequate revenues to meet community needs, including adequate funding for all public schools, even those in the poorest areas? Do the children from poor and lower middle class families in your state have a reasonable opportunity to better their situation by achieving an adequate education?

If your state broadly resembles Alabama, even if the degree of unfairness in your state is not nearly as bad, Alabama's story speaks directly to you.

Susan Pace Hamill
Tuscaloosa, Alabama
April 2003

than 15,000 copies of this pamphlet have been printed and distributed and the demand for more pamphlets keeps growing.

Another op-ed editorial, also reprinted in Chapter 3 and published in many Alabama newspapers, focuses on the moral responsibilities of political leaders, urging the Alabama Legislature to deal with the state's current fiscal crisis by enacting fair taxes, rather than just adopting another temporary solution that leaves the unfair taxes in place.

How to Read This Book

As you read the first section of the law review article in Chapter 1 do not be intimidated by the footnotes documenting the details of Alabama's unfair taxes. The research reflected in these footnotes (and the 30 pages of empirical tables following the conclusion and prayer) was extremely important in order to document an iron-clad case to the churches, civic and political organizations, and to the citizens that Alabama's taxes are in fact indisputably and grossly unfair. Most readers should ignore the footnotes because the text explains the facts documenting Alabama's unfair taxes in a very clear and user-friendly manner. My father, who has no background in law or tax, understood it very well. So will you.

Once you get through the basic introduction to tax policy principles in the second section of the law review article, you will find the biblically based ethical evaluation of Alabama's unfair taxes even more accessible than the tax section. Readers who are interested in exploring the depth of my biblical analysis will find these footnotes far more user-friendly than they initially appear. Those of you who love the Bible will find this portion of the article, including the footnotes, a pure joy.

As you read the law review article and the supporting materials, I urge you to contemplate how it speaks to you. My article and supporting materials clearly speak to Alabama readers, especially those who are Christians, telling them that they have a moral duty to join the fight for fair taxes in Alabama.

What about readers living in other states? Can Alabama's story as it unfolds in the rest of the book speak to people living elsewhere? Even more essential, can the moral lessons of Alabama's story speak to people living in other states who are not Christians? Does Alabama's story have any relevance in states that do not have a substantial Christian population or that have much more diversity in the religious preferences adopted by the people? The answer to all of these questions is yes.

Remember that tax fairness is an ethical question that ultimately must look to moral values for answers. All legitimate moral values for solving ethical questions, even those not based on a religious faith, forbid oppression of the poor and require that the poor enjoy at least a minimum opportunity to better their situation. Therefore regardless what values serve as the moral compass for you and the people living in your state, these two broad ethical principles central to Alabama's story apply to you and your state.

Governing Magazine, which focuses on state and local issues, reports that most states could significantly improve the fairness of their tax structures, and

My masters thesis, *An Argument For Tax Reform Based on Judeo-Christian Ethics* (reprinted in its entirety in Chapter 1) is a 112-page law review article published in the Fall 2002 edition of the *Alabama Law Review*. In order to thoroughly document both the degree and the complexities of the unfairness embedded in Alabama's tax structure, especially the property tax structure, I harnessed the resources of the law school. Six student research assistants and key members of the law library staff labored with me for over a year, building the case against Alabama's unfair taxes with empirical facts.

The superb education I received at the Beeson Divinity School empowered me to ethically condemn Alabama's unfair taxes as contrary to biblical principles, and impose an absolute moral responsibility on Alabama's Christians to use their powers and resources, which at a minimum includes the right to vote, to remedy the unfair taxes poisoning our state. In my ethical evaluation of Alabama's unfair taxes, I consulted more than one hundred biblical commentaries and other works authored by the finest evangelical scholars, and developed two broad moral principles using accepted techniques of biblical hermeneutics (the interpretation of the Scriptures). These two broad moral principles forbid the oppression of the poor and require that the poor enjoy at least a minimum opportunity to better their situation.

I completed the requirements for a masters in theological studies (MTS) degree from the Beeson Divinity School in May of 2002. Although the officially published version of my thesis was not released until January of 2003, an interested reporter convinced me to let him see the draft of August 8, 2002 that I had submitted to the law review for the publication process. A few days later he published a story in the *Mobile Register* and immediately interest in my thesis exploded. Numerous requests for copies flooded into my office, prompting us to make the August 8 draft available on the internet. Numerous newspaper editorials and stories, a few of which are reprinted in Chapter 2, culminating with a story in *The Wall Street Journal* on February 12, 2003, evaluated my thesis, expressing hope that the biblically based Judeo-Christian moral arguments just might provide enough ammunition to break down the wall that has kept Alabama's taxes unfair for decades.

In addition to heavily emphasizing the arguments imposing moral duties on Alabama's Christians to affirmatively fight for tax fairness, these stories and editorials also highlighted the empirical research of my article. The most shocking empirical data proves that timber acres, which cover 71% of Alabama's real property and earn substantial profits, pay less than 2% of Alabama's meager property taxes, averaging less than one dollar per acre.

Responding to requests made by Alabama's major newspapers, I published a summary of the thesis in the form of an op-ed editorial, which is reprinted in Chapter 3 of this book. In order to reach the people in the churches on a massive scale, the Samford University Press reprinted this summary in a user-friendly pamphlet form with a cover showing Jesus ministering to the poor. To date more

and corporations. I failed to notice certain signs that should have alerted me to Alabama's abysmally unfair taxes and their devastating effects on the poorest Alabamians. These signs included the property taxes on my home being unbelievably low, the sales tax rate (imposed on even groceries) seeming awfully high, and finally the public school my children attended (one of only a handful that gets barely minimum adequate funding) constantly begging for donations to cover school expenses that should have been covered by the budget.

As I approached the end of the promotion and tenure process I started to plan my upcoming sabbatical. Instead of using the time to complete a book on the evolution of business organizations, I yearned to broaden my background with more education that would lead me to ethics. I had a sense that my areas of tax and business law both badly needed ethics. On a deeply personal level, I had a nagging feeling that I was only partially meeting my fiduciary duties to the state. My minister and I cooked up the idea to send me to the Beeson Divinity School at Samford University in Birmingham. After all, surely I would find ethics at a seminary. And on a personal and spiritual level, a seminary would be the best place to figure out how to be a better servant to the state of Alabama. Most certainly, a seminary would offer a far more interesting, challenging, and different experience than staying at home and writing a book about limited liability companies, partnerships, and corporations. Finally, the Beeson Divinity School was an easy commute from home.

Even though my religious background was that of a main-line Protestant, I became immersed in the rich evangelical tradition of the Beeson Divinity School. My education proceeded at lightning speed, covering Old and New Testament studies (including study of the New Testament in the Greek), theology, church history, and spirituality. For the first time in many years I was not surrounded by lawyers, law professors, and law students; and for the first time in seven years I was able to see the unfairness of Alabama's taxes.

A small newspaper article informing me that Alabama's income taxes reach deep into poverty prompted me to look further. A cursory investigation revealed ridiculously low property taxes, oppressively high sales taxes, and outrageously low funding for most of Alabama's public schools. As a tax professional I was shocked. I did not think this much unfairness existed anywhere in the United States. Because of my education at the Beeson Divinity School and the fact that most Alabamians practice Christianity, I immediately focused on the gap between Alabama's unfair taxes and the moral values most of us have adopted.

The professors I consulted at the Beeson Divinity School said that, based on biblical ethics, I had an iron-clad case against Alabama's unfair taxes. They also told me that I should pursue this topic because I was probably the only person in Alabama with both extensive tax background and a seminary education. I promptly changed my masters thesis from the corporate theory topic I had planned, and committed my research to helping stamp out the injustice caused by Alabama's unfair taxes.

Alabama's shamefully unfair taxes date back to 1901. In that year a group of wealthy and powerful planters designed Alabama's constitution to keep taxes low, inadequate, and regressive. Low taxes require very little from those most able to pay, while inadequate taxes fail to raise the minimum amount of revenues needed to support the community. Regressive taxes impose a greater proportional tax burden on those with a lesser ability to pay.

For many readers, the concept of regressive taxation needs further explanation. A simple example helps. Compare a family earning $10,000 with a $500 tax bill to a family earning $100,000 with a $1,000 tax bill. These taxes are regressive because the family with less must give up 5% of their earnings to pay taxes (5% of $10,000 equals $500), while the family with more only has to give up 1% of their earnings to pay taxes (1% of $100,000 equals $1,000). At first glance these taxes may appear fair because the family with more pays more taxes when measured in actual dollars. However, because of the larger proportional burden (5% verses 1%) imposed on the family with less earnings, these taxes are unfair. Think of it this way: a family earning less cannot afford to pay as much tax, not just in terms of actual dollars, but also in terms of the proportional size of their tax burden given their total earnings.

All legitimate tax policy models, even the most politically conservative, condemn regressive taxes as conclusively wrong. Alabama's wealthy and powerful planters of 1901 had an immoral purpose for the low, inadequate, and regressive taxes enshrined in the 1901 constitution. In order to reverse the limited success enjoyed by some blacks and poor whites after the Civil War, they sought to deny all blacks and poor whites minimum health care and education.

The devastating consequences of their immoral vision continue to this day. Many blacks and poor whites sunk deeper into poverty and the economic well-being of the entire state suffered greatly. In order to alleviate the suffering inflicted on the poorest Alabamians and improve the state's economic situation, for decades reformers made traditional tax policy and equity arguments against Alabama's unfair taxes. Primarily due to the relentless and often dishonest lobbying of powerful special interest groups, especially those representing owners of Alabama's vast acres of timber property, the hard work of these reformers failed, leaving Alabama starting the 21st century with horrendously unfair taxes, a backward and depressed economic environment, and a large population of poor people with little chance of escaping poverty.

How the Alabama Movement Got Started

I arrived in Alabama in 1994 as a newly appointed assistant professor at the University of Alabama School of Law, in the areas of tax and business law. Despite my vast knowledge of and experience practicing tax law, in both the private sector and government, I had no idea that I was sitting on the worst, most unfair state and local tax structure in the country.

For six years I labored through the promotion and tenure process at the law school focusing on business organizations, especially limited liability companies

addition to providing support that everyone in the community needs, revenues raised from taxes also care for the poor and allow them a chance to better themselves. Nobody likes paying taxes, yet few people want to give up the benefits taxes provide. Can you imagine the cost and anxiety if you had to protect your own life and property without the police department? Without taxes civilization would quickly descend to anarchy. In the United States, citizens pay two distinct levels of tax (federal taxes meet national needs, and state and local taxes meet needs within the borders of the particular state, county, and city). Alabama's story involves unfair taxes at the state and local levels.

Why are taxes compulsory? Why do we have to legally require people to pay their taxes and impose fines or even prison terms on those who fail to pay? Why not just rely on voluntary charitable giving to raise the needed level of revenues? The answer is simple. Virtually all people, if given the choice,would pay less than their fair share. Many people would pay nothing at all. More bluntly, everyone wants the community benefits taxes provide (good public schools, well-maintained roads, a competent and responsive police force, an infrastructure supporting healthcare, to name just a few), but nobody wants to pay their fair share of the costs.

Russell B. Long captured this well when he said "Don't tax you, don't tax me, tax the fellow behind the tree." This attitude stems from basic human greed, which is present to some degree in all of us. Those practicing Christianity and Judaism attribute basic human greed to the effects of the Fall as revealed in the third chapter of *Genesis* in the Bible. Although charitable giving can be an important supplement to a community that already has a fair tax structure, we simply cannot rely exclusively on charitable giving to raise adequate revenues to meet most community needs.

Why must the yardstick measuring the fairness of taxes ultimately rely on moral standards? The compulsory nature of taxes (the fact that taxes must be legally enforced) exalts the evaluation of tax fairness to a moral question. Taxes tend to provoke a visceral reaction in otherwise rational people, especially when they believe that the taxes are unfair. In order to meet the test of fairness, the system for imposing taxes must satisfy two broad standards.

First, the taxes must raise adequate revenues that efficiently meet the minimum needs of those in the community subject to the tax. The level of "minimum needs" is defined by the norms of the community and will differ among communities. Second, the taxes must be based on ability to pay. Taxpayers with the same ability to pay should pay the same amount, while taxpayers with a greater ability to pay should carry a higher tax burden than those with less. Truly poor people should pay no taxes.

The judgement of "fairness" under the standards of adequacy and ability to pay ultimately comes down to the moral values adopted by the people subject to the tax. More plainly, there is a right way and a wrong way to impose taxes. Taxes that raise revenues in a right way reflect a morally healthy society, while taxes that raise revenues in a wrong way reflect an immoral society.

INTRODUCTION

How Alabama's Story Gives All Americans a Moral Blueprint for Tax Reform

This book tells the story of one state's struggle to overcome the terrible injustice caused by its unfair taxes. It shows how the tragedy of this one state morally urges everyone, everywhere, to demand fair taxes. The state of Alabama, the subject of this story, forces low income Alabamians to pay an unacceptably large portion of their meager resources in state and local taxes, and at the same time allows the wealthiest Alabamians to get away with not paying their share. Alabama's unfair taxes leave critical services, including most of Alabama's public schools, grossly underfunded. Children from poor and lower middle class families have little opportunity to better their situation, and Alabama remains at or near the bottom in all measurements of quality of life. In Alabama we crush the poor by heavily taxing them. Then we keep them poor by denying them any reasonable chance of escaping poverty.

Unfortunately, Alabama is not the only state that imposes unfair taxes on those least able to pay. And Alabama is not the only state with inadequately funded public schools that happen to be in the poorest areas. So, what could possibly be going on in Alabama that offers moral guidance to people living outside Alabama?

The scenario in Alabama is unprecedented. Alabamians practicing Christianity are demanding that Alabama's taxes meet the moral standards of justice required by their faith. Inspired by a law review article, (*An Argument For Tax Reform Based on Judeo-Christian Ethics*), more and more Alabamians are recognizing that taxes are a moral issue that must exemplify Judeo-Christian values as revealed in the Bible, because those are the ethical standards most of us have adopted. Because of this movement, the fight against Alabama's unfair taxes is no longer confined to the exclusive circle of tax professionals and other intellectuals. Alabama's unfair taxes are now everyone's business, and challenge our moral credibility as a religious people. Alabama's story teaches all Americans that the moral standards of faith, or other ethical models adopted by the people, offer the best moral compass guiding us to fair taxes.

Why Mix Morality with Taxes?

Before we get too deep into Alabama's story, it is worth exploring what taxes are, why we have taxes, and finally why the fairness of taxes must be tested by moral standards. A tax is a compulsory payment imposed by a government to meet public needs. Governments use tax revenues to pool resources so that all, even those in the community the least well off, will collectively benefit. In

allows owners of Alabama timber acres to account for less than two percent of all property taxes, averaging less than one dollar per acre. Although all classes of property pay inadequate property taxes, timber acres, which make up approximately seventy-one percent of Alabama's landmass and constitute one of the most important sources of profits in Alabama's economy, contribute substantially less than their proportionate share when compared to the other classes of property.

Part I finally illustrates how Alabama's property tax structure itself is primarily responsible for the inadequate funding of primary and secondary public education, arguably the most important state and local governmental function needed to foster the well-being of Alabama's children. Because the state provides insufficient funds for education, largely due to the state's dependence on revenues from income and sales taxes, the local areas must raise substantial additional revenues for their individual school systems. The vast majority of the local areas across the state, however, are not able to raise sufficient revenues from additional property taxes. Because these areas enjoy no significant commercial or industrial activity, they have very little valuable commercial property and personal residences, the two classes of property most capable of raising at least a tolerable level of revenues under the current property tax structure. Moreover, because the property tax structure allows only a *de minimis* portion of the value of the numerous timber acres present in these areas to be available for taxation, the property tax structure itself bars these areas from imposing fair taxes on their most significant source of wealth and represents an important reason why close to ninety percent of Alabama's public schools are inadequately funded. Alabama's failure to adequately fund its public schools denies children from low-income families a minimum opportunity to achieve an adequate education, which represents their only reasonable chance of enjoying a better future.

Part II first identifies and discusses the two primary traditional tax policy tools used to evaluate the fairness of tax structures. Vertical equity, which primarily focuses on the taxpayer's ability to pay the tax, seeks to define how to fairly apportion the tax burden among taxpayers with different levels of income and wealth. Progressive taxes significantly factor in ability to pay by requiring taxpayers with a greater ability to pay to bear a higher burden, while regressive taxes disregard ability to pay by imposing a heavier burden on taxpayers with less ability to pay. Horizontal equity states that taxpayers with similar abilities to pay should bear a similar tax burden, and deems tax preferences that vary the tax burden among similarly situated taxpayers inequitable unless the particular tax preference more accurately measures ability to pay or creates important benefits beyond the immediate taxpayer that are best achieved through the tax structure. Part II then determines that the fairness of tax structures is ultimately an ethical issue that can only be resolved by using value judgments with a philosophical or theological foundation, and discusses the principles of vertical and horizontal equity in the context of income, sales, and property tax structures generally.

In order to develop the theologically based Judeo-Christian ethical principles that can be used to evaluate the fairness of economic structures, Part II then explores the relevant biblical texts of the Old and New Testaments. These biblical texts include many parts of the Old Testament, which link a genuine responsibility to God with proper treatment of poor, vulnerable, and powerless persons, and strong language in the New Testament, both affirming and re-establishing under the teachings of Jesus Christ, the Old Testament's message concerning the proper treatment of those persons. From these biblical texts two broad moral principles of Judeo-Christian ethics emerge, which provide a theological foundation for the ethical evaluation of the tax structure and funding of the public schools in Alabama. These ethical principles forbid the economic oppression of low-income Alabamians and require, not only that their basic needs be met, but also that they enjoy at least a minimum opportunity to improve their economic circumstances and, consequently, their lives.

Part II then illustrates that Alabama's tax structure not only fails to meet a reasonable definition of fairness under any legitimate ethical model, but also specifically violates the moral principles of Judeo-Christian ethics. By imposing the heaviest burdens on the taxpayers least able to pay, both Alabama's income and sales tax structures economically oppress low-income Alabamians. By being largely responsible for Alabama's inadequate tax revenues, the property tax structure is both directly responsible for the state's inadequate public services and indirectly contributes to economic oppression of the poorest Alabamians by forcing local areas to raise the sales tax rates within their borders. In addition to exacerbating the state's inadequate tax revenues, the property tax structure's substantially different treatment accorded to different types of property, which allows timber acres, an important source of profits and wealth, to enjoy the lightest tax burden, cannot be justified under the ability to pay principle and only fosters the self serving interests of powerful lobby groups. Moreover, by significantly impairing the ability of most areas to adequately fund their public schools, Alabama's property tax structure, especially the features allowing timber acres to pay only *de minimis* property taxes, denies the poorest, most vulnerable, and powerless segment of Alabama's population, children from low-income families, a minimum opportunity to achieve an adequate education, which represents their only chance of improving their economic circumstances and their lives.

Finally, Part II concludes that Alabama's citizens, especially those of faith, who are empowered by virtue of that faith to live according to moral principles of Judeo-Christian ethics, have a moral responsibility to affirmatively exercise their constitutional rights and support comprehensive tax reform in order to eliminate the vast amount of injustice created by Alabama's tax structure. When voting, all Alabamians have a moral duty to carefully consider whether candidates seeking public office plan to support a plan for tax reform that addresses these injustices. However, by virtue of possessing more education, wealth, or status than the average Alabamian, some Alabamians have a greater moral responsibility to foster tax reform by seeking to educate others and to challenge positions taken by those distorting the truth for their own self interest. Additionally, Alabama's elected members of the House and the Senate, and the Governor of Alabama, by virtue of their direct access to the legislative process, have an even greater moral duty to work towards securing a fair and just tax structure for all Alabamians, even when pressured by special interests groups who, for their own self interest, seek to maintain the status quo. And finally, as ministers of God's word, Alabama's religious leaders have the greatest moral responsibility to faithfully preach the word that the injustices perpetuated by Alabama's tax structure are immoral and cannot be defended under any reasonable interpretation of Judeo-Christian ethics, and therefore individuals claiming to be part of the People of God can no longer complacently tolerate Alabama's tax structure as it currently operates.

I. ALABAMA'S TAX STRUCTURE ECONOMICALLY OPPRESSES LOW-INCOME ALABAMIANS AND FAILS TO RAISE ADEQUATE REVENUES

The tax structure adopted and enforced by any governmental entity will foster great good for the community if the taxes imposed are fair to all citizens and raise adequate revenues. Because the federal income tax imposed by the United States government plays only a minor role towards supporting the community of citizens living in a particular state, adequate revenues from state and local taxes are vitally important for the well-being of citizens living in that state.[8] States that impose unfair tax structures in a

---

8. *See* STATE AND LOCAL SOURCEBOOK 40 (Peter A. Harkness ed.) (2001) [hereinafter SOURCEBOOK]; STATE RANKINGS 2001: A STATISTICAL VIEW OF THE 50 UNITED STATES 275 (Kathleen O'Leary Morgan & Scott Morgan eds.) (12th ed. 2001) [hereinafter STATE RANKINGS] (showing that 18.1% of Alabama's revenue to meet state needs came from federal aid, while only 15.1% of the revenue to meet state needs came from federal sources nationally, and that no state received enough federal aid to even approach 25% of its total revenue). The portions of state revenues that do not come from federal funds presumably come largely from state and local tax revenues. Considering that state and local taxes in Alabama provide approximately 80% of Alabama's total revenue, and that state and local taxes represent at least 75% of states' total tax revenues nationally, a sound state and local tax structure is probably the most important factor ensuring the long term well being of citizens in any given state. In their respective studies of economic trends, tax revenues, and funding patterns in all fifty states, both the SOURCEBOOK, *supra*, and the STATE RANKINGS, *supra*, use 1997 figures (or for limited categories 1999 figures). Because each of these studies was published in 2001, the 1997 (or 1999 figures) represent the most current figures available for providing meaningful comparisons be-

manner that fails to raise adequate revenues cannot adequately support the citizens living in that state, resulting in great hardships, especially to those citizens at lower income levels. In evaluating Alabama's tax structure, both from a fairness and ability to raise adequate revenues perspective, this Article focuses in detail on the three most important sources of tax revenue for state and local governments—the income tax, the sales tax, and the property tax.[9]

---

tween Alabama and the other states. However, because this Article focuses on broad comparisons of tax and spending patterns between Alabama and other states, the studies in these sources provide useful information supporting the argument presented in this Article: that Alabama's tax revenues, especially property tax revenues, are inadequate and severely compromise Alabama's vital programs benefiting its citizens.

9.   *See* JOEL SLEMROD & JON BAKIJA, TAXING OURSELVES: A CITIZEN'S GUIDE TO THE GREAT DEBATE OVER TAX REFORM 18-19 (1996) (providing a table and text for the United States tax struc- ture and the states in general). With figures from 1994, the three largest sources of state revenues are income taxes (contributing 17.6%), sales taxes (30.3%), and property taxes (25.6%). *Id.* At the state level, well over half of the $6.2 billion (this figure includes $6,056,442,562.13 in revenue collected at the state level with the exception of net property taxes, *see id.* at 62, and state net property taxes of $191,852,437, *see id.* at 67, for a total of $6,248,294,999.13, rounded to $6.2 billion) in total state tax revenues raised in Alabama for the fiscal year ending on September 30, 2000 came from income, sales, and property taxes. *See* STATE OF ALA. DEP'T OF REVENUE, 2000 ANNUAL REPORT 62-67 (2000), *available at* http://www.ador.state.al.us (on file with author) [hereinafter 2000 ANNUAL REPORT OF ALABAMA]. Individual income, sales, and property taxes produced $4,130,970,779.54 (66.12%) of the roughly $6.2 billion collected. *Id.* The $4,130,970,779.54 figure is the sum of $2,409,067,979.67 (38.56%), which came from individual income tax collections, $1,530,050,362.87 (24.49%), which came from state imposed sales tax collections, and $191,852,437 (3.07%), which came from state imposed property tax collections. *Id.* The sum of all other taxes collected at the state level came to $2,117,324,219.59 (33.88%). *Id.* This $2,117,324,219.59 figure is the sum of the revenue from business taxes totaling $444,666,980.95 (7.11% of total state taxes), privilege taxes and licenses revenue totaling $624,547,901.54 (10.00% of total state taxes), and revenue from all other taxes totaling $1,048,109,337.10 (16.77% of total state taxes). *Id.* Business taxes represent taxes imposed on business organizations legally organized as C corporations, S corporations, or other busi- ness forms, and include the Business Privilege Tax, the Corporate Shares Tax, the Corporate Entrance Fee, the Corporate Franchise Tax, the Corporation Permit Fee, Corporate Income Tax, and Registra- tion of Securities. Privilege taxes and licenses are imposed for the opportunity and ability to operate in certain industries or perform certain activities, and include the Agent's Occupational Licenses, the Automotive Dismantler's License, the Automotive Reconditioners/Rebuilders Fee, the Bulk Storage Withdrawal Fee, the Coal Severance Tax, the tax on Contractors' Gross Receipts, the Financial Insti- tutions' Excise Tax, the Forest Products' Severance Tax, the Freight Line R.R. Equipment Hazardous Waste Fee, Hydro-Electric KWH, IRP Registration Fees, Medicaid Nursing Facility, Medicaid Phar- maceutical Services, Motor Carrier Mileage, the Oil and Gas Privilege License, Oil and Gas Produc- tion, Oil Lubricating, Oil Wholesale License, Pari-Mutuel Pool, Store Licenses, Utility Gross Re- ceipts, and Utility License. Other taxes consist of taxes on Cellular Telecommunications, Deeds and Assignments, Estate and Inheritance, Gasoline, Gasoline (Aviation & Jet Fuel), Illegal Drugs, Lodg- ings, Miscellaneous Tags, Motor Fuels (Diesel), Motor Vehicle Title Fees, Playing Card, Rental or Leasing, Salvage Vehicle Inspection Fees, Tobacco Products, and T.V.A. Electric and Use. The taxes were categorized by using the names of the taxes and the descriptions of the taxes in a book published by the Alabama Department of Revenue. *See id.* at 62; *see also* ALA. DEP'T OF REVENUE, GENERAL SUMMARY OF STATE TAXES (2000), *available at* http://www.ador.state.al.us (on file with author) (providing a "concise handbook of the revenue sources for the state of Alabama"). Because individual counties and municipalities impose additional sales and property taxes within their borders, the $6.2 billion does not include all tax collected in Alabama. *See infra* notes 46-48 and 87-89 and accompany- ing text.

Alabama's income tax collects a percentage of the taxpayer's taxable income, which includes, for example, all wages, salaries, dividends, and interest received by the taxpayer less certain allowable deductions.[10] Alabama's sales tax, which in its most significant form is known as the general retail sales tax, collects a percentage of the purchase price of consumer expenditures.[11] Alabama's property tax, which covers real property, such as personal residences, timber, and agriculture, and personal property, such as automobiles, collects a percentage of the assessed value, which will always be significantly less than true fair market value of the taxpayer's property.[12]

A. Alabama's Income and Sales Tax Structures Economically Oppress Low-Income Alabamians

Although greatly affected by the complexities of the constitutional amendment process, the Alabama legislature bears ultimate responsibility for setting the income tax rate,[13] defining the income items that appear in

---

10.   *See* MARVIN A. CHIRELSTEIN, FEDERAL INCOME TAXATION 1-2 (9th ed. rev. 2002). During the nineteenth century, the states imposed income taxes, but due to administrative failures these income taxes produced only meager revenues. *See* 2 JEROME R. HELLERSTEIN & WALTER HELLERSTEIN, STATE TAXATION ¶ 20.01 (1st ed. 1992). However, by the early twentieth century after the federal income tax, first enacted in 1913 following the Sixteenth Amendment, had a few years to operate, the states learned how to centrally administer the income tax and produce significant revenues. *Id.* By 1991, forty-one states, including Alabama, Arkansas, Georgia, Kentucky, Louisiana, Mississippi, North Carolina, and South Carolina, and the District of Columbia imposed broad-based income taxes. *Id.* Under current law, of the Southeastern states, only Florida fails to impose an income tax, and Tennessee imposes an income tax on only selected types of income. *Id.* at 20-3 n.5.

11.   2 HELLERSTEIN, *supra* note 10, ¶ 12.01. In addition to the retail sales tax, the term "sales tax" also includes the "compensatory use tax," "gross receipts tax," "manufacturer's excise tax," and "gross income tax." *Id.* ¶ 12.01. Because the retail sales tax, which covers groceries, medicine, and all other consumer items, has the greatest effect on Alabama's citizens, this Article exclusively focuses on the retail sales tax when analyzing the role of sales taxes within the larger Alabama state tax structure. The increasing reliance of states on sales taxes is one of the most significant developments of the twentieth century in state finance. *See id.* The sales tax was born out of the Depression era, a time when states needed another form of revenue to pay for basic functions because income and property taxes were producing lower yields. *Id. See also* RUSSELL W. MADDOX & ROBERT F. FUQUAY, STATE AND LOCAL GOVERNMENT 315-16 (3d ed. 1975) (providing a historical overview showing that twenty-nine states imposed retail sales taxes between 1932 and 1937, including Alabama, which first introduced a retail sales tax in 1936). By 1999 the general sales tax was in effect in forty-five states and the District of Columbia. In that year Alaska, Delaware, Montana, New Hampshire, and Oregon were the only five states that did not have a general sales tax. *See* 2 HELLERSTEIN, *supra* note 10, ¶ 12.01.

12.   *See infra* notes 60-89 and accompanying text (discussing in detail the Alabama state property tax structure). The general property tax was first imposed by the democratic New England communities of Colonial America. 1 HELLERSTEIN, *supra* note 10, ¶ 1.01. Although the property tax was a major source of state tax revenue in the early twentieth century, and gradually declined in importance, property taxes continue to bring in a substantial portion of local government tax revenue around the nation. *Id.* ¶ 1.02.

13.   *See* ALA. CONST. amend. 25 (stating that the income tax rates on individuals shall not exceed 5%); *see also* Bryce, *supra* note 1, at 544 (stating that a constitutional amendment would be needed to increase Alabama's individual income tax rate above 5%).

the base,[14] and defining the lowest level of income subject to the income tax.[15] Although the nationwide trend among the states has been to elimi-nate, or at least reduce, the income tax burden on low-income families,[16] Alabama imposes the most regressive income taxes in the United States, which in addition to requiring those taxpayers least able to pay to bear the greatest burden, produces revenues among the lowest in the southeast and the nation.[17] Structurally, Alabama's extremely low exemptions and flat rates work together to produce an income tax system that is the most un-fair tax system in the United States to poor citizens.[18] Of all the states in the nation, Alabama provides the lowest exemptions. Exemptions grant every taxpayer a defined minimum amount of income, which never enters the tax base, in order to allow the taxpayer to meet basic needs without being overburdened by income taxes.[19] Larger exemptions help low-income taxpayers by allowing a greater portion of their income to be to-tally available to meet basic expenses rather than being taxed.[20] Married

14.   See Bryce, supra note 1, at 545 (noting that the present Alabama income tax scheme computes income tax based on Alabama rules); see also ALA. CODE §§ 40-18-1 to 40-18-176 (1998); ALA. CONST. amend. 25 (limiting the top income tax rate to 5% for individuals, but leaving to the legisla-ture the discretion of defining the income tax base).

15.   See ALA. CODE § 40-18-5 (1998) (providing the tax rates imposed on individuals and the income levels to which they apply); see also ALA. CONST. amend. 25 (requiring that individual tax-payers be granted the following exemptions: $1500 for unmarried persons; $3000 for married couples filing jointly; and $300 for each dependent). Because the language of the constitution establishes these exemption amounts as a minimum, presumably the legislature could increase the exemptions without going through the constitutional amendment process.

16.   See THE CTR. ON BUDGET AND POLICY PRIORITIES, STATE INCOME TAX BURDENS ON LOW-INCOME FAMILIES IN 2000: ASSESSING THE BURDEN AND OPPORTUNITIES FOR RELIEF 9 (2001) [here-inafter TAX BURDENS] (noting that "[o]f the 24 states with below-poverty thresholds for families of four in 1991, 23 states—all but Alabama—raised those thresholds between 1991 and 2000").

17.   See PARCA REPORT, supra note 1, at 98 (noting that Alabama has the highest income tax burden for low-income families among the forty-two states that have an income tax); see also TAX BURDENS, supra note 16, at 5 (observing that adequate revenue from income taxes can be raised without taxing the poor because six of the ten states that receive the largest shares of tax revenues from income taxes exempt poor families); see also STATE RANKINGS, supra note 8, at 306 (ranking Alabama thirty-eighth in per capita revenues raised from income taxes out of the forty-one states that impose broad based income taxes, indicating that Alabama collects less per capita in income taxes than North Carolina, Kentucky, Georgia, South Carolina, and Arkansas, but more per capita than Louisi-ana and Mississippi); see also SOURCEBOOK, supra note 8, at 42 (ranking Alabama thirty-seventh in per capita income tax collections, and showing the same per capita collection patterns as STATE RANKINGS for the Southeastern states).

18.   See PARCA Report, supra note 1, at 8 (stating that Alabama places the highest income tax burden on low-income families among the states with an income tax); ALABAMA POLICY INSTITUTE, supra note 1, at 32; see also TAX BURDENS, supra note 16, at 6.

19.   See TAX BURDENS, supra note 16, at 47 (noting that personal exemptions are subtractions from income that reduce the amount of income that is subject to tax); see also SLEMROD & BAKIJA, supra note 9, at 38 (noting that exemptions are subtracted directly from adjusted gross income in order to determine taxable income, with the personal exemption and standard deduction creating an extra tax bracket at the bottom of the income scale with a zero tax rate).

20.   SLEMROD & BAKIJA, supra note 9, at 38-39 (noting that a higher tax-exempt threshold—accomplished through deductions and exemptions—helps remove many low-income people from the income tax rolls, and makes the system more progressive by reducing average tax rates on low- and moderate-income individuals); see also Bryce, supra note 1, at 547 (noting that adopting the federal

taxpayers filing jointly have a mere combined exemption of $3000, and taxpayers with dependents are allowed an exemption of only $300 for each dependent.[21] Nearly every other state in the nation, as well as most of Alabama's neighboring Southeastern states, allow exemptions, or the equivalent of exemptions, that far exceed those provided by Alabama.[22] For example, Georgia allows married couples filing jointly a personal exemption of $5400 and an exemption of $2700 per dependent.[23] Mississippi allows married taxpayers filing jointly a $12,000 personal exemption and an exemption of $1500 for each dependent.[24]

Alabama's low level of exemptions forces Alabamians whose earnings fall well below the poverty line to use a portion of their scarce resources to pay income taxes, greatly exacerbating the negative effects of poverty. The mere $3000 personal exemption for married taxpayers and the $300

---

personal exemption—which is higher than Alabama's—has the effect of removing low-income individuals from the income tax rolls).

21.   See ALA. CODE § 40-18-19(a)(8) to (9) (1998); Alabama Department of Revenue, *Alabama Individual Income Tax Return Form 40* (2001) [hereinafter *Alabama Form 40*]; ALA. DEP'T OF REVENUE, ALABAMA FORM 40 BOOKLET 9-10 (2001) [hereinafter ALABAMA FORM 40 BOOKLET]. Other filing statuses, besides married filing jointly, receive the following personal exemptions: single person $1500, married and not living with husband or wife $1500, head of household $3000, and married and living together but filing separate returns, $1500. *Id.*

22.   See TAX BURDENS, *supra* note 16, at 16 (noting that states with the lowest thresholds for taxing citizens tend to have very low personal and dependent exemptions). Alabama has the lowest threshold in the nation for taxing single-parent families of three, and two-parent families of four. *See id.* at 14-15. "[I]n the ten states with the lowest thresholds for a single-parent family of three, the combined amount of the personal and dependent exemptions and standard deduction averages only $6,138." *Id.* at 16. The other thirty-two states with an income tax have an average combined amount of the personal and dependent exemptions and standard deduction of $11,497. *Id.* A very similar pattern exists for two-parent families of four. *Id.* at 16-17. Further, the median combined value of the personal and dependent exemptions and the standard deduction in the twelve states with the highest income tax thresholds for a single-parent family of three and a two-parent family of four is higher than the poverty line. TAX BURDENS, *supra* note 16, at 18. The poverty lines for a single-parent family of three and a two-parent family of four are $13,737 and $17,601, respectively. *Id.* at 14-15.

23.   See GA. CODE ANN. § 48-7-26(b)(1), (b)(3)(C) (2002). A person who files as "head of household" in Georgia gets a personal exemption of $2700. *See id.* § 48-7-26(b)(2) (2002). Although it is difficult to compare the other Southeastern states, besides Georgia and Mississippi, with Alabama on this issue of personal exemptions, all of the other Southeastern states except Kentucky, build in comparable provisions to ensure that their state income tax thresholds significantly exceed those of Alabama. *See* TAX BURDENS, *supra* note 16, at 14-15. Arkansas gives tax credits of $40 to both those "married filing jointly" and those filing as "head of household." ARK. CODE ANN. § 26-51-501 (2)(A)(i) (Michie 1997 & Supp. 2001). Kentucky gives a tax credit of $40 for those persons "married filing jointly" and a $20 tax credit for head of household. KY. REV. STAT. ANN. § 141.020(3) (Michie 1991). Louisiana figures the personal exemption into the amount of tax charged on the state's tax table. *See* State of Louisiana, *Individual Income Tax Form IT-540* (2000). In South Carolina taxable income is determined the same way it is under the Internal Revenue Code. S.C. CODE ANN. § 12-6-560 (Law. Co-op. 2000). North Carolina computes state taxable income based on one's federal taxable income and slightly reduces the effect of the personal exemption from the federal return. N.C. GEN. STAT. §§ 105-130.5, -134.5, -134.6 (2001); *see also* North Carolina Department of Revenue, *Individual Income Tax Return Form D-400* (2000). Florida does not have an income tax and Tennessee only taxes dividend and interest income; therefore, it is not relevant to do an income tax comparison involving those two states.

24.   See MISS. CODE ANN. § 27-7-21(c), (e) (1999 & Supp. 2002). In Mississippi, a person with the filing status of "head of family" will have a personal exemption of $9500. *Id.* § 27-7-21(d).

exemption per dependent results in a family of four—two parents and two children—starting to pay income taxes at an income level of only $4600 a year,[25] which represents the lowest level in the nation for the minimum income tax base to start, and falls well below the poverty line of $17,601 for a family of four.[26] This same family would not start paying state income taxes until their income level reached $21,400 in South Carolina and $19,600 in Mississippi; both of these amounts exceed the poverty line.[27] On the federal level, this hypothetical family of four must reach an income level exceeding $18,550 of income to incur any federal income tax liability.[28] Even though the federal system deems this family too poor to bear federal income tax liability, a family of four with an income level of $18,550 must pay nearly $500 in Alabama state income taxes.[29]

---

25.   TAX BURDENS, *supra* note 16, at 15. The $4600 of income refers to adjusted gross income, which is similar to federal adjusted gross income. The income tax threshold includes earned income tax credits, other general tax credits, exemptions, and standard deductions. *Id.* In Alabama, if a two-parent family of four has $4600 of adjusted gross income (line 11 of *Alabama Form 40*), the family takes the standard deduction of $920 (line 12); the family will get a personal exemption of $3000 (line 14); the family will get a $600 dependent exemption ($300 for each of the two children) (line 15); the family then has taxable income of $80 (line 17). This amount of taxable income creates a tax liability of $1 (line 18). *See Alabama Form 40, supra* note 21. The figures are just as disturbing for a single parent with two children. In Alabama, this single parent begins to pay tax when he or she has $4600 of income. *See* TAX BURDENS, *supra* note 16, at 14; *Alabama Form 40, supra* note 21 (showing that if a single parent family with two children has $4600 of income (line 11), the family takes the standard deduction of $920 (line 12); the single parent will get a personal exemption of $3000 (line 14); the family will get a $600 dependent exemption ($300 for each of the two children) (line 15); the family then has taxable income of $80 (line 17), creating a tax liability of $1 (line 18)).

26.   TAX BURDENS, *supra* note 16, at 15 (noting that the 2000 poverty line is a Census Bureau estimate based on the actual 1999 line adjusted for inflation).

27.   *Id.* A hypothetical family of four begins paying state income taxes when adjusted gross income reaches $17,000 in North Carolina, $15,600 in Arkansas, $15,300 in Georgia, and $13,000 in Louisiana. *Id.* The state with an income structure almost as regressive as Alabama's, Kentucky, starts imposing income taxes on a family of four at the $5400 adjusted gross income level. *Id.* Tennessee and Florida are not listed because they do not have comparable income tax systems to the other eight Southeastern states. A single parent with two children does not begin to pay tax until she has $17,700 of income in South Carolina, $14,400 of income in Mississippi, $13,900 of income in North Carolina, $13,000 of income in Arkansas, $12,100 of income in Georgia, and $11,000 in Louisiana. *Id.* at 14. Kentucky starts imposing income taxes on a single parent with two children at the $5000 adjusted gross income level. TAX BURDENS, *supra* note 16, at 15.

28.   *See* Department of the Treasury Internal Revenue Service, *Form 1040 U.S. Individual Income Tax Return* (2000) [hereinafter *IRS Form 40 for either 2000 or 2001*]. Assuming that a family of four (married taxpayers filing a joint return with two children) has $18,550 of wages (line 7), and assuming the family has no adjustments to income (lines 23 through 32), the family will have $18,550 of adjusted gross income (lines 33 and 34). The family will get a standard deduction of $7350 (line 36) and personal exemptions of $11,200 (line 38) (4 exemptions (one for husband, one for wife, one for each child) multiplied by $2800), therefore having taxable income of $0 (line 39). This, in turn, will lead to $0 federal income tax liability. The family could actually have income of $18,554 and still pay no taxes, but $18,550 was used for rounding purposes.

29.   *See Alabama Form 40, supra* note 21. If a family of four (married taxpayers filing a joint return with two children) has $18,550 of adjusted gross income (which is very similar to the federal adjusted gross income figure) (line 11), the family will get a standard deduction of $3710 (line 12), a personal exemption of $3000 (line 14), and a dependent exemption of $600 (line 15- $300 for each child). The family will then have taxable income of $11,240 (line 17). This will create an income tax liability of $483 (line 18). ALABAMA FORM 40 BOOKLET, *supra* note 21, at 25. Although several

While greatly burdening those taxpayers at the lowest income levels, three features of the Alabama income tax structure work together to effectively minimize the tax burden on those taxpayers at the highest income levels—those taxpayers having the greatest ability to pay. Alabama allows all taxpayers, regardless of income level, to reduce income subject to tax by the full exemption amount.[30] Because exemptions represent one of the mechanisms to avoid imposing income taxes below a taxpayer's ability to pay,[31] the benefit of an exemption should be phased out, or gradually denied, as the taxpayer's income, representing their ability to pay, increases.[32] The federal tax system contains a schedule that gradually phases the exemption out, eventually completely denying the exemption at very high income levels.[33] Because Alabama's income tax system never phases out personal exemptions, the wealthiest taxpayers, of whom the federal

---

Southeastern states also impose state income taxes at income levels below the minimum threshold for incurring federal income tax liability, Alabama's income taxes impose the highest level of tax on these poor families. For example, the same family of four has a tax liability of only $102 in Georgia. *See* Georgia Department of Revenue, *Georgia Individual Income Tax Form 500 and Instructions* (2001) [hereinafter *Georgia Form 500*]. This tax liability for the family of four is calculated as follows: the family has $18,550 of federal adjusted gross income and Georgia adjusted gross income (lines 8 and 10); the family gets a total standard deduction of $3000 (line 11c) and personal exemptions of $10,800 (line 14) (4 exemptions at $2700 each); the family thus has taxable income of $4750 (line 15). The family has a tax liability of $102 (line 16). *Id.* In Arkansas, the same family of four has a tax liability of $373 when it has $18,550 of income. *See* Arkansas Department of Finance and Administration, *Form AR1000 Arkansas Individual Income Tax Return* (2000) [hereinafter *Arkansas Form AR1000*]. *See also* ARK. DEP'T OF FIN. AND ADMIN., ARKANSAS INDIVIDUAL INCOME TAX BOOKLET (2000) [hereinafter ARKANSAS BOOKLET]. The tax liability of the family of four in Arkansas is calculated as follows: the family has a total income of $18,550 (line 22); the family has adjusted gross income (an item similar to the concept of federal adjusted gross income) of $18,550 (line 34 and line 35); the family gets a standard deduction of $4000 (line 36); the family has net taxable income of $14,550 (line 37); the family has total tax of $453 (line 42); the family gets a personal tax credit of $80 (line 43); the family has net tax of $373 (line 52); and the family has total tax due of $373 (line 64C). In Louisiana, the family of four has an income tax liability of $395. *See* Louisiana Department of Revenue, *Form IT-540 Louisiana Resident* (2000) [hereinafter *Louisiana Form IT-540*]. The tax liability of the family of four in Louisiana is calculated as follows: the family has federal adjusted gross income of $18,550 (line 7); the family has Louisiana taxable income of $18,550 (line 10); the family has Louisiana income tax of $395 (line 11); the family has zero credits (line 12); the family has adjusted Louisiana income tax of $395 (line 13A); the family has total payments of $0 (line 14D); therefore, the family has a balance due to Louisiana of $395 (line 15).

30.   ALA. CODE § 40-18-19(a)(8) to (9) (1975) (providing for personal and dependent exemptions and not calling for any phasing out of these exemptions); *see also* ALABAMA FORM 40 BOOKLET, *supra* note 21, at 9 (instructions for personal and dependent exemptions, lines 14 and 15, respectively, providing for no phasing out of exemption amounts).

31.   TAX BURDENS, *supra* note 16, at 45 (noting that personal and dependent exemptions, the standard deduction, and credits are the basic features of a standard income tax structure that states use to reduce or eliminate the income tax burden on low-income families).

32.   *Id.* at 47 (noting that a way to target low-income tax relief more effectively is to reduce and phase out the value of the exemption at higher income levels).

33.   I.R.C. § 151(d)(3)(C)(i) (2001) (providing that the federal personal exemption begins to be phased out when the adjusted gross income (on a joint return) reaches $150,000 and is completely phased out when adjusted gross income (on a joint return) reaches $275,000).

system denies any benefit of exemption, are permitted to claim the full exemption under the state income tax.[34]

The rate schedule represents another feature of Alabama's income tax structure that benefits taxpayers at higher income levels. Although Alabama's rate structure, which ranges from two to five percent, gives the illusion of mild progressivity, in substance Alabama essentially has a flat rate structure.[35] Because the top rate of five percent starts applying at income levels as low as $12,000, which is well below the poverty line,[36] the same income tax rate applies to both the wealthiest Alabamians and those at the lowest end of the income spectrum.[37] All of Alabama's Southeastern neighbors have more progressive rate structures than Alabama's, either

---

34. ALA. CODE § 40-18-19(a)(8) to (9) (1998); *see also Alabama Form 40, supra* note 21, at lines 14-15; *see also* ALABAMA FORM 40 BOOKLET, *supra* note 21, at 9-10 (containing instructions for lines 14 and 15). Among Alabama's Southeastern neighbors, Georgia and Mississippi also fail to phase out their personal exemptions. GA. CODE ANN. § 48-7-26 (1995 & Supp. 2001); *Georgia Form 500, supra* note 29, at lines 6-14, and 7-8 (containing instructions for lines 6 and 14); MISS. CODE ANN. § 27-7-21 (1999 & Supp. 2001). North Carolina and South Carolina incorporate the federal personal exemption phase-out into their own tax systems. TAX BURDENS, *supra* note 16, at 49. Arkansas, Kentucky, and Louisiana use personal or dependent credits as an alternative to personal or dependent exemptions. *Id.* at 47; *see also* LA. REV. STAT. ANN. § 47:79 (West 2001).

35. *See* ALA. CODE § 40-18-5 (1998). The tax rate on married persons filing a joint return progresses as follows: 2% on taxable income not in excess of $1000; 4% on taxable income in excess of $1000 and not in excess of $6000; and 5% of taxable income in excess of $6000. *Id.* For single individuals in Alabama, the tax rate progresses as follows: 2% on taxable income not in excess of $500; 4% on taxable income in excess of $500 and not in excess of $3000; and 5% on taxable income in excess of $3000. *Id.* Taxable income consists of all the income of a taxpayer less adjustments to that income, less the standard deduction or itemized deductions, less the personal exemption, and less any dependent exemptions. *See Alabama Form 40, supra* note 21, at lines 1-17. Because there is so little spread between the bottom income levels of $500 for a single individual and $1000 for a married couple filing jointly for the lowest rate and the top income levels of $3000 and $6000, respectively, for the highest rate, Alabama's income tax is effectively flat. *See* Bryce, *supra* note 1, at 546 (noting that the present rate structure in Alabama is essentially flat).

36. *See Alabama Form 40, supra* note 21 (computation on return will show that an Alabama family of four (a married couple with two children) filing a joint return will pay income tax at Alabama's highest rate well below the poverty line). The poverty line for a family of four is set at an adjusted gross income of $17,601. TAX BURDENS, *supra* note 16, at 15. The top rate of 5% takes effect in Alabama as soon as adjusted gross income exceeds $12,000 as follows: The family has $12,000 in wages from jobs (line 6a); the family has no interest, dividend income, nor income from any other source (lines 7 and 8); the family has no adjustments to income for IRA deductions, payments to a Keogh retirement plan and self-employment SEP deduction, penalties on early withdrawal of savings, alimony paid, adoption expenses, moving expenses, or self-employed health insurance (line 10 and page 2, part II, line 8); this leads to adjusted gross income of $12,000 (line 11); the family then takes the standard deduction of $2400 (20% times adjusted gross income of $12,000 equals $2400) (line 12); the family has zero federal tax liability deduction (line 13); the family gets a personal exemption of $3000 (line 14); the family gets a dependent exemption of $600 (2 dependents times the $300 dependent exemption equals $600) (line 15); this creates total deductions of $6000 (the $2400 standard deduction from line 12, plus the $3000 personal exemption from line 14, plus the $600 dependent exemption from line 15 equals $6000) (line 16); taxable income equals $6000 ($12,000 adjusted gross income from line 11 less the $6000 of deductions from line 16 equals $6000). *See Alabama Form 40, supra* note 21; *see also* ALABAMA FORM 40 BOOKLET, *supra* note 21. The top rate of 5% takes effect for a married couple filing a joint return on taxable income in excess of $6000. ALA. CODE § 40-18-5 (1998).

37. *See infra* notes 151-58 and accompanying text (discussing flat and progressive income tax rates).

because of higher top rates, or because the highest rate takes effect at a higher level of income.[38] Finally, as one of the very few states that allow a full and unlimited deduction for a taxpayer's federal tax liability, the Alabama state income tax structure allows the wealthiest taxpayers to further reduce their state tax burden.[39] The deduction for federal taxes paid clearly

---

38.   2 STATE TAX GUIDE (CCH) ¶ 15-100 (2d ed. 2001) [hereinafter STATE TAX GUIDE]. Mississippi, North Carolina, and South Carolina have the most progressive income tax systems in the southeast. *See* TAX BURDENS, *supra* note 16, at 14-17 (identifying these three Southeastern states as having the most progressive income tax systems among the southeast). Mississippi imposes income tax on individuals (including married couples filing jointly) as follows: 3% on the first $5000 of taxable income; 4% on the next $5000 of taxable income; 5% on all taxable income in excess of $10,000. MISS. CODE ANN. § 27-7-5 (1999); *see also* STATE TAX GUIDE, *supra*. North Carolina imposes income tax on a married couple filing jointly as follows: 6% on taxable income up to $21,250; 7% on the amount of taxable income over $21,250 and up to $100,000; 7.75% on the amount of taxable income over $100,000 and up to $200,000; and 8.25% on the amount of taxable income over $200,000. N.C. GEN. STAT. § 105-134.2 (2001); *see also* STATE TAX GUIDE, *supra*. It should be noted however, that a married couple filing jointly with two children must have $17,000 of gross income before the couple owes any North Carolina income tax. TAX BURDENS, *supra* note 16, at 15. South Carolina imposes income tax on individuals as follows: 2.5% on the first $2400 of taxable income; 3% on taxable income over $2400 but not over $4800; 4% on taxable income over $4800 but not over $7200; 5% on taxable income over $7200 but not over $9600; 6% on taxable income over $9600 but not over $12,000; and 7% on taxable income over $12,000. S.C. CODE ANN. §§ 12-6-510, -520 (Law. Co-op. 2000); *see also* STATE TAX GUIDE, *supra*. Arkansas, Georgia, and Louisiana have income tax systems that are not as progressive as the three noted above, but still more progressive than Alabama's. Kentucky's income tax, although slightly better than Alabama's, has been also harshly criticized as unjust to low-income citizens. TAX BURDENS, *supra* note 16, at 14-17. Arkansas imposes income tax on individuals under the following rate structure: on the first $2999 of net income or any part thereof, 1%; on the next $3000 of net income, 2.5%; on the next $3000 of net income, 3.5%; on the next $6000 of net income, 4.5%; on the next $10,000 of net income, 6%; on net income of $25,000 and above, 7%. ARK. CODE ANN. § 26-51-201 (Michie 1997). Georgia imposes income tax on a couple that is married filing jointly as follows: 1% on taxable net income not over $1000; $10 plus 2% of amount of taxable net income over $1000 but not over $3000; $50 plus 3% of amount of taxable net income over $3000 but not over $5000; $110 plus 4% of amount of taxable net income over $5000 but not over $7000; $190 plus 5% of amount of taxable net income over $7000 but not over $10,000; $340 plus 6% of amount of taxable net income over $10,000. GA. CODE ANN. § 48-7-20 (1995); *see also* STATE TAX GUIDE *supra*. Kentucky imposes income tax on individuals as follows: 2% on the amount of net income not exceeding $3000; 3% on the amount of net income in excess of $3000 but not in excess of $4000; 4% on the amount of net income in excess of $4000 but not in excess of $5000; 5% on the amount of net income in excess of $5000 but not in excess of $8000; and 6% on the amount of net income in excess of $8000. KY. REV. STAT. ANN. § 141.020 (Michie 1991); *see also* STATE TAX GUIDE, *supra*. Louisiana imposes income tax on individuals at the following rates (for a married couple filing jointly the tax is computed by using the same rates as those for individuals and then doubling the amount of tax): 2% of the first $10,000 of net income in excess of the credits provided by the state; 4% on the next $40,000 of net income; and 6% on any amount of net income in excess of $50,000. LA. REV. STAT. ANN. § 47:32 (West 2001); *see also* STATE TAX GUIDE, *supra*. Florida and Tennessee cannot provide any meaningful comparison with Alabama's system because Florida does not impose an income tax, and Tennessee imposes a 6% tax upon interest and dividend income of individuals. *See id.*
39.   ALA. CONST. amend. 225; ALA. CODE § 40-18-15(a)(3) (1998); *see also* Federation of Tax Administrators, State Individual Income Taxes, *available at* http://www.taxadmin.org/fta/rate/ind_inc.pdf (Jan. 1, 2002) (noting that among Alabama's Southeastern neighbors, only Louisiana allows a deduction for federal income taxes paid). The only other states that allow a deduction for federal income taxes paid are as follows (with any limitation on the deduction in parentheses): Iowa, Missouri (up to $10,000 on a joint return and $5000 on an individual return); Montana, North Dakota (only long form filers can take deduction); Oklahoma, Oregon (up to $3000); and Utah (one-half of federal taxes are deductible). *Id.*; *see also* LA. CONST. art. 7, § 4; IOWA CODE ANN. § 422.9 (West 1998 &

favors those taxpayers with more income, because the total amount allowed as a deduction increases as the taxpayer's federal income tax liability increases.[40] In addition to favoring the wealthiest Alabamians, the deduction for federal taxes paid costs the state substantial lost revenues every year.[41]

Of the three most important state and local revenue sources, income, sales, and property taxes, sales taxes potentially impose the greatest burden on low-income citizens.[42] Alabama relies on sales taxes for more than fifty percent of its total tax revenue, imposing sales tax rates among the highest in the United States.[43] Although the state's four percent rate,[44] which can be raised or lowered by the legislature without going through

---

Supp. 2002); MO. ANN. STAT. § 143.171 (West 1996); MONT. CODE ANN. § 15-30-121 (2001); N.D. CENT. CODE § 57-38-01.2 (2000 & Supp. 2001); OKLA. STAT. ANN. tit. 68 § 2358D(8)(a) (West 2001); OR. REV. STAT. § 316.680 (2001); UTAH CODE ANN. § 59-10-114(2)(a) (2000 & Supp. 2001).

40.   CITIZENS FOR TAX JUSTICE AND THE INST. ON TAXATION & ECON. POLICY, WHO PAYS? A DISTRIBUTIONAL ANALYSIS OF THE TAX SYSTEMS IN ALL 50 STATES 1 n.1 (1996) [hereinafter CITIZENS FOR TAX JUSTICE] (stating that a deduction for federal income taxes paid greatly reduces the degree of progressivity within the state's income tax structure); Bryce, supra note 1, at 547 (noting that the federal income tax deduction is undesirable from the standpoint of vertical equity, because to the extent the federal income tax is progressive, high-income taxpayers are allowed proportionally larger deductions than low-income taxpayers).

41.   This deduction costs Alabama about $450 million in lost revenue each year. Chaney, supra note 1, at 260 n.231.

42.   See infra notes 170-72 and accompanying text (discussing the general regressive nature of sales taxes).

43.   See SOURCEBOOK, supra note 8, at 41, 45, 147. Alabama sales taxes for 1997 (including not only the general sales tax revenue, but also selective sales and gross receipts taxes on alcoholic beverages, amusements, insurance, motor fuels, parimutuels, public utilities, and tobacco products) accounted for 51% of total tax revenue ($4,037,000,000 divided by $7,958,000,000), while the national average shows only 35% ($261,734,000,000 divided by $728,594,000,000) of total revenue coming from sales taxes. Of the Southeastern states, Georgia, Kentucky, North Carolina, and South Carolina relied substantially less on sales taxes than Alabama (they are much more consistent with the national average percentage); while Arkansas, Florida, Louisiana, Mississippi, and Tennessee, like Alabama, relied heavily on sales taxes. See id; see also STATE RANKINGS, supra note 8, at 302, 309 (Alabama's sales tax revenue in 1999 (excluding sales and gross receipts taxes on special items such as alcohol, gasoline, and tobacco) contributed 27% to Alabama's total tax revenue ($1,649,120,000 divided by $6,032,234,000)). See also SLEMROD & BAKIJA, supra note 9, at 19 (discussing state and local taxes and indicating that in 1994 state and local governments relied on sales taxes for 30.3% of their revenues).

44.   See ALA. CODE § 40-23-2(1) (1975) (establishing the 4% state rate). Certain activities have a sales tax rate below 4%. The state imposes a sales tax rate of 1.5% on every person, firm, or corporation engaged in the business of selling at retail machines used in mining, quarrying, compounding, processing, and manufacturing of tangible personal property within Alabama, id. § 40-23-2(3); 2% on the gross proceeds from the sale of automotive vehicles or truck trailers, semi-trailers, house trailers, or mobile home set-up materials and supplies when the buyer is engaged in those businesses and the re-sale of those goods and products, id. § 40-23-2(4); and 3% on the cost of the food, food products, and certain beverages sold through machines when the buyer is engaged in those businesses and the re-sale of those goods and products, id. § 40-23-2(5). For fiscal year 2000, Alabama's sales tax imposed at the state level collected just over $1.5 billion, representing almost 25% of all revenue collected by state imposed taxes. See 2000 ANNUAL REPORT OF ALABAMA, supra note 9, at 62 (sales tax revenues equaled $1,530,050,362.87, representing 25.26% of Alabama's state tax revenue ($1,530,050,362.87 divided by total state tax revenues of $6,056,442,562.13)).

the constitutional amendment process,[45] appears deceptively reasonable, Alabamians pay an average overall sales tax rate exceeding eight percent[46] because individual counties and municipalities significantly increase the state's four percent rate within their borders.[47] A few areas impose sales tax rates as high as ten and eleven percent.[48] Moreover, Alabama's ex-

---

45.   *See* ALA. CODE §§ 11-51-200, 40-12-4 (1975) (allowing an increase of the state sales tax rate); *see also* PARCA REPORT, *supra* note 1, at 3, 6 (noting that the Alabama Constitution does not address the issue of sales taxes, thus permitting the state legislature to raise or lower the 4% state rate or change the structure of exemptions without going through the constitutional amendment process).

46.   *See infra* app. B, Range of Alabama Sales Tax by County, and underlying compilation of data on file with author [hereinafter Comp. & app. B] (containing the sales tax rate for each of Alabama's sixty-seven counties and 389 municipalities listed in 1 ALABAMA STATE TAX REPORTER ¶¶ 60-120 (2001)). The research team computed Alabama's average sales tax of 8.14% by using these figures listed in the Alabama State Tax Reporter. The average county figure of 1.79% was computed by adding the sales and use tax "general rate" for each of Alabama's sixty-seven counties and then divid-ing that sum by sixty-seven. The average municipal jurisdiction rate of 2.35% was computed by add-ing "sales and use" and "gross receipts" general rates for each of the 389 cities listed in ¶¶ 60-120 and dividing that sum by 389. The average total rate of 8.14% is the sum of Alabama's general sales tax rate of 4%, the average county rate of 2.35%, and the average municipal jurisdiction rate of 1.79%. The average sales tax rate of 8.14% does not measure the complete impact of the sales tax because the averaging process weighs each of the sixty-seven counties and the 389 cities equally (rather than at-tempting to weigh the sales taxes in the averaging process in accordance with their true impact on the sales tax revenues) when calculating those respective averages. It should also be noted that not every town and city imposes a sales tax, in which case only the state and county rates apply. *See* Comp. & app. B, *supra* (using the sales tax rates from the Compilation to document the highest and lowest sales tax rates imposed within the borders of each of Alabama's sixty-seven counties).

47.   *See* ALA. CODE § 11-51-200 (1975) (authorizing the council or other governing body of all incorporated cities and towns within the State of Alabama to provide by ordinance for the levy and assessment of sales taxes paralleled to the state levy of sales taxes, and not requiring a vote of the people for the adoption of a sales tax); ALA. CODE § 40-12-4 (1975) (authorizing the governing body of an Alabama county to levy a sales tax which parallels, except for rate, the sales tax imposed by the state, and leaving to the discretion of the governing body whether to submit the adoption of such a tax to a vote of the qualified electors of the county). *See also* 1 ABA SALES & USE TAX DESKBOOK § 1-132 (D. Michael Young & Gregg D. Barton eds., 2000-2001 ed.) [hereinafter SALES & USE DESKBOOK] (noting that Alabama allows cities and counties to impose additional taxes, even at rates higher than the state's 4% rate, as long as the rules of applicability and exemption are consistent with the state sales and use taxes). Although Alabama's Southeastern neighbors impose a state sales tax rate and allow their counties and municipalities to impose additional rates, several of these states explicitly limit how high these additional rates can climb, which effectively ensures that their total sales tax rates remain lower than Alabama's sales tax rates. For example, three Southeastern states, Georgia, North Carolina, and South Carolina, which rely less heavily on sales taxes, *see supra* note 43 and accompa-nying text, all have significant caps on how high the sales tax rates can be raised locally, which effec-tively limits the total sales tax rate to 6%. *See* 1 SALES & USE DESKBOOK, *supra*, §§ 11-131, 132 (Georgia's 4% sales tax rate cannot be raised beyond 6%); 2 SALES & USE DESKBOOK §§ 34-131, 34-132 (North Carolina's 4% sales tax rate cannot be raised beyond 6%); *id.* §§ 41-131, -132 (South Carolina's 5% rate can only be increased by 1%). The other Southeastern states limit to a far lesser degree the local increases in sales tax rates. *See id.* § 4-132 (discussing Arkansas); *id.* §§ 10-131, -132 (discussing Florida); *id.* §§18-131, -132 (discussing Kentucky); 2 SALES & USE DESKBOOK §§19-131, -132 (discussing Louisiana); *id.* §§ 25-131, -132 (discussing Mississippi); *id.* §§ 43-131, -132 (dis-cussing Tennessee).

48.   Within the City of Arab the sales tax rate reaches 11% (consisting of the general state rate of 4%, the Cullman County rate of 4%, and the Arab city rate of 3%). *See* Comp. & app. B, *supra* note 46; 1 ALABAMA STATE TAX REPORTER, *supra* note 46, at 6113. In the City of Prichard, the sales tax rate reaches 10% (consisting of the general state rate of 4%, the Mobile County rate of 1%, and the Prichard city rate of 5%). In the City of Bibb, the sales tax rate reaches 10% (consisting of the 4% general state rate, the 3% Bibb County rate, and the 3% rate for the City of Bibb). *Id.* at 6112-16. *But*

tremely unfair rules concerning sales tax exemptions result in low-income Alabamians bearing the heaviest burden relative to their available income. Unlike most states, which exempt the purchase of certain necessities, Alabama fully taxes the purchase of clothing, over-the-counter medicines, and even basic food items purchased at the grocery store such as bread and milk.[49]

B. Alabama's Property Tax Structure Fails to Raise Adequate Revenues and Favors the Wealthiest Land Interests

Alabama's minimum property taxes, which are the lowest in the nation,[50] in addition to favoring wealthier Alabamians, leave the state chronically revenue-starved and represent one of the single most important reasons why the state is unable to adequately fund many of its services. The nationwide average of property tax collections per capita imposed at the state, county, municipal, and school district levels, exceeded Ala-

---

see Comp. & app. B, *supra* note 46 (illustrating that parts of Randolph and Washington counties impose sales taxes as low as 4%, the required state sales tax rate).

49.   *See* ALA. CODE §§ 11-54-96, 11-92A-18, 40-9-9 to 40-9-33, 40-23-4, 40-23-5 (1975) (providing exemptions for sales taxes, and not providing such an exemption for food, clothing, and over-the-counter medicine); *see also* Bryce, *supra* note 1, at 567 (noting that the Alabama sales tax applies to food and clothing based on the holding of Boswell v. Gen. Oils, Inc., 368 So. 2d 27 (Ala. Civ. App. 1978)). Among the Southeastern states, Florida, Georgia, Kentucky, Louisiana (beginning July 1, 2002), and North Carolina (which exempts food that can be purchased under the food stamp program from the state, but not local, sales taxes), exempt food from sales tax. *See* FLA. STAT. ANN. ch. 212.08 (2001); GA. CODE ANN. § 48-8-3(57) (2002); KY. REV. STAT. ANN. § 139.485 (Michie 1991); LA. REV. STAT. ANN. § 47:305 (West 2001); N.C. GEN. STAT. § 105-164.13B (2001); *see also* Federation of Tax Administrators, State Sales Tax Rates & Food & Drug Exemption, *at* http://www.taxadmin.org/fta/rate/sales.pdf (last visited Sept. 27, 2002) (as of Jan, 1, 2002, around the nation, twenty-seven states fully exempted food from sales tax). In general, Alabama's sales tax exemptions can be viewed as arbitrary. For example, sales of admission tickets into recreational facilities (such as movie theaters, bowling alleys, amusement parks, athletic contests, skating rinks, race tracks, and any other place of amusement or entertainment) are not exempted from sales tax, *see* ALA. CODE § 40-23-2(2) (1975), but all services other than those listed in ALA. CODE § 40-23-2(2) are nontaxable services. 1 SALES & USE DESKBOOK, *supra* note 47, § 1-428.02. Alabama provides many sales tax exemptions for business-related transactions, on at least some of which it would be fairer to impose a sales tax than it is to impose a sales tax on food. For example, the sale of containers, pallets, crowns, caps, and tops, intended for one-time use only, are exempt. *See id.* § 1-421.06. The sales tax does not apply to the gross proceeds of sales of fuel and supplies for use or consumption aboard ships, vessels, towing vessels or barges, or drilling ships, rigs, or barges using the high seas, intercoastal waterways, or Alabama ports. *See* ALA. CODE § 40-23-4(10) (1975). Sales of real estate are not subject to sales tax in Alabama. *See* 1 SALES & USE DESKBOOK, *supra* note 47, § 1-427. http://www.taxadmin.org/fta/rate/sales.pdf.

50.   *See* SOURCEBOOK, *supra* note 8, at 46; STATE RANKINGS, *supra* note 8, at 284 (indicating that Alabama ranked 50th for property tax revenues, collecting a mere $240 in property taxes per person). Per capita figures are a meaningful way to make revenue comparisons between states because they allow for the elimination of population differences. If one were to just look at the total property tax revenue collected in one state and compare it to the total property tax revenue collected in another state, it would not provide a fair comparison because states with smaller populations would tend to have less revenues, not because the property tax burden is actually less, but because the population is smaller.

bama's per capita property tax collections by more than three times.[51] The top three ranked states in the nation collected over six times more property tax per person than Alabama,[52] and among the Southeastern states, Florida collected almost four times, while Georgia collected almost three times more property taxes per person than Alabama.[53] Mississippi, North Carolina, South Carolina, Tennessee, and Kentucky each collected around twice as much property tax per person as Alabama.[54]

When focusing on the percentage that property taxes contribute to total state government revenues, Alabama's property taxes accounted for as little as five percent of Alabama's total revenue, a percentage that reflects the smallest contribution among the Southeastern states and the nation,[55] nearly three times less than the national average.[56] The contribution made by property tax revenues in the Southeastern states often constituted significantly higher percentages of those states' total revenues than the comparable contribution made by Alabama's property taxes. For example, Georgia's and South Carolina's property taxes contributed more than twice as much to those states' total revenues.[57] Florida's property taxes contrib-

---

51.   See SOURCEBOOK, *supra* note 8, at 46; STATE RANKINGS, *supra* note 8, at 284 (Alabama's $240 of total property taxes collected per capita divided into the national average of $817, equals 3.4).

52.   See SOURCEBOOK, *supra* note 8, at 46 (Alabama's $240 of property taxes collected per capita divided into New Jersey's $1,586 equals 6.6; New Hampshire's $1,549 equals 6.45; and Connecticut's $1,501 equals 6.25); *see also* STATE RANKINGS, *supra* note 8, at 284 (identifying the same top three property tax collecting states with minor variations of a dollar or two in their actual per capita figures).

53.   See SOURCEBOOK, *supra* note 8, at 46 (Alabama's $240 of property taxes collected per capita divided into Florida's $840 equals 3.5; Georgia's $660 equals 2.8); *see also* STATE RANKINGS, *supra* note 8, at 284 (showing only minor variations of a dollar or two in per capita amounts).

54.   See SOURCEBOOK, *supra* note 8, at 46 (Alabama's $240 of property taxes collected per capita divided into Mississippi's $460 equals 1.9; North Carolina's $512 equals 2.1; South Carolina's $553 equals 2.3; Tennessee's $434 equals 1.8; Kentucky's $391 equals 1.6); *see also* STATE RANKINGS, *supra* note 8, at 284. Arkansas ($323) and Louisiana ($330) also collected more property tax per person than Alabama. *Id.*

55.   See STATE RANKINGS, *supra* note 8, at 285 (ranking Alabama 50th, meaning Alabama's state and local property tax revenue, which accounts for 4.9% of state and local government total revenue (which includes all sources of revenue including federal aid) constitutes the smallest in the nation); *see also* SOURCEBOOK, *supra* note 8, at 41, 46 (ranking Alabama 49th in total property tax collections (with New Mexico ranked 50th) with Alabama's total property tax collections accounting for 13% of Alabama's total tax revenues ($1,035,000,000 divided by $7,958,000,000), which does not include other non tax sources such as federal aid).

56.   See STATE RANKINGS, *supra* note 8, at 285 (Alabama's 4.9% of revenues coming from property taxes divided into the national average of 13.6% equals 2.78); *see also* SOURCEBOOK, *supra* note 8, at 41, 46 (Alabama's 13% of tax revenues coming from property taxes ($1,035,000,000 divided by $7,958,000,000) divided into the national average of 30% ($218,827,000,000 divided by $728,594,000,000) equals 2.3); *see also* SLEMROD & BAKIJA, *supra* note 9, at 19 (discussing state and local taxes, and indicating that in 1994 state and local governments relied on property taxes for 25.6% of their revenues).

57.   See STATE RANKINGS, *supra* note 8, at 285 (Alabama's 4.9% of revenues coming from property taxes divided into Georgia's 12.4% equals 2.53; South Carolina's 10.5% equals 2.14); *see also* SOURCEBOOK, *supra* note 8, at 41, 46 (Alabama's 13% of tax revenues coming from property taxes divided into Georgia's 27.2% ($4,946,000,000 divided by $18,171,000,000) equals 2.1; South Carolina's 26.8% ($2,095,000,000 divided by $7,802,000,000) equals 2.1).

uted almost three times more to its revenues.[58] Property tax revenues in Mississippi, North Carolina, and Tennessee contributed almost twice as much to their respective total tax revenues than the comparable contribution made by Alabama's property taxes. Property tax revenues in the remaining Southeastern states, Arkansas, Kentucky and Louisiana, contributed significantly more to their total revenues than Alabama.[59]

The extremely low revenues raised from property taxes are one of the most important reasons why Alabama's state and local taxes as a whole raise woefully inadequate revenues. The comparison of Alabama's total state and local tax revenues with that of other states reveals patterns similar to those found in the property tax revenues comparison. When focusing on total revenues collected from all state and local taxes per person, Alabama collects the lowest revenues in the United States.[60] States collecting tax revenues per person in the range of the national average approached

---

58.   *See* STATE RANKINGS, *supra* note 8, at 285 (Alabama's 4.9% of revenues coming from property taxes divided into Florida's 16.2% equals 3.31); *see also* SOURCEBOOK, *supra* note 8, at 41, 46 (Alabama's 13% of tax revenues coming from property taxes divided into Florida's 34.6% ($12,330,000,000 divided by $35,633,000,000) equals 2.7).

59.   *See* STATE RANKINGS, *supra* note 8, at 285 (Alabama's 4.9% of revenues coming from property taxes divided into: Mississippi's 9.5% equals 1.94; North Carolina's 9.7% equals 1.98; Tennessee's 8.1% equals 1.65; Arkansas' 6.8% equals 1.39; Kentucky's 7.5% equals 1.53; and Louisiana's 6.1% equals 1.24); *see also* SOURCEBOOK, *supra* note 8, at 41, 46 (Alabama's 13% of tax revenues coming from property taxes divided into Mississippi's 23.4% ($1,257,000,000 divided by $5,362,000,000) equals 1.8; North Carolina's 21.5% ($3,807,000,000 divided by $17,741,000,000) equals 1.7; Tennessee's 21.9% ($2,333,000,000 divided by $10,626,000,000) equals 1.7; Arkansas' 15.9% ($816,000,000 divided by $5,120,000,000) equals 1.2; Kentucky's 17.2% ($1,528,000,000 divided by $8,896,000,000) equals 1.3; Louisiana's 14.9% ($1,435,000,000 divided by $9,630,000,000) equals 1.2).

60.   *See* SOURCEBOOK, *supra* note 8, at 41; STATE RANKINGS, *supra* note 8, at 279 (Alabama collected $1841 and $1842, per person, respectively, and was ranked 50th among the states in revenue collected per person). In their argument that Alabama's tax system produces inadequate revenues, especially for education, the Public Affairs Research Council of Alabama states that tax reform should produce more revenues, primarily raised from a reformed property tax structure, and also recognizes that earmarking of funds must be substantially eliminated in order to allow more efficient spending of the funds. *See* PARCA REPORT, *supra* note 1, at 5-10. In their argument that tax reform should offer a revenue neutral plan, the Alabama Policy Institute does not discuss the inequities of, or the extremely low revenues raised by, the property tax structure and states that inefficient government spending and earmarking of funds are the major reason why the state constantly faces budget crises and funding shortages in important services. They also cite to a study claiming that Alabama is a high revenue state relative to the size of its government and that the percentage of income Alabamians pay in taxes has risen. *See* ALABAMA POLICY INSTITUTE, *supra* note 1, at 28-29. Given the highly regressive nature of Alabama's state tax structure and the fact that the burden on low-income Alabamians has continued to increase, it is not surprising that the tax burden of Alabamians as a group has increased. Consequently, an examination of the relative tax burden treating Alabamians at all income levels as one group does not address the argument that upper-income Alabamians are not paying their fair share of Alabama's taxes. Although addressing inefficient spending patterns, especially the pervasive earmarking of funds, must be part of a comprehensive tax reform package, by ignoring the inequities and unacceptably low contribution to the revenue base from property taxes and downplaying Alabama's unacceptably low per capita revenues, the Alabama Policy Institute fails to recognize the importance of adequate revenues to meet the minimum needs of the citizens and the harsh injustices suffered, especially by low-income Alabamians, when these needs are not met.

collecting twice as much per person as Alabama,[61] while the top three states collected even more than two times as much per person than Alabama.[62] Although all of the Southeastern states collect less revenue per person than the national average, these states collected more, and in most cases substantially more, revenue per person than Alabama.[63]

Alabama's inadequate property tax revenues largely result because only a fraction of the property's fair market value is subject to the tax. Owners of real and personal property within Alabama pay property taxes based on the assessed value of the land or property, which represents only a small percentage of the property's fair market value.[64] A property's fair market value is established by the monetary price hypothetically negotiated between a willing buyer and a willing seller, both fully aware of all relevant facts and circumstances while seeking to maximize their economic self interests.[65] Alabama law explicitly requires that the hypothetical price take into account any willing buyer, including willing buyers interested in changing the use of the property to maximize the property's development potential.[66]

The Alabama Constitution divides property into four classes and each class calculates the property's assessed value at a different percentage.[67] Class I, which assesses property at thirty percent of fair market value, the highest assessment ratio of the four classes, consists of all property of utilities used in the business of the utility. Property owned by Alabama Power would fall within this classification.[68] Class II, which assesses property at twenty percent of fair market value, consists of all real and

---

61.   *See* SOURCEBOOK, *supra* note 8, at 41; STATE RANKINGS, *supra* note 8, at 279 (Alabama's total tax revenues collected per capita of $1841.50 (averaging the dollar difference between the two sources) divided into the national average per capita total tax revenues per person of $2721 equals 1.48).

62.   *See* SOURCEBOOK, *supra* note 8, at 41 (Alabama's $1841 per capita total tax revenues divided into Connecticut's $4205 equals 2.28; New York's $4159 equals 2.26; Alaska's $3953 equals 2.15); *see also* STATE RANKINGS, *supra* note 8, at 279 (showing minor variations in the per capita figures by a dollar or two).

63.   *See* SOURCEBOOK, *supra* note 8, at 41 (compare Alabama's $1841 per capita total tax revenues to: Georgia's $2426; Florida's $2428; North Carolina's $2387; Kentucky's $2275; Louisiana's $2212; South Carolina's $2060; Arkansas' $2029; Tennessee's $1978; and Mississippi's $1963); *see also* STATE RANKINGS, *supra* note 8, at 279 (showing minor variations by a dollar or two in the per capita amounts).

64.   ALA. CONST. amend. 373 (1978) (amending ALA. CONST. § 217).

65.   Robert Reilly, *Property Tax Valuation Service,* THE CPA JOURNAL ONLINE, May 1989, *available at* http://www.nysscpa.org/cpajournal/old/070505278.htm.

66.   ALA. CODE § 40-1-1(12) (1998). The requirement that the willing buyer standard take into account the price a willing developer will pay tends to increase the property's appraised fair market value.

67.   ALA. CONST. amend. 373 (1978) (amending ALA. CONST. § 217); *see also supra* text accompanying note 4 (four classes of property and their assessment ratios explicitly required by the constitution making a constitutional amendment necessary to alter the assessment ratios for the property tax); PARCA REPORT, *supra* note 1, at 10; Chaney, *supra* note 1, at 239-240.

68.   ALA. CONST. amend. 373 (1978) (amending ALA. CONST. § 217).

personal property that does not fit in the definitions for Classes I, III, or IV.[69] Class II includes most commercial and industrial property, including ordinary businesses such as restaurants and malls, as well as factories.[70] Class III, which assesses property at ten percent of fair market value, the lowest assessment ratio of the four classes, covers timber acres, other agricultural property, single-family owner-occupied residential property, as well as historic buildings and sites.[71] Class IV, which assesses property at fifteen percent of fair market value, contains all private passenger automobiles and motor trucks owned and operated by an individual for personal or private use.[72]

In addition to having the lowest assessment ratio of all the classes of property, Class III property enjoys additional opportunities to further reduce the portion of the property's value subject to the tax.[73] As required by the Alabama Constitution, the Alabama Code allows owners of Class III property to elect an alternate method of appraising the property's fair market value that abandons the price that any willing buyer will pay, and instead values the property according to its current use, reducing the assessed value to a smaller figure than what a fair market value appraisal would provide.[74] The alternate method of valuing Class III property in accordance with its current use does serve legitimate policy goals. The current use election of valuation protects owners of Class III property from unreasonably high property taxes that would result if property values were artificially inflated by prospective developers.[75] For example, if a homeowner elects current use status, the value of the house and lot must

---

69.   *Id.*

70.   *See id.* Alabama has no specific definition of business property, but all taxable property of a business would be Class II property.

71.   *Id.* Apartments are excluded from Class III, which causes them to be included into Class II by default.

72.   *Id.* Class IV excludes automobiles and trucks for hire, causing them to fall within Class II by default.

73.   ALA. CODE § 40-7-25.1(a) (1975).

74.   *See id.* (providing that the alternate method of valuing Class III property will not appraise the property at its true fair market value, but will base valuation on the "use being made of that property on October 1 of any taxable year; provided, that no consideration shall be taken of the prospective value such property might have if it were put to some other possible use"); *see also* L. Louis Hyman, *Current Use Taxes in Alabama*, ALABAMA'S TREASURED FORESTS, Spring 1996, at 12-13, *available at* http://www.members.aol.com/jostnix/curntuse.htm. Although the Alabama Constitution requires that the legislature establish criteria and procedures for current use valuation of eligible Class III property, the details of the current use formula are left to the discretion of the legislature, presumably allowing the legislature to alter the current use formula without going through the constitutional amendment procedure. ALA. CONST. amend. 373 (1978) (amending ALA. CONST. § 217).

75.   *See* Mike Kilgore, *Tax Reform or Tax Increase?*, NEIGHBORS, Aug. 2001, at 16-18, *available at* http://www.AlfaFarmers.org/page.cfm?view=119&docID=2587; *see also* Steve Nix, *Current Use Values Reassessed for Forestland*, ALABAMA'S TREASURED FORESTS, Winter 2001, at 20; Hyman, *supra* note 74, at 12-13 (stating that most property taxes are figured using the market value of the property and that one major difference in Alabama is that timber is only taxed on the bare value of the land rather than the market value).

reflect only what a willing buyer will pay for the house to be used as a house and cannot reflect a higher price a willing developer would offer to convert the house to commercial use.[76]

In order to preserve Alabama's forests and agricultural property, the Alabama Code also allows owners of timber acres and agricultural property to elect the alternative method of valuation based on the property's current use.[77] Unlike the current use valuation procedure for personal residences and historic sites, the current use valuation procedure for timber acres and agricultural property is designed to consider productivity factors only, and does not examine what a willing buyer would pay to purchase the land.[78] The actual valuation formula characterizes the acres of timber acres as "good," "average," "poor," or "nonproductive," based on which of ten different soil groups set by the U.S. Soil Conservation Services the property best fits into.[79] The character of the soil assigned to the property,

---

76.   ALA CODE § 40-7-25.1(d)(3) (1998) (providing that residential property and historic buildings and sites electing current use are valued according to what the willing buyer would pay for a residence or a historic building without any reference to the property's productivity).

77.   ALA. CODE § 40-7-25.1(b) (1998) (identifying forestlands and agricultural property as eligible to elect current use valuation and providing separate formulas for each). Moreover, the intent of the legislature in enacting the Current Use Act was to preserve Alabama's "agricultural and forest property . . . through [Alabama's] property tax structure . . . by providing additional preferential tax treatment for such property." Weissinger v. White, 733 F.2d 802, 806 (11th Cir. 1984).

78.   See ALA. CODE § 40-7-25.1(d)(2) (1998) (providing details concerning the current use valuation formula for timber property); see also supra note 77. The procedure for valuing agricultural property under its current use formula broadly resembles the current use valuation procedure applicable to timber property. ALA. CODE § 40-7-25.1(d)(1), (2) (1998). Like owners of timber property, owners of agricultural property must elect current use valuation and submit evidence to the property tax assessor identifying to which of the ten soil groups the agricultural property belongs. Id. The soil groups for identifying agricultural property are the same as the soil groups identifying timber property. Id. In order to determine "the current use standard value" for agricultural property, every year the Department of Revenue identifies the three crops that produced the most harvest on a per acre basis. Id. § 40-7-25.1(d)(1)(a). The Department of Revenue must also determine the "seasonal average price" of these top three crops for each of the most recent 10 years. Id. § 40-7-25.1(d)(1). The Department of Revenue must then multiply the total production in the entire state during the current year for each of these top three crops by the "seasonal average price" for each of the ten years and then divide by "acreage harvested for each crop for each year." ALA. CODE § 40-7-25.1(d)(1) (1998). This formula reveals the gross return for each of the 10 years for each of the current year's top three crops. Id. The net return is determined by subtracting production expenses from each of these gross returns. Id. § 40-7-25.1(d)(1)(c). The net returns for each of the ten years for each of the current top three crops are then converted into a figure estimating the total yielding income flow per acre, which is then divided by an interest rate factor, detailed in the statute, which resembles the procedure applicable to timber property. Id. § 40-7-25.1(d)(1)(d)-(e). This figure represents the statewide value per acre applicable to all owners of agricultural property. Id. § 40-7-25.1(d)(1). In order to calculate the "current use standard values per acre" the individual owner of agricultural property with a soil rate of "good" must increase the statewide value by 20%. ALA. CODE § 40-7-25.1(d)(1) (1998). Owners of agriculture with soil rates of "poor" or "unproductive" are allowed to decrease the statewide value by 30% and 75% respectively. Id. The "current use standard values per acre" are equal to the statewide values per acre for owners with "average" soil ratings. Id. Finally, the owner of agricultural property multiplies their "current use standard value[s] per acre" by the number of acres they actually own. Id. Because agricultural property is Class III property, only 10% of this total is assessed for property tax purposes. ALA. CONST. amend. 373(a)-(b); see also ALA. CODE § 40-7-25.1(c) (1998) (detailing the ten soil groups used for rating productivity for both timber and agriculture).

79.   See   National   Timber   Tax   Web   site,   at

along with other parts of the formula designed to roughly consider productivity factors, determines the appraised value of the land.[80]

As Class III property, only ten percent of the appraised value under the current use formula becomes the assessed value subject to the property tax according to the applicable millage rates. For the 1999-2000 fiscal year, the assessed value of timberland rated "good" equaled fifty-three dollars an acre, the assessed value of timberland rated "average" equaled forty dollars an acre, the assessed value of timberland rated "poor" equaled twenty-nine dollars an acre, and the assessed value of timberland rated "nonproductive" equaled twenty-three dollars an acre. When applying the millage rate, which equals just over one half of one percent, im-

---

http://www.timbertax.org/state_laws/states/protax/Alabama.asp?id=statelaws+topic=protax   (last visited Sept. 27, 2002). There are ten different soil groups ranging in productivity rating from good, average, poor, to nonproductive. For a complete description of the soil groups, see ALA. CODE § 40-7-25.1(c) (1998). The assessor is responsible for determining which of the ten different soil groups best characterizes the acres of forestlands being valued. *Id.*; *see also* Nix, *supra* note 75, at 20.

80.   ALA. CODE § 40-7-25.1(d)(2) (1998). Every year using Timber Mart South reports, the Alabama Forestry Commission determines the average pulpwood price per cord. The average pulpwood price per cord takes into account the weighted averages of pulpwood prices of both pine and hardwood. This process is designed to calculate an average price per cord for all property owners actually harvesting and selling their timber received for a cord of wood during the particular year. A cord is the basic unit for estimating pulpwood in trees. *See* Charles A. Blinn & Thomas E. Burk, *Sampling and Measuring Timber in the Private Woodland*, at www.extension.umn.edu/distribution/naturalresources/components/DD3025-06.html (last visited Sept. 27, 2002). It is the equivalent of a stack of wood eight feet long, four feet high, and four feet wide (128 cubic feet). *Id.* Thus, the average pulpwood price per cord will change every year. The tax assessor determines the productivity rating of each property owner's forestland based on which of ten possible soil groups the property fits into. Each owner of forestland acres is assigned a productivity class value of "good," "average," "poor," or "nonproductive" based on which of these ten soil groups the property fits into. The productivity class tells the owner of forestlands their annual yield per acre in cords, "Good," 1.38 cords per acre; "Average," 1.05 cords per acre; "Poor," .75 cords per acre; and "Nonproductive," .6 cords per acre. The tax assessor then multiplies the property owner's assigned productivity class by the average pulpwood price per cord and then subtracts out the expense ratio (fixed by law at 15% of annual income from timber sales), which results for that particular owner of forestland their imputed net income per acre. National Timber Tax Web site, *at* http://www.timbertax.org/state_laws/states/protax/Alabama.asp?id=statelaws&topic=protax   (last visited Sept. 27, 2002). The imputed net income per acre is then divided by an interest rate factor set by law. *Id.* This interest rate factor is "the average of the annual effective interest rates charged on new Federal Land Bank loans by the New Orleans District Federal Land Bank for the 10 most recent calendar years since 1973" minus "the lesser of 4.5% or the difference between such [average interest] rate and 2%." *Id.* This formula provides all owners of forestland with a "current use standard value" for each of the four productivity ratings. *Id.* Each property owner of forestland must then multiply their particular "current use standard value" by the total number of acres of timber they own within each productivity class to determine the current use value of the property subject to the 10% assessment ratio for Class III property. *Id.*; *see also* ALA. CODE § 50-7-25.1 (1998).

Using the above formula, the current use values for the 2000 tax year for the four productivity classes of timberland property were as follows:

Categories of Timberland	2000 Current Use Values
Good Timberland:	$529 per acre
Average Timberland:	$403 per acre
Poor Timberland:	$288 per acre
Nonproductive Timberland:	$230 per acre.

Nix, *supra* note 75, at 20. *See* National Timber Tax Web site *at* www.timbertax.org/state_laws (last visited Sept. 27, 2002).

Although Alabama property owners, overall, pay the lowest property taxes in the nation, certain property owners in Alabama disproportionately pay even lower property taxes relative to other property owners in Alabama. Among the four classes of property, great percentage disparities exist when comparing the amount of property taxes assessed to that class.[90] Class II, with commercial property as the most important example, was

---

bama's state millage rate of 6.5 mills, the average county rate of 12.99 mills, the average school district rate of 12.05 mills, and the average municipality rate of 8.80 mills. *See* Comp. & app. D, *supra* (providing property tax millage rates imposed by the school districts supporting each of Alabama's 128 school systems).

90. *See infra* app. C, Property Tax Revenues Assessed by Classes of Property and Total Landmass and Total Timber Landmass for the State of Alabama for Each County, and underlying compilation of data on file with author [hereinafter Comp. & app. C] (including a separate assessment for Class III Property (timber acres and agricultural property) electing to be valued according to the current use formula, focusing on productivity in each of Alabama's sixty-seven counties at the state, county, municipal, and school district levels, and documenting for each of Alabama's sixty-seven counties the property tax assessments for each of Alabama's classes of property). All footnotes providing numerical documentation for the property tax revenue contributions made by Alabama's four classes of property are supported by this compilation. The total property taxes collected at the state, county, municipal, and school district levels, as reported by the Alabama Department of Revenue for the 1999-2000 fiscal year, while providing revenue figures collected by each county, fails to further break down the relative revenue contributions made by each of Alabama's four classes of property. In order to determine the proportional contributions made by each of Alabama's four classes of property, the research team, using figures obtained from the Alabama Revenue Department, Property Tax Division (which provided separate categories for each of Alabama's four classes of property, including a separate category within Class III for current use property valued with respect to productivity (forestland and agricultural property) and other Class III property (personal residences and historic sites)), first assembled the property tax assessments made at the state, county, municipal, and school district levels. The research team then, for each of Alabama's sixty-seven counties, applied the applicable millage rates, at the state, county, municipal, and school district levels, to each class of property in order to determine the property tax assessed to each of the four classes of property. Because this process of calculating the property taxes assessed did not factor in any exemptions enjoyed by property owners or assessments of property tax not collected, the property tax assessed using this process will show a greater figure for property taxes assessed than was reported as being collected by the Alabama Department of Revenue for the 1999-2000 fiscal year. For example, this Compilation computes total property taxes assessed by each of the sixty-seven counties at the state level (applying the state's 6.5 millage rate), to each of the state's four classes of property, to be $245,203,485, while the Alabama Department of Revenue reports total property tax collected at the state level to be $191,852,437. *See supra* note 9. This Compilation also computes total property taxes assessed by each of the sixty-seven counties at the county, municipality, and school district levels at $1,236,778,401, while the Alabama Department of Revenue reports the total property taxes collected at these three levels to be $1,226,634,616. *See supra* note 9. Finally, this Compilation computes total property taxes assessed at the state, county, municipality, and school district levels to be $1,481,981,886, while the Alabama Department of Revenue reported a total property tax collection at $1,418,487,053. *See supra* note 9 (documenting revenue figures reported by the Alabama Department of Revenue for the 1999-2000 fiscal year). Although the property taxes assessed under the process the research team used to create this Compilation do not perfectly match the property taxes reported as collected by the Alabama Department of Revenue, this Compilation provides compelling evidence that allows for meaningful comparisons between the proportional shares of the total property tax revenues being contributed by each of the four classes of property. Because no evidence exists that any one of the four classes of property disproportionately claims exemptions beyond what the law legally allows, or disproportionately has lower or higher collection ratios, the property taxes assessed to each of the classes of property shed meaningful light on the relative proportional burdens each class carries for the property tax and the effect this burden has on the ability of a particular area to fund services at the county, municipal, and school district levels.

assessed at approximately fifty-six percent, providing the greatest share of Alabama's total property tax revenues. The property in Class III that is not valued by the current use productivity formula, residential homes being the most important example, was assessed approximately at twenty-nine percent, a significant share of Alabama's total property taxes. Of the remaining classes of property, Class I, consisting of public utilities, and Class IV, consisting only of motor vehicles, were assessed approximately at nine and four percent, respectively, representing minority, but not insignificant, shares of Alabama's total property taxes.[91]

However, timber acres and agriculture, the property within Class III that can use a current use formula that roughly considers productivity factors, was assessed as the smallest portion by far, less than two percent, of Alabama's total property taxes.[92] This extremely low percentage is starkly illustrated from another perspective by computing the average property tax assessed per acre for timber acres, which equals less than one dollar per acre,[93] considerably less than comparable timber acres in neighboring Georgia and Mississippi.[94] Moreover, timber acres represent a highly visi-

---

91. See Comp. & app. C, *supra* note 90.

92. See *id*. When evaluating the shares of the property tax borne by timber acres, this Article assumes that the overwhelming majority of eligible owners of timberland elect current use valuation. See L. Louis Hyman, *Current Use Taxes in Alabama, reprinted in Alabama's Treasured Forests*, Spring 1996, at 12-13 (indicating the average current use value of Alabama timber is lower than the average fair market value based on what a willing buyer would pay to use the property as forestland). Because a reasonable timber owner would only switch back to a fair market valuation if this standard produced a lower assessed value, and given the extremely low assessed property taxes for all "current use" Class III property when compared to "other" Class III property, any timber property not electing current use would contribute a very insignificant portion of the assessed revenues of "other" Class III property. Moreover, when evaluating the shares of the property tax borne by owners of timber property, this Article generously estimates their contribution because the assessment of property tax for current use property includes property taxes borne by owners of agricultural property electing current use status. However, because Alabama's landmass data only identifies timber acres, rendering it impossible to determine how much of Alabama's land can be classified as agriculture, and because the Property Tax Division of Alabama Revenue Department does not distinguish between assessments made for timber and agriculture electing current use, but treats the two combined as one assessment for current use property, it is not possible to separate the revenue contributions made by timber and agricultural property valued according to current use formulas. In order to avoid underestimating the proportional contributions to property tax revenues made by the owners of timber property, this Article treats timber as contributing the entire share of property tax assessed to Class III current use property, which includes the share of property tax contributed by agriculture. See also *id*. (showing forestry industry estimates that timber paid an average property tax of eighty-three cents an acre).

93. See Comp. & app. C, *supra* note 90. The estimate of the average property tax per acre borne by timber is generous because it factors in the share borne by agriculture. See *supra* note 92. For a number of reasons, including technical variations related to the current use productivity formula, as well as different millage rates applied at the county, municipal, and school district levels within each of the sixty-seven counties, the average property tax contributed per acre by timberland varies, sometimes significantly, from the statewide average of $.96. See Comp. & app. C, *supra* note 90; *see also supra* notes 77-81 and accompanying text (discussing how the process of valuing forestland for the productivity factor varies based on soil type which determines whether the wood is deemed good, average, poor, or non-productive); *supra* notes 87-89; Comp. & app. D, *supra* note 89 (discussing variations in millage rates).

94. Although Alabama's neighbor, Georgia, has a wood composition, *see* Georgia State Inven-

ble feature of the landmass in every county across Alabama. Timber acres account for approximately seventy-one percent of the total landmass of Alabama's real property.[95]

tory, at http://www.srsfia.1.fia.sus.fs.fed.us (on file with author) (showing that Georgia's timberland produces approximately 44.7% pine, 15% oak, 38% bottomland, and 2.3% non typed), similar to Alabama's, *see* Alabama State Inventory, *at* http://www.srsfia.1.fia.sus.fs.fed.us (on file with author) (showing that Alabama's timberland produces approximately 34% pine, 55.5% oak, 10% bottomland timber, and 0.5% non typed), and uses a current use formula strongly resembling Alabama's, Georgia assessment ratio is substantially higher. *See* GA. CODE ANN. § 48-5-7, -269 (2002) (showing that Georgia assesses the value of timberland for property tax purposes at 40% of its current use value, uses an income capitalization that looks at the land's net income before property taxes, and applies a capitalization rate based on interest rates factor); *see also* DAVID NEWMAN, ET AL., TAX POLICY AND SUSTAINABLE FORESTRY IN GEORGIA (indicating that timber in Georgia pays an average property tax of approximately $4 an acre) (PowerPoint presentation on file with the author); Joe Sumners, *The Case for a New Alabama Constitution*, AUBURN UNIVERSITY NEWS, Feb. 12, 1996, at 2 (demonstrating that contiguous timber property over the Georgia and Alabama lines shows Georgia timber paying almost six times more per acre in property tax than the Alabama timber); Chaney, *supra* note 1, at 248 (discussing property taxes paid by contiguous timber property in Cleburne County, Alabama, and Haralson County, Georgia, and showing that Georgia's timber property pays nearly four times as much per acre). Similarly, Mississippi has a wood composition like Alabama's, *see* Mississippi State Inventory, *at* http://www.srsfia.1.fia.sus.fs.fed.us (on file with author), and also uses a current use formula like Alabama's, *see* National Timber Tax Web site, State Laws, The Treatment of Timber Income and Expenses for Each State, *at* http://www.timbertax.org/state_laws/state_laws.asp?id=statelaws (last visited Sept. 29, 2002) (providing information on each state's property tax structure), but Mississippi's assessment ratio is higher. MISS. CONST. art. 4, § 112 (1998); MISS. CODE ANN. § 27-35-50 (1998) (showing Mississippi, like Alabama, divides property into three classes, but assesses timber property at 15% and uses a current use value that looks at the soil types and the net income of the land along with a capitalization factor); *see also* Editorial, *Blessed are the Privileged*, MOBILE REG., Oct. 17, 2000, at 6A (demonstrating contiguous timber property over the Mississippi and Alabama lines shows Mississippi timber paying 2.5 times more per acre in property tax than the Alabama timber).

95.   Different sources list slightly different figures for both total landmass and total forestland. For 1997, the National Resources Inventory conducted by the Department of Agriculture's Natural Resources Conservation Service showed 21.261 million acres of forestland, 33.4238 million acres of total surface area, 12.2232 million acres of water areas, 32.2006 million acres of total land area (representing total water area subtracted from total surface area), and 28.9504 million acres of rural land in the state. U.S. DEP'T OF AGRIC., NATURAL RESOURCES CONSERVATION SERV., SUMMARY REPORT, 1997 NATIONAL RESOURCES INVENTORY, tbls. 2 & 3 (1999, revised Dec. 2000), *available at* http://www.nrcs.usda.gov/technical/NRI/1997/summary_report (on file with the author). Using these figures, forestland accounts for 63.61% of Alabama's total surface area (21.261 divided by 33.4238 equals .6361), 66.02% of total land area (21.261 divided by 32.2006 equals .6602), and 73.44% of total rural land (21.261 divided by 28.9504 equals .7344). However, more recent statistics from the U.S. Forest Service indicate that forestland makes up an even greater percentage of the state's landmass. For 2001, these statistics list 22.9905 million acres of forestland, and 32.4802 million acres of total land area in the state. *See* Andrew J. Hartsell & Mark J. Brown, *Forest Statistics for Alabama, 2000*, USDA SOUTHERN RESOURCE STATION RESOURCE BULLETIN SRS-67, 19 tbl. 1, (2002) (on file with author). These figures demonstrate that forestland accounts for 70.78% of Alabama's landmass (22.9905 divided by 32.4802 equals .7078). *See also* Comp. & app. C, *supra* note 90 (showing timber acres and total landmass for the state and each of its counties and regions and listing timber acres by private, industry, or government ownership).

Two of Alabama's closest neighbors, Georgia and Mississippi, also have substantial concentrations of forestland within their landmasses, with timber constituting well over half of the total land area in those states. *See* U.S. DEP'T OF AGRIC., NATURAL RESOURCES CONSERVATION SERV., SUMMARY REPORT, 1997 NATIONAL RESOURCES INVENTORY, tbls. 2 & 3 (1999, revised Dec. 2000), *available at* http://www.nrcs.usda.gov/technical/NRI/1997/summary_report (showing that for 1997 Georgia had 21.5598 million acres of forestland, which represented 57.13% of its 37.7405 million acres in total surface area, 58.70% of its 36.7288 million acres in total land area (surface area minus

The massive presence of timber acres significantly enhances Alabama's economy in most counties across Alabama. Nationally, Alabama ranks among the top states in forestry and logging,[96] forestry support,[97] and woods products industries,[98] causing some industry experts to charac-

---

1.0117 million acres of water areas), and 70.35% of its 30.6475 million acres in total rural land; and showing that for 1997 Mississippi had 16.2088 million acres of forestland, which represented 53.10% of its 30.5273 million acres in total surface area, 54.63% of its 29.6723 million acres of total land area (surface area minus 0.855 million acres of water areas), and 61.33% of its 26.4286 million acres of total rural land).

96.   The forestry and logging industry (NAICS code 113) involves the actual growing, harvesting, and selling of wood. *See infra* app. E, Statistics Illustrating the Impact of Timber on Alabama's Economy and Depicting Business and Forest Activity in Alabama Counties, and underlying compilation of data on file with author [hereinafter Comp. & app. E]. According to the Census Department's statistics for the year 2000, Alabama ranked second among all states in the number of forestry and logging establishments in operation (Oregon ranks first), and ranked third in both the number of forestry and logging employees (Oregon ranks first and Washington ranks second) and total payroll for these employees (Washington ranks first and Oregon ranks second). *Id*. More comprehensive data from the 1997 economic census show that the Alabama logging industry (NAICS code 113310—a subset of code 113, "forestry and logging") consisted of 1048 establishments (of these, 45 had 20 or more employees), employed 7109 people, paid $145,407,000 in payroll, provided $437,946,000 of value added by manufacturing, and enjoyed a total value of shipments of $913,593,000. *Id*. For 2000, the Bureau of Economic Analysis reported $88,491,000 in private earnings from forestry for Alabama (ranking Alabama fifth in the United States behind Oregon, Washington, California, and Georgia, respectively). *Id*. Finally, the 2000 statistics from the Alabama Agricultural Service showed total cash receipts of $877,722,000 for forestry in Alabama, equaling 19.1% of all cash receipts from agriculture and forestry in Alabama and the second highest total receipts for any single commodity (after broilers). *See id*.

97.   Forestry support activities (NAICS code 1153) involve merchants dealing in goods and services needed by those engaged in forestry and logging. *See* Comp. & app. E, *supra* note 96. For the year 2000, the Census Department's statistics (NAICS code 1153) ranked Alabama second in total annual payroll for forestry support (Oregon was first), fifth in the number of forestry support establishments (behind Oregon, Washington, Georgia, and California, respectively), and among the top six in the number of forestry support employees (totals for some states are reported as ranges, making it impossible to get a precise ranking for forestry support employment; the other states in the top six are Oregon, Georgia, Washington, Arkansas, and New York, respectively). *See id*.

98.   For purposes of this Article, the wood products industries include wood product manufacturing (NAICS code 321), paper manufacturing (NAICS code 322), and furniture and related product manufacturing (NAICS code 337). This list of wood product industries closely corresponds to that used in KAREN LEE ABT ET AL., SOCIO-5: LOCAL ECONOMIC IMPACTS OF FORESTS, in U.S. FOREST SERV., SOUTHERN RESEARCH STATION, SOUTHERN FOREST RESOURCE ASSESSMENT, DRAFT REPORT at 5.3 (Nov. 2001), *available at* http://www.srs.fs.fed.us/sustain/report/index.htm (on file with author) (defining the "wood products sector" using SIC codes 24 ("lumber and wood products"), 25 ("furniture"), and 26 ("pulp and paper")). While the Forest Service report uses SIC (Standard Industrial Classification) codes to define these industries, the census department has moved to the newer NAICS (North American Industrial Classification System) codes for its current statistics. This Article uses those NAICS codes that most closely correspond to the SIC codes chosen by the Forest Service to represent the wood products industries (excluding logging, which is reported separately). *See also* John Bliss & Ken Muehlenfeld, *Timber and the Economy of Alabama*, ALA. COOPERATIVE EXTENSION SYS. PUBLICATION NO. ANR-602 at tbl. 6 (June 1995), *available at* http://www.aces.edu/department/extcomm/publications/anr/anr-602/anr-602.html (relying on the same SIC codes to define the "forest products sectors" of the economy).

Under the Census Department's 2000 statistics, Alabama ranks eighth in the number of employees, ninth in annual payroll, and seventeenth in the number of establishments for wood products manufacturing (NAICS code 321). *See infra* Comp. & app. E, *supra* note 96. In paper manufacturing (NAICS code 322), Alabama ranks fourteenth in the number of employees, ninth in total annual payroll, and twenty-third in the number of establishments. *Id*. In furniture manufacturing, Alabama ranks

terize Alabama's timber industry profits as "Alabama's #1 industry" and "the backbone of the state economy."[99] In addition to generating substantial profits for traditional timber industry firms, Alabama's timber acres also generate significant profits for farmers and other private landowners throughout the state.[100] A legitimate tax structure that apportions the burden of property taxes in a fair manner between timber acres and other types of property necessitates a balancing of several competing and complex factors. Nevertheless, given the overwhelming dominance of timber acres over both Alabama's landmass and economy, a proportional share of less than two percent of property taxes assessed, averaging less than one dollar per acre, is *de minimis* and fails to even approach representing a fair share of Alabama's total property taxes.[101]

---

fifteenth in number of employees, seventeenth in total annual payroll, and nineteenth in number of establishments. *Id.* According to data from the 1997 economic census, these industries in combination accounted for 19.2% of Alabama's manufacturing establishments, 17.9% of manufacturing shipments, 17.0% of manufacturing employees, and 18.7% of total payroll for manufacturing. *See id.* For 2000, the Bureau of Economic Analysis reported private earnings in Alabama from the wood products industries totaling $2,684,740,000, which represented 19.5% of total Alabama earnings from manufacturing in 2000. *See id.*

99.   Alabama Forestry Association, *Alabama Forestry Facts*, at www.alaforestry.org/facts.htm (last visited Sept. 29, 2002) (citing facts on the forestry industry's impact on Alabama's economy); John Bliss & Ken Muehlenfeld, *Timber and the Economy of Alabama*, ALA. COOPERATIVE EXTENSION SYS. PUBLICATION NO. ANR-602, at 1 (1995), *available at* http://www.aces.edu/department/extcomm/publications/anr/anr-602/anr-602.html. The large number of timber acres in Georgia and Mississippi contributes substantially to those states' gross products and profits. *See* America's Forest & Paper People, *Why the Forest & Paper Industry is Important to Georgia*, at www.afandpa.org/pdfs/gaw.PDF (last visited Sept. 29, 2002); America's Forest & Paper People, *Why the Forest & Paper Industry is Important to Mississippi*, at www.afandpa.org/pdfs/msw.PDF (last visited Sept. 29, 2002).

100.   Statistics on farm marketing for 2000 from the Alabama Agricultural Statistics Service show that farmers and other private non-industry landowners generate two-thirds ($585,302,000, representing the total of receipts for "farm forest products" and "private, non-farm timber") of the cash receipts for forestry in the state ($877,732,000), while the traditional forest industry accounts for less that 30% ($254,172,000) of this total. *See* Comp. & app. E, *supra* note 96 (defining cash receipts and the various ownership classes and tabulating statistics on cash receipts). Since the forest industry owns just 16% of Alabama's timberland, the industry obviously averages higher cash receipts per acre than other private landowners. *See* Comp. & app. C, *supra* note 90 (providing statistics on timberland ownership for the state, its regions, and individual counties). Nonetheless, the sheer volume of cash receipts flowing to non-industry owners conclusively demonstrates that forestland generates significant income across all ownership classes. *See id.*; Comp. & app. E, *supra* note 96 (showing cash receipts for each of Alabama's counties).

101.   A proportionate share that equals less than 2% of the property taxes, averaging less than $1.00 per acre, is per se a grossly inadequate share and is therefore unfair to all other taxpayers who do not own timber property under the principle of *res ipsa loquitur*, meaning "the thing speaks for itself." *Res ipsa loquitur* is a commonly understood doctrine of tort law that can appropriately be used by analogy here, where the nature of the plaintiff's injury and the immediate events surrounding the injury can by itself show that the defendant was negligent. *See* RESTATEMENT (SECOND) OF TORTS § 328(d) & cmt. (American Law Institute Publishers 1965); PROSSER & KEETON ON THE LAW OF TORTS 243 (W. Page Keeton et al. eds., 5th ed., West Publishing Co. 1984); DAN B. DOBBS, THE LAW OF TORTS 370 (West Group 2000).

A determination of precisely the proportionate share of property taxes timber acres should bear, and the technical changes to the law that would best accomplish that result, are beyond the scope of this Article. *See infra* notes 173-75 and accompanying text (discussing the complexities of designing a fair

C. Inadequate Tax Revenues for Public Schools
Deny Children From Low-Income Families Minimum
Opportunities to Achieve an Adequate Education

Although an unsound tax structure that raises inadequate revenues will negatively affect many vital services, this Article focuses on the funding of primary and secondary public education. An adequately funded public school system is arguably the most critical state and local function for ensuring that Alabama's children, the most powerless and voiceless segment of the population, enjoy a minimum opportunity to achieve an adequate education and improve their lives.[102] Although inadequate funding of pub-

---

property tax structure using the tools of vertical and horizontal equity); *infra* notes 272-73 and accompanying text (discussing general factors that should be considered when designing a fair property tax structure for all property owners and determining the proportion that should be borne by timber acres). Although this Article expresses no opinion of whether owners of timber acres in Georgia are paying their fair share of Georgia's property taxes, Georgia's property tax structure requires owners of Georgia timber acres to pay, on average, at least four times more in property taxes than owners of Alabama timber acres, and could serve as a starting point for the analysis. *See supra* note 94 (discussing Georgia's property taxes that apply to timber).

102.   While some may argue that Alabama students' average score of 56 on the Stanford Achievement Test (SAT), compared to a national average of 50, (*See* Comp. and app. D, *supra* note 89), independently indicates that the state provides an adequate education, this Article maintains that inadequate funding materially compromises the ability of individual students, particularly students from low-income families, to achieve an adequate education. Standardized tests are designed to determine the knowledge or skill levels of individual students and may not legitimately measure the quality of schools   or   school   systems.   W.   James Popham, *Why Standardized Tests Don't Measure Educational Quality*, EDUCATIONAL LEADERSHIP, Mar. 1999, at 10 (describing such attempts as "measuring temperature with a tablespoon"). Furthermore, the success of Alabama students on the SAT is not matched on other measures of student performance, for example the NAEP (National Assessment of Educational Progress), which at least some educators argue is a better measure of performance than the SAT. Alabama students consistently score below the national average in all subjects on the NAEP, a set of tests given to a sample of third and sixth graders across the country. *See* U.S. Dep't of Educ., Nat'l Ctr. for Educ. Statistics, *The Nation's Report Card: State Mathematics 2000, the Nation's Report Card for Alabama, available at* http://nces.ed.gov/nationsreportcard/states/profile.asp?state=. Indeed, on the latest NAEP math exam for which results are available, only one state—Mississippi—had an average score statistically lower than Alabama's. *See* U.S. Dep't of Educ., Nat'l Ctr. for Educ. Statistics, *The Nation's Report Card: State Mathematics 2000, The Nation's Report Card for Alabama*, No. NCES 2001-519 AL, at 17 fig. 2A (2001), *available at* http://nces.ed.gov/nationsreportcard/pdf/stt2000/2001519AL.pdf (showing that thirteen states had scores statistically equivalent to Alabama's and nine states either did not participate in the assessment or did not meet the guidelines for reporting).

Another reason to reject the state's average SAT score as an indication of educational adequacy is that this average camouflages substantial disparities between the scores of individual students, schools, and school systems. Statistics show that students who receive free or reduced price lunches (a nationally recognized poverty indicator) scored substantially lower on the SAT exam than other students. *See* Joseph Morton, Ala. Dep't of Educ., Stanford Achievement Test: 2001 (Apr. 9, 2002) (unpublished report provided by Dr. Joseph Morton, Deputy State Superintendent of Education for Instructional Services on file with author) [hereinafter ALABAMA SAT REPORT] (showing that 43.2% of Alabama students receive free or reduced price lunch and that their average SAT scores are below the national average; third graders receiving free lunch averaged an overall score of 33 on the SAT, those receiving reduced price lunch averaged 46, and those paying full price averaged 62; by 11th grade, average scores had dropped to 23 for students receiving free lunch, 31 for those receiving reduced price lunch, and 47 for those paying full price). Similarly, data from the Public Affairs Research Council of Alabama indicates that schools with a higher percentage of students receiving free or reduced price

lic schools impacts all of Alabama's children to some degree, children from low-income families suffer the greatest negative effects, including a substantial risk of welfare dependency, imprisonment,[103] a lack of em-

---

lunches tended to have lower average SAT scores. Pub. Affairs Research Council of Ala., *Performance Comparisons for Alabama Schools*, 2001, *available at* http://parca.samford.edu/k-12.htm. Moreover, while virtually all of Alabama's adequately funded school systems had average SAT scores above, sometimes well above, the national average, 30% (34 of 113) of inadequately funded systems had scores below the national average. *See infra* note 89.

Finally, even though it is difficult to precisely measure the impact of school funding on educational quality, Alabama's education funding falls so short of any reasonable definition of minimum adequacy that the performance, at least of the low-income students, is bound to be negatively affected. Experts on education funding disagree vehemently on the extent to which increases in school resources yield corresponding gains in student performance, *compare* Eric A. Hanushek, *School Resources and Student Performance, in* Does Money Matter? The Effect of School Resources on Student Achievement and Adult Success 43-70 (Gary Burtless ed., Brookings Inst. Press 1996) (finding no positive relationship between funding and performance) *with* Larry V. Hedges et al., *Does Money Matter? A Meta-Analysis of Studies of the Effects of Differential School Inputs on Student Outcomes*, Educational Researcher 5-14 (Apr. 1994) (rejecting the conclusions of an earlier Hanushek study and arguing for a link between resources and performance), or improvements in students' long-term earnings potential. *Compare* David Card & Alan B. Krueger, *Labor Market Effects of School Quality: Theory and Evidence, in* Does Money Matter? The Effect of School Resources on Student Achievement and Adult Success 97-140 (Gary Burtless ed., Brookings Inst. Press 1996) (linking school resources to earnings potential), *with* Julian R. Betts, *Is There a Link between School Inputs and Earnings? Fresh Scrutiny of an Old Literature, in* Does Money Matter? The Effect of School Resources on Student Achievement and Adult Success 141-91 (Gary Burtless ed., Brookings Inst. Press 1996) (criticizing Card & Krueger and finding their results internally inconsistent). *See generally* Does Money Matter? (Gary Burtless ed. 1996) (presenting research articles on both sides of these debates).

The debate addressing the impact of funding on the quality of education also addresses how new funds should be spent; evidence exists indicating that wisely spent new funds will positively enhance student performance, especially that of low-income students. *See* Lawrence O. Picus, *Does Money Matter in Education? A Policymaker's Guide, in* U.S. Dep't of Educ., Nat'l Ctr. for Educ. Statistics, Selected Papers in School Finance, 1995, 19, 29, 31-32 (William J. Fowler ed., 1997), *available at* http://nces.ed.gov/pubsearch/pubsinfo.asp?pubid=97536; *see also* Opinion of the Justices No. 338, 624 So. 2d 107, 140 (Ala. 1993) (accepting as true a study of Alabama's public school system by Dr. Ronald Ferguson, Professor of Public Policy, Harvard University, finding a systematic, positive correlation between student achievement and certain specific expenditures, including money spent to secure smaller class sizes, teachers with more experience, and teachers who themselves had better test scores). Moreover, even if spending levels have no effect on overall student performance, research indicates that greater funding can reduce the performance gap between disadvantaged students and their peers. *See* David Card & A. Abigail Payne, School Finance Reform, the Distribution of School Spending, and the Distribution of SAT Scores (Nat'l Bur. of Econ. Research, Working Paper No. 6766, 1998), *available at* http://www.nber.org/papers/w6766 (finding that court-ordered spending equalization reduced disparities in test scores between children of well-educated and poorly-educated parents); David Grissmer et al., *Does Money Matter for Minority and Disadvantaged Students? Assessing the New Empirical Evidence, in* U.S. Dep't of Educ., Nat'l Ctr. for Educ. Statistics, Developments in School Finance, July 1997, at 15-30 (William J. Fowler ed., 1998) (concluding that increased spending narrows the gap between the test scores of black and white students and speculating that this is true for "disadvantaged" students generally). Although the issue of whether Alabama has a moral obligation to fund the public schools at a level above minimum adequacy, or to ensure equal funding for each of the individual school systems is beyond the scope of this Article, the connection between poverty, poor SAT scores, and the credible evidence indicating that increases in funding spent in an appropriate way can enhance student, especially low-income student, performance proves that education funding that fails to meet at least a minimum level of adequacy denies low-income children a minimum opportunity to achieve an adequate education.

103.   Opinion of the Justices No. 338, 624 So. 2d at 138-39 & n.31 (containing testimony of Dr.

ployment skills,[104] and little access to a higher education.[105] Middle and upper income Alabamians, however, have the ability to mitigate the negative consequences of funding shortages and ensure that their children still receive an adequate education by using their personal resources to pay for private school or other educational needs their children may have that the public school cannot provide, such as reading and math tutoring.[106]

Wayne Flynt, University Professor of History at Auburn University, stating that 65% to 70% of welfare program recipients (defined as food stamp and Medicaid recipients), and 90% of Alabama state prisoners, did not finish high school).

104.   *Id.* at 138-39. Dr. Flynt's testimony also states that the cycle of failure to invest in education by the State of Alabama has denied Alabama the pool of talent necessary to make it competitive in the global economy, or even in the Southeast. *Id.; see also id.* at 139 (containing testimony of Dr. Harold Elder, economics professor, The University of Alabama, finding a positive relationship between funding levels for primary and secondary schools and state income and employment growth, and concluding that increased educational support will lead to higher incomes and increased employment); Mahendra Lai Joshi, Industrial Recruitment Policy and Rural Development: A Case Study of the Pulp and Paper Industry in Alabama at 26, 57-59, 68-69, 72 and 80 (1997) (unpublished Ph.D. dissertation, Auburn University) (on file with Auburn University and author) (stating that many of the poorly funded schools in rural Alabama fail to adequately prepare students with low-income backgrounds in basic skills such as math, reading, and computer competence, which are needed for meaningful employment in industry, and arguing that increased school funding will help these low-income students learn these skills).

105.   The opportunity to receive a quality education at college and even higher levels represents a very important step beyond primary and secondary education for a person to improve his or her economic circumstances and general well-being. *See Alabama Coll. & Univ., A Case Study on Higher Education in Alabama, at* http://www.higheredpartners.org/thinkalabama/did_you_know.html (Aug. 12, 2002) (stating that the higher the degree obtained, the larger the increase in earnings). Because of lower tuition, a sound system of public higher education allows low-income Alabamians a better opportunity to afford the tuition. *Id.*

Until Alabama's public primary and secondary schools reach a minimum standard of adequate funding, many low-income children are deprived of an opportunity to achieve a higher education. *See id.* (ranking Alabama forty-ninth in the nation with only 14% of low-income students attending college). In arguing that comprehensive tax reform is essential to adequately fund Alabama's primary and secondary schools, this Article recognizes that higher education would greatly benefit from tax reform and that a well-funded, high quality, and affordable higher education system for in-state residents is also needed to ensure that low-income Alabamians enjoy adequate opportunities to further improve their financial situation and general well-being. *See id.* (stating that first, over the last ten years the percentage of state appropriations for Alabama's higher education has decreased while revenues received by Alabama's higher education institutions from tuition and fees paid by students has increased; second, higher education's share of the Education Trust Fund is still below the amounts received in fiscal year 1993-1994; and finally, Alabama's faculty salaries for four-year institutions of higher educations rank forty-fourth in the nation).

106.   *See* STATE RANKINGS, *supra* note 8, at 119-20 (stating that Alabama ranks twenty-sixth in the percentage of children who attend private school and twenty-fifth in the number of private schools). *See also* U.S. DEP'T OF EDUC., NAT'L CTR. FOR EDUC. STATISTICS, PRIVATE SCHOOL UNIVERSE SURVEY: 1999-2000, at 26 (Aug. 2001), *at* http://nces.ed.gov/pubs2001/2001330.pdf (showing that Alabama ranks twenty-second in number of private elementary and secondary schools, twenty-third in enrollment at private elementary and secondary schools, twenty-second in the number of teachers at private elementary and secondary schools, and twentieth in the number of high school graduates from private schools). Given the relatively small size of Alabama's population and the rural nature of most of the state, a middle of the pack ranking for private schools indicates that proportionally, private schools are extraordinary factors in Alabama education, which suggests that many families with the personal resources to send their children to private schools do so. *See also* Robert D. Wrinkle, Joseph Stewart, Jr. & J.L. Polinard, *Public School Quality, Private Schools, and Race*, 43 AM. J. POL. SCI. 1248, 1250 (1999) (concluding, in their study of schools in Texas, that median family income measures resources available to families within a school district and that generally both private school

The Alabama Department of Education provides report cards that individually evaluate all 128 school systems in the state.[107] The amount of spending per student is one of several categories evaluated by the report card and given a traditional "A" to "F" grade that can be used to evaluate the state as a whole, and to make meaningful comparisons of the school systems within a state. These report cards represent one of the most important means of evaluating the adequacy of any school, and the report cards include grades for the amount of money spent per student by each system.[108] For the state as a whole, the report card gave Alabama's schools a spending per student grade of "D," which means that the funding level for the schools are under "caution."[109] Although no consensus has developed defining precisely the minimum amount of spending necessary to reach adequate funding, arguably the lowest spending per student grade possible indicating a minimum level of adequate funding should be a "C," which means that the funding level for the schools is "average," an intermediate level without anything extra, unusual, or special.[110] However,

---

enrollment and public school performance both increase as family resources increase within a school district increase). Although much anecdotal evidence suggests that race has played a substantial role in the development of private schools, and that race is currently a significant factor explaining why so many of Alabama's public schools are inadequately funded, a full examination as to whether the inadequate funding of the schools is the result of racial discrimination is beyond the scope of this Article. However, if the inadequate funding of the public schools can be at least partially linked to racial discrimination, the moral principles of Judeo-Christian ethics even more strongly condemn it. *See supra* note 2.

107.   *See* Comp. & app. D, *supra* note 89. The research team used the system-wide school report cards published by the Alabama Department of Education for each of Alabama's 128 school systems during the 1998-1999 school year, which evaluate each school system using a traditional "A" to "F" grading scale, based on spending per student, overall performance, safety and discipline, and academic performance to create a spreadsheet containing the spending per student, total spending, overall performance, and percent of funding by source for each school system.

108.   *See* sources cited and discussion *supra* note 102.

109.   *See* Comp. & app. D, *supra* note 89 (stating that Alabama averaged $5303 per student for the 1998-1999 school year, with the "D" ranges for the national grading scale being $5000 to $5499, and for the Southeastern grading scales being $5264 to $5463); *see also* U.S. DEP'T OF EDUC., NAT'L CTR. FOR EDUC. STATISTICS, STATISTICS IN BRIEF: REVENUES AND EXPENDITURES FROM PUBLIC ELEMENTARY AND SECONDARY EDUCATION: SCHOOL YEAR 1998-99, tbl. 5 (July 19, 2001), *at* http://nces.ed.gov/pub2001/2001321.pdf (listing Alabama's average spending per student to be $5188, lower than the $5303 figure stated by the Alabama Department of Education). Alabama's average spending per student is considerably less than the national average of $6508 per student for 1998-1999, *see id.*, which earns a grade of "C" in the national scale. *See* Comp. & app. D, *supra* note 89 (showing a range of $6434 to $6934 for a "C," qualifying as a "B-," which means "good," on the Southeastern scale); *see id.* (showing a range of $6465 to $6665 for a "B-"). Although the Alabama Department of Education did not provide a definition for "caution," the NEW AMERICAN HERITAGE DICTIONARY 305 (3d ed. 1992), defines caution as "[a] warning or admonishment, especially to take heed." *See also* STATE RANKINGS, *supra* note 8, at 137 (for 1997) and 139 (for 2000) (ranking Alabama forty-fifth out of the fifty states in the amount of spending per student for public primary and secondary schools).

110.   *See* Comp. & app. D, *supra* note 89 (providing a spending per student range of $6434 to $6934 on the national scale and $5864 to $6264 on the Southeastern scale to earn a "C"). Although the Alabama Department of Education did not provide a definition of "average," the AMERICAN HERITAGE DICTIONARY OF THE ENGLISH LANGUAGE 127 (3d ed. 1992), defines average as "[a]n intermediate level or degree."

in order to avoid debating the merits as to where the line should be precisely drawn, and without conceding that substantively a "C-" level of funding is in fact adequate, for purposes of evaluating Alabama's schools, this Article treats a spending per student grade of "C-," a funding level under "moderate caution," as the minimum level for adequate funding of any school system.[111] Alabama's statewide spending per student grade of "D" indicates that Alabama fails to provide Alabama's children a funding level for primary and secondary education that meets a minimum level of adequacy, seriously jeopardizing the opportunity for children from low-income families to achieve an adequate education.[112]

Even though Alabama's overall grade of "D" presents a discouraging report of the state's situation, it still suggests a funding situation better than what the majority of the 128 individual school systems enjoy. Across the state several small areas exist with schools funded at a minimum level, while the rest of the schools fall below, often substantially below, a level indicating minimum adequate funding. With the exception of a cluster of school systems in Greater Birmingham,[113] all of the school systems in Northeast Alabama[114] fail to receive minimum adequate funding with well over two-thirds of them receiving a spending per student grade no better than a "D-," representing a funding level under "extreme caution," and over one-third receiving a "F," representing a funding level that is "failing."[115] With the exception of the City of Tuscaloosa,[116] the spending per

---

111.   By treating school systems earning a spending per student grade of "C-," with the designation "moderate caution," as the minimum level of adequate funding, this Article is not taking the substantive position that a "C-" grade for spending per student is actually adequate. Rather than debate the merits of whether a "C-" funded school substantively meets the minimum standard of adequate funding, this Article focuses on the most desperately funded schools, those below "C-," and those even below the statewide average of "D." Moreover, Alabama's overall failure to meet even a moderate cautionary level of spending leaves no room for argument that Alabama adequately funds its public schools.

112.   See sources cited and discussion supra notes 102-05.

113.   Four school systems in the Greater Birmingham area received the following grades on the national and Southeastern scales: Mountain Brook City: C+, A-; Homewood City: C, B+; Hoover City: C-, C+; and Tarrant City: C-, C. Comp. & app. D, supra note 89; see also infra notes 135, 138, 143 (explaining why these school systems receive adequate funding under the current tax structure).

114.   For purposes of this Article the following counties are defined as being located in Northeast Alabama: Jackson, Marshall, DeKalb, Etowah, Cherokee, Cullman, Jefferson, Shelby, Talladega, St. Clair, Blount, Calhoun, Clay, Randolph, and Cleburne. This Article recognizes that this division is somewhat arbitrary and that other reasonable groupings of the state's counties will differ from this one.

115.   The spending grades, the first reflecting the national scale and the second reflecting the Southeastern scale, are as follows for the thirty-seven school systems in these counties (the following spending grades do not include the cities of Mountain Brook, Homewood, Hoover, and Tarrant, located in the northeast section of Alabama, see supra note 113): Blount County: D-, F; Calhoun County: D, D-; Cherokee County: D, D-; Clay County: D, F; Cleburne County: D, D-; Cullman County: D, D-; DeKalb County: D-, F; Etowah County: D-, F; Jackson County: D, D; Jefferson County: D, D; Marshall County: D, D-; Randolph County: D-, F; Shelby County: D+, D+; St. Clair County: D-, F; Talladega County: D-, F; Oneonta City (in Blount County): D, D-; Anniston City (in Calhoun County): D+, C-; Jacksonville City (in Calhoun County): D-, F; Oxford City (in Calhoun County):

student grades are even more dismal in West Alabama.[117] In addition to all of these school systems showing funding levels below the minimum level of adequacy, a greater percentage, more than three-quarters of the school systems, received a spending per student grade no better than "D-," with well more than one-third of these receiving a "F."[118] Outside of the City of Auburn,[119] the school systems in the Black Belt region[120] are inade-

D-, F; Piedmont City (in Calhoun County): D, F; Cullman City (in Cullman County): D, F; Fort Payne City (in DeKalb County): D, D; Attalla City (in Etowah County): D, F; Gadsden City (in Etowah County): D+, C-; Scottsboro City (in Jackson County): D+, C-; Albertville City (in Marshall County): D, D; Arab City (in Marshall County): D, F; Guntersville City (in Marshall County): D, D+; Roanoke City (in Randolph County): D-, F; Pell City (in St. Clair County): D, D-; Sylacauga City (in Talladega County): D, D; Talladega City (in Talledega County): D+, D+; Vestavia Hills City: D+, C-; Bessemer City: D+, C-; Fairfield City: D-, F; Midfield City: D, D; and Birmingham City: D, D- (these last five all in Jefferson County). *See id.* Out of thirty-seven school systems, fifteen (15 divided by 37 equals 0.41, as rounded 41%), well over one-third of the school systems, received an "F" in the spending per student category for the Southeastern grading scale and an additional ten received a "D-" in the spending per student category for the national scale, for a total of twenty-six school systems receiving either a "D-" or an "F" (25 divided by 37 equals 0.676, as rounded 68%), over two-thirds of the total. *See id.*

116.   The Tuscaloosa City school system (in Tuscaloosa County) and the Linden City school system (in Marengo County) each received national and Southeastern spending per student grades of "C-" and "C+." *See Id.* The evidence indicates that the Linden City school system receives large amounts of funds from sources not typical of other adequately funded school systems and therefore is more like the inadequately funded schools because it is located in an area with little ability to raise sufficient additional property and sales taxes. *See id.* (showing that this system receives 64% of its funding from the state (the largest percentage among the adequately funded school systems, and well over the state-wide average of 56%), only 19% from local sources (substantially less than other adequately funded schools and well under the statewide average of 27% even though this figure includes revenue from additional property and sales taxes), and 17% from federal sources (significantly more than any other adequately funded school system, and well over the statewide average of 9%)); *see infra* note 135 (Marengo County is among the fifty-four rural counties showing only approximately one-third of the state's employment activity, low property tax assessments for commercial property and personal residences, and low gross retail sales). *See infra* notes 135, 138, 143 (explaining why the Tuscaloosa City school system receives adequate funding under the current tax structure).

117.   For purposes of this Article, the following counties are defined as being located in West Alabama: Winston, Marion, Lamar, Fayette, Pickens, Tuscaloosa, Greene, Hale, Bibb, Perry, Marengo, Sumter, Choctaw, Clarke, Washington and Walker counties. This Article recognizes that this division is somewhat arbitrary and that other reasonable groupings of the state's counties will differ from this one.

118.   The spending grades, the first reflecting the national scale and the second reflecting the South-eastern scale, are as follows for the twenty-one school systems in these counties (the following spending grades do not include the City of Tuscaloosa and the City of Linden, both located in West Alabama, *see supra* note 116): Winston County: D, D; Marion County: D, F; Lamar County: D-, F; Fayette County: D-, F; Pickens County: D, D; Tuscaloosa County: D-, F; Greene County: D+, C; Hale County: D, F; Bibb County: D-, F; Perry County: D, D; Marengo County: D, D-; Sumter County: D, D+; Choctaw County: D, D; Clarke County: D, D-; Washington County: D, D; Walker County: D+, C-; Winfield City (in Fayette County): D-, F; Demopolis City (in Marengo County): D-, F; Thomasville City (in Clarke County): D, D-; Jasper City (in Walker County): D+, C; and Haleyville City (in Winston County): D-, F. *See* Comp. & app. D, *supra* note 89. Out of twenty-one school systems, nine (9 divided by 21 equals 0.4285, as rounded 43%), just under half the school systems, received an "F" in the spending per student category for the Southeastern grading scale, and an additional seven received a "D-" in the spending per student category for the national scale, for a total of sixteen school systems receiving a "D-" or an "F" (16 divided by 21 equals .7619, as rounded 77%), just over three-quarters of the total. *See id.*

119.   The Auburn City school system (in Lee County) and the Barbour County school system each received national and Southeastern spending per student grades of "C-" and "C." *See id.* The evidence

quately funded with almost half of the systems receiving grades no better than a "D-."[121] In Lower Alabama,[122] not one school system in the entire region met the minimum standard for adequate funding. Almost two-thirds of these school systems received a spending per student grade no better than a "D-," with well over one-third of them receiving a "F."[123] Only in Northwest Alabama[124] did a significant percentage of the school systems,

---

indicates that the Barbour County school system receives large amounts of funds from sources not typical of other adequately funded school systems and therefore is more like the inadequately funded schools because it is located in an area with little ability to raise sufficient additional property and sales taxes. *See id.* (showing that this system receives only 11% from local sources (substantially less than other adequately funded schools and well under the statewide average of 27%, even though this figure includes revenue from additional property and state taxes), but receives 12% from federal sources (greater than the statewide average of 9%), and 27% from other sources (significantly greater than the statewide average of 8%)); *infra* note 135 (Barbour County is among the fifty-four rural counties showing only approximately one-third of the state's employment activity, low property tax assessments for commercial property and personal residences, and low gross retail sales); *see also infra* notes 135, 138, 143 (explaining why the Auburn City school system receives adequate funding under the current tax structure).

120.   Historically, the term "Black Belt" refers to the dark, nutrient-rich soil commonly existing in this area. For purposes of this Article, the following counties are defined as being in the Black Belt region: Autauga, Barbour, Butler, Bullock, Chambers, Chilton, Coosa, Crenshaw, Dallas, Elmore, Lee, Lowndes, Macon, Montgomery, Pike, Russell, Tallapoosa, and Wilcox. This Article recognizes that this division is somewhat arbitrary and that other reasonable groupings of the state's counties will differ from this one.

121.   The spending grades, the first reflecting the national scale and the second reflecting the Southeastern scale, are as follows for the twenty-five school systems in the counties located in the Black Belt (the following list does not include the City of Auburn and Barbour County, *see supra* note 119): Autauga D-, F; Butler: D, D-; Bullock: D, D-; Chambers: D, D-; Chilton: D, F; Coosa: D, F; Crenshaw: D, D; Dallas: D, D-; Elmore: D-, F; Lee: D, F; Lowndes: D+, C-; Macon: D, D-; Montgomery: D, F; Pike: D+, C; Russell: D, D-; Tallapoosa: D, D; Wilcox: D+, D+; Eufaula City (in Barbour County): D, D-; Lanett City (in Chambers County): D, D- ; Selma City (in Dallas County): D, D-; Tallassee City (in both Elmore and Tallapoosa Counties): D-, F; Opelika City (in Lee County): D, D; Troy City (in Pike County): D, F; Phoenix City (in Russell County): D, D; Alexander City (in Tallapoosa County): D, D. *See* Comp. & app. D, *supra* note 89. Out of twenty-five school systems, eleven (eight receiving a spending per student grade of "F" in the Southeastern scale and three receiving a spending per student grade of "D-" on the national scale) school systems (11 divided by 25 equals 0.44, 44%), almost half, received spending per student grades of either "D-" or "F." *See id.*

122.   For purposes of this Article the following counties are defined as being in Lower Alabama: Baldwin, Coffee, Conecuh, Covington, Dale, Escambia, Geneva, Henry, Houston, Mobile, and Monroe. This Article recognizes that this division is somewhat arbitrary and that other reasonable groupings of the state's counties will differ from this one.

123.   The spending grades, the first reflecting the national scale and the second reflecting the Southeastern scale, are as follows for the twenty school systems in the counties located in Lower Alabama: Baldwin: D, D; Coffee: D, D-; Conecuh: D, D; Covington: D, F; Dale: D, F; Escambia: D, D; Geneva: D-, F; Henry: D, D; Houston: D-, F; Mobile: D, F; Monroe: D, D-; Elba City (in Coffee County): D+, D+; Enterprise City (in Coffee County): D, D-; Andalusia City (in Covington County): D-, F; Dothan City (in Houston County): D+, D+; Opp City (in Covington County): D, D- ; Daleville City (in Dale County): D-, F; Ozark City (in Dale County): D, D; Brewton City (in Escambia County): D, D-; and Geneva City (in Geneva County): D-, F. Out of twenty school systems, eight (8 divided by 20 equals 0.40, 40%), well over one-third, received an "F" in the spending per student category for the Southeastern scale, with an additional five receiving a "D-" in the spending per student category for the Southeastern scale, for a total of thirteen (13 divided by 20 equals 0.65, 65%), almost two-thirds of the total. *See id.*

124.   For purposes of this Article the following counties are defined as being in Northwest Alabama: Colbert, Franklin, Lauderdale, Lawrence, Limestone, Madison, and Morgan. This Article

which are in the Quad-Cities and Greater Huntsville area, receive adequate funding.[125] The handful of adequately funded school systems are an exception to the pattern of inadequate funding that prevails across the state. Close to ninety percent of Alabama's individual school systems are inadequately funded with a spending per student grade below a "C-."[126]

Although a reform of the income tax structure could increase available revenues and improve the shortage of funding for Alabama's schools,[127] the woefully inadequate property tax revenues raised from all classes of property, especially timber acres, is the principal reason why Alabama's public schools as a whole are inadequately funded. Primarily because of extremely low property taxes imposed at the state level for education funding in general, all of Alabama's individual school systems receive insufficient funding from the state.[128] Although at the state level, and especially at the local level, property taxes normally provide the backbone of funding

---

recognizes that this division is somewhat arbitrary and that other reasonable groupings of the state's counties will differ from this one.

125.   Of the seventeen school systems in Northwest Alabama, seven of them (41%) receiving national and Southeastern spending per student grades at or above the minimum adequate level of funding. Those systems are: Florence City (in Lauderdale County): C, B; Athens City: C-, C+ (in Limestone County); Decatur City: C-, C (in Morgan County); Huntsville City: C-, C+ (in Madison County); and Tuscumbia City: C-, C; Sheffield City: C-, C; and Muscle Shoals City: C-, C (all three in Colbert County), were adequately funded. Moreover, these seven adequately funded school systems account for almost half of the state's fifteen adequately funded school systems. The ten inadequately funded school systems in Northwest Alabama received national and Southeastern spending per student grades of: Lauderdale County: D, D-; Limestone County: D, D-; Colbert County: D+, C-; Franklin County: D, D; Lawrence County: D, D-; Madison County: D, F; Morgan County: D+, C-; Russellville City (in Franklin County): D+, D+; Madison City (in Madison County): F, F; and Hartselle City (in Morgan County): D, D+. *See id.*; *see also infra* notes 135, 138, 143 (explaining why the seven school systems in the Quad Cities and Greater Huntsville area receive adequate funding under the current tax structure).

126.   *See* Comp. & app. D, *supra* note 89 (showing that of the 128 school systems in Alabama only fourteen (12%) received a spending per student grade of C-, C, or C+ on the national scale, while 113 (88%) received spending per student grades below a "C-" on the national scale).

127.   *See supra* note 17 (discussing the low revenues raised by Alabama's income tax structure); *supra* notes 30-41 and accompanying text (discussing how Alabama's income tax structure favors upper income taxpayers).

128.   *See* Comp. & app. D, *supra* note 89 (showing that on average Alabama's school systems relied on the state for 56% of their total funding which indicates that state provided funds will never be sufficient to even bring a school system's spending per student grade close to a "C-"). On average, Alabama's schools relied on local sources for 27% of their funding, other sources for 9% of their funding, and federal sources for 8% of their funding. *Id.* Local sources of funds include all local taxes (such as ad valorem, sales, gasoline, alcohol taxes, county commission, or city council appropriations), and non-federal food service income (such as daily lunch sales, tuition and revenues from other school systems, earnings on investments, revenues from rentals, charges for services, fines, fees, textbooks sales, athletic gate receipts, concession receipts, donations, fund raisers, and Helping Schools car tags). Other sources of revenues include bonds and warrants, sales and dispositions of fixed assets, reimbursements from Medicaid, proceeds of debt, refunds and rebates received on prior year expenditures, proceeds from indirect costs charged on federal programs, and payments made on the LEA's behalf (such as county commission debt service payments on bond issues and E-Rate payments for telephone and Internet services). E-mail from Mitch Edwards, Alabama State Department of Education, to Leslie Patton, The University of Alabama School of Law (Sept. 24, 2001, 15:31:16 CST) (on file with author).

for public education in general,[129] Alabama collects only sparse revenues for schools from property taxes,[130] while largely relying on income and sales taxes to provide the state's contribution for public school funding.[131] Because revenues raised from income and sales taxes often decline unexpectedly with economic changes, those taxes are generally regarded as inferior to the property tax as a tool to build solidly funded public schools.[132] A reform of Alabama's property tax structure that both requires a greater portion of the fair market value of all classes of property, especially of timber acres, to be subject to the millage rates and increases the state's millage rate supporting schools would empower the state to make greater contributions to the funding of the individual school systems and bring the state closer to adequately funding public schools.

In addition to being largely responsible for the inadequate public school funding as a whole from state sources, the property tax structure itself substantially limits the ability of most local areas to adequately supplement the state's insufficient contributions and bring their individual school systems up to a minimum level of adequate funding.[133] The vast

---

129.   *See* H.C. HUDGINS & RICHARD S. VACCA, LAW AND EDUCATION: CONTEMPORARY ISSUES AND COURT DECISIONS 145 (6th ed. 1995) (recognizing that while federal and state revenues support public education, local property taxes still remain "the backbone of public school financ[ing]."); Roy Bahl et al., *School Finance Reform and Impact on Property Taxes*, 83 PROC. OF THE ANN. CONF. ON TAX'N 163, 163 (1990) ("The property tax has long been the mainstay of revenue sources for public education in this country.").

130.   Alabama only allots three mills, which translates to well under one-half of 1% of the assessed value of the property, to education funding. GUIDE TO TAXES, *supra* note 82, at 4 (indicating three mills of ad valorem tax are distributed to the public school fund).

131.   The Alabama Education Trust Fund collected $4.1 billion in fiscal year 2000. GUIDE TO TAXES, *supra* note 82, at 371 (providing that 54% of the money in the Education Trust Fund came from income taxes, 32% came from state imposed sales taxes, and 14% came from other sources generated through beer, hydroelectric, insurance premium, rental/leasing, tobacco use, utility taxes, and store licenses). State sources outside the Alabama Education Trust Fund, which included $92,532,864 from the Alabama General Fund, came from taxes, fees, and charges collected by state agencies, but does not include bond proceeds, interagency transfers, or federal funds. *Id.* at 364.

132.   *See* PARCA REPORT, *supra* note 1, at 6-7 (discussing the financial crisis of proration that regularly threatens public school funding and identifying low level of local support due to "frequent proration of state income and sales tax dollars" as a major reason for the financial crisis); *id.* at 8-9 (indicating that due to Alabama's constitutional controls over local property taxes, most cities have made sales taxes their primary source of revenue although most states rely on the property tax for local support of schools because property taxes provide a stable source of revenues that enhance property values due to the support for schools and also create accountability within the community). *But see* ALABAMA POLICY INSTITUTE, *supra* note 1, at 28-29 (failing to discuss the low revenues raised from Alabama's property taxes and the usual pattern of states funding schools primarily with property tax revenues, arguing that the proration of Alabama's education funding is caused by expenditures increasing without a matching budget increase due to a slow economy, and arguing that inefficient spending patterns contributes to proration without specifying details concerning the nature of the inefficiency).

133.   *See supra* notes 64-81 and accompanying text (discussing Alabama's classes of property and the percentage of the property's fair market value subject to the property tax being only 10% for personal residences and timber acres, with further reductions for timber by the current use formula, and being only 20% for commercial property); *see also infra* notes 134 and 141 (subjecting a greater portion of a property's fair market value to the property tax and citing data to show the relation be-

majority, more than eighty percent, of the inadequately funded school sys-tems[134] are located in areas of the state that enjoy no significant commer-cial or industrial activity,[135] and have a significant number of low-income Alabamians among the population.[136] Without the valuable commercial, industrial, and residential property that accompanies business develop-ment, property taxes in these rural areas, even at millage rates exceeding

---

tween Alabama's under-funded schools and economically depressed communities).

134.   Of Alabama's 113 inadequately funded school systems, 91 of them (81%) are located in areas showing insignificant levels of commercial and industrial activity. *See infra* notes 135, 138, 143. However, twenty-two of these inadequately funded school systems only 19% of the 113 total, are located in areas that enjoy at least some, and in a few cases significant levels of, commercial and industrial activity. *See id.* These twenty-two school systems include the following schools: seven systems in the Northeast area: Jefferson County, Shelby County, Vestavia Hills City, Bessemer City, Fairfield City, Midfield City, Birmingham City (all five in Jefferson County); one system in West Alabama: Tuscaloosa County; three systems in the Black Belt: Lee County, Opelika City (in Lee County), and Montgomery County; four systems in Lower Alabama: Houston County, Baldwin County, Mobile County, and Dothan City (in Houston County); and seven systems in the Northwest area: Lauderdale County, Limestone County, Colbert County, Madison County, Morgan County, Madison City (in Madison County), and Hartselle City (in Morgan County). *See id.* The greater than marginal presence of business activity in the areas where these twenty-two school systems are located makes the reasons for the inadequate funding patterns more complex than just primarily being due to the property tax structure. However, a strong argument can be made that these school systems would benefit greatly from tax reform by at least being able to receive greater state funding for education.

135.   Only nine counties—Jefferson, Mobile, Madison, Montgomery, Tuscaloosa, Shelby, Houston, Morgan, and Baldwin—enjoy approximately two-thirds of Alabama's commercial and industrial activ-ity. *See* Comp. & app. E, *supra* note 96. These counties alone account for 62% (1,024,728 people) of the state's total employment and 67% ($29,492,204,000) of the total payroll in the state. *See id.* (tabu-lating data and citing source materials). Four of the remaining counties in the state fall below this top tier, but nonetheless enjoy significant development flowing from identifiable industries. *Id.* Lee County (ranking thirteenth in both employment and payroll) benefits from the activity generated by Auburn University and by companies like Briggs & Stratton and Uniroyal-Goodwrench. *See also* Economic Development Partnership of Alabama, *Alabama Community Profiles*, *at* http://www.edpa.org/frameset-commprofilesh.htm (last visited Sept. 23, 2002) (providing in-depth economic information on Alabama's communities). The counties of Lauderdale (fourteenth in both employment and payroll), Colbert (nineteenth in employment and twentieth in payroll), and Limestone (twentieth in employment and sixteenth in payroll), experience substantial levels of business activity connected, respectively, to the textiles, aluminum processing, and steering components industries. *See* Comp. & app. E, *supra* note 96. The economic data suggests that the remaining fifty-four counties, 81% of Alabama's sixty-seven total counties, have little or no significant commercial or industrial activity independent of timber.

136.   Of the fifty-four counties showing insignificant levels of commercial and business activity, *see id.*, the school systems in thirty-seven of those counties had more than half, often substantially more than half, of the children receiving free and reduced price lunch assistance, which is a poverty indica-tor. *See* ALABAMA SAT REPORT, *supra* note 102. The remaining seventeen of those counties had more than one-third, often close to half, of the children receiving free and reduced price lunch assistance. *See id.* Moreover, the latest U.S. census figures indicate that in all fifty-four of these counties, more than 12.4% of the population (the percentage of the population of the entire United States below the poverty line) is below the poverty line. U.S. Census Bureau, *2000 Census*, *at* http://www.census.gov/hhes/poverty/2000census/poppvstat.html. Even worse, in thirty-nine of the fifty-four counties, more than 16.1% of the population (the percentage of all Alabamians below the poverty line), is below the poverty line, and in twenty-one of those counties more than 20% of the population is below the poverty line. *Id.* Of the thirteen counties showing significant levels of com-mercial and industrial development, only four (Lee, Mobile, Montgomery and Tuscaloosa) showed a higher percentage of the population living in poverty than the 16.1% for Alabama as a whole, with only Lee County showing a percentage greater than 20%. *Id.*

the statewide average,[137] will not raise substantial revenues from commercial property and personal residences. Under the current property tax structure, only areas with significant commercial and industrial development, which include the few areas with adequately funded school systems, are able to raise more than marginal property taxes from commercial property and personal residences—the two classes of property that account for approximately eighty-five percent of Alabama's property taxes.[138]

Timber acres, however, which form the backbone of the economy and constitute the state's most important source of wealth, especially in areas that would otherwise have little or no commercial and industrial develop-

---

137.   Although the locally imposed property tax millage rates supporting inadequately funded schools tend to be lower than the adequately funded schools, a significant range exists with some of these millage rates being greater, sometimes substantially greater, than the statewide average of 12.05 mills. *See* Comp. & app. D, *supra* note 89. The following school systems, among the ninety-one inadequately funded school systems located in areas with insignificant business activity, are supported by millage rates between 13 and 22 mills. *Id.* In Northeast Alabama: Blount County, Oneonta City (in Blount County), Calhoun County, Piedmont City, Oxford City, Jacksonville City, Anniston City (all four in Calhoun County), Cherokee County, Clay County, Cleburne County, DeKalb County, Fort Payne City (in DeKalb County), Etowah County, Attalla City (in Etowah County), St. Clair County, Pell City (in St. Clair County), and Talladega County; In West Alabama: Clarke County, Thomasville City (in Clarke County), and Sumter County; In the Black Belt: Eufalula City (in Barbour County), Bullock County, Russell County, Phoenix City (in Russell County), Alexander City (in Tallapoosa County), Tallassee City (in Elmore and Tallapoosa Counties), and Macon County; and in Lower Alabama: Coffee County, Elba City, and Enterprise City (both in Coffee County). *Id.* Comparing the millage rates to the state's average of 12.05 only provides trends within the state and does not conclusively indicate if, given the particular size of the school system and the population which will vary greatly from place to place, the millage rate is in fact in a high range. By way of illustration, among the school systems with a spending per student grade of "C-," the millage rates range from 8 to 28.5 mills. *Id.*

138.   The thirteen counties with substantial commercial and industrial development, *see supra* note 135, also are assessed substantial levels of property taxes for commercial property (Class II) and personal residences (Class III (other)) property, while the remaining fifty-four counties showed very low property tax assessments in these categories. *See* Comp. & app. C, *supra* note 90. With the exception of Talladega County (probably related to the Talladega Superspeedway), all the counties in Northeast Alabama, except for Jefferson (showing approximately $210 and $125 million, respectively) and Shelby (showing approximately $38 and $31 million, respectively), showed low property tax assessments for commercial property (often well under $10 million) and for personal residences (often less than $5 million). *Id.* In West Alabama, all the counties, except for Tuscaloosa (showing approximately $28 and $13 million, respectively), showed extremely low property tax assessments for commercial property (almost always well under $5 million, and sometimes not even $2 million, and in four counties less than $1 million) and for personal residences (almost always less than $2 million and in five counties less than $1 million). *Id.* In the Black Belt, all the counties, except for Lee (showing approximately $19 and $10 million, respectively) and Montgomery (showing approximately $35 and $18 million respectively), showed insignificant property tax assessments for commercial property (most of the counties showed less than $5 million with four showing more than $5 but less than $10 million) and for personal residences (only one county showed more than $5 million). *Id.* In Lower Alabama, except for Baldwin (showing approximately $48 and $20 million, respectively), Houston (showing approximately $12 and $6 million respectively), and Mobile (showing approximately $82 and $35 million, respectively), most of the remaining counties showed substantially less than $5 million for commercial property and well under $1 million for personal residences. *Id.* In Northwest Alabama, the counties of Colbert, Lauderdale, Limestone, Madison, and Morgan showed assessments of at least $5 million, sometimes substantially more, for both commercial property and personal residences, while Franklin and Lawrence Counties showed assessments for both commercial property and personal residences of well under $5 million. *See* Comp. & app. C, *supra* note 90.

ment,[139] yield only *de minimis* corresponding property tax revenues for the local governments.[140] By severely limiting the ability of these areas to impose fair taxes on timber acres, their only significant source of wealth, the property tax structure bears primary responsibility for the inadequately funded state of the local public schools, thus denying children from low-income families the opportunity to break out of the cycle of economic poverty by achieving an adequate education.[141]

Moreover, by failing to raise adequate revenues in Alabama's rural areas, the property tax structure also causes the local governments to increase sales tax rates to oppressively high levels, which often exceed the statewide average of just over eight percent.[142] Because those rural areas show low, sometimes extremely low, levels of gross retail sales due to

---

139. For the importance of timber to the overall economy of the state, see *supra* notes 96-100 and accompanying text. In the year 2000, Alabama timber producers took in $877,732,000 in total cash receipts from the sale of timber. *See* Comp. & app. E, *supra* note 96. The presence of these cash receipts across Alabama counties does not follow the same economic pattern as commerce and industry, which is concentrated in only a few areas in the state. Thus, every county in the state benefited to some extent from cash receipts from timber, ranging from a low of just over $1 million for Limestone County to more than $50 million for Clarke County. *See id.* The nine counties that enjoy two-thirds of the state's payroll and employment activity received only 11% ($100,349,000) of total cash receipts from timber sales, while the remaining fifty-eight counties—counties that account for only one-third of the payroll and employment in the state—received 89% ($777,383,000) of the state's timber receipts. *Id.* Of the twenty-five counties at the very bottom of the rankings for total payroll, seventeen (Bibb, Butler, Chilton, Choctaw, Conecuh, Coosa, Crenshaw, Fayette, Greene, Hale, Lamar, Lowndes, Perry, Pickens, Sumter, Washington, and Wilcox) are in the top half of counties for cash receipts from forestry with more than $9,600,000 each in cash receipts. *Id.* Clarke County, the county with the highest level of cash receipts from timber at over $50 million, ranks in the bottom half of counties for both payroll (thirty-eighth) and employment (fortieth). *Id.* More dramatically, Hale County, the county receiving the second highest level of cash receipts for forestry ($46,476,000), ranks fifty-seventh and fifty-eighth out of the state's sixty-seven counties for payroll and employment, respectively. *See* Comp. & app. E, *supra* note 96. Obviously, timber plays a critical role throughout the state and often dominates the economy in poorer areas. *See* William David Dawson, Timber Dependency and Persistent Poverty: Examination from the Theoretical Perspectives of Human Capital and Community Power 53 (unpublished M.S. thesis) (on file with Auburn University and author) (highlighting timber dependency in the economies of Alabama's rural counties).

140. In all counties across the state, timber acres (Class III, current use property) by far showed the lowest property tax assessments. No county (other than Jefferson County, showing an assessment of just over $1 million) showed assessments for timber acres exceeding $1 million and only ten counties showed assessments exceeding $500,000, while twenty-one counties showed assessments of less than $200,000. *See* Comp. & app. C, *supra* note 90. Moreover, because these property tax assessments also include the share assessed to agricultural land, these figures generously estimate the actual property tax paid by owners of timber acres. *See supra* note 92.

141. Comprehensive tax reform allowing a greater portion of a property's fair market value to be subjected to the property tax represents only the first step for the state and the local governments to raise sufficient funds to adequately fund Alabama's schools. A longstanding cultural bias against even reasonable property taxes has kept the millage rates too low in all but a few places across the state. *See* Comp. & app. D, *supra* note 89 (showing that many school systems are supported by millage rates below, and sometimes well below, the statewide average of 12.05). However, the persistent resistance to reasonable property tax rates represents a different problem and does not justify keeping the property tax base so low that increases in millage rates are largely ineffective.

142. Of the fifty-four counties showing low levels of commercial and industrial activity, twenty-seven showed sales tax rates within their borders exceeding the state's average rate of just over 8%, while only four showed sales tax rates less than this average. *See* Comp. & app. B, *supra* note 46.

limited commercial and industrial activity, these additional sales taxes cannot raise sufficient revenues to make up for the shortage of funds due to inadequate property tax revenues.[143] However, these additional sales taxes greatly exacerbate the disproportionately heavy and unfair tax burden imposed on Alabama's poorest citizens, who account for a large portion of the population in these rural areas.[144]

II. Alabama's Tax Structure Fails to Meet Any Reasonable Definition of Fairness and Violates the Moral Principles of Judeo-Christian Ethics

A. Traditional Tax Policy Evaluates Fairness Using Concepts Focusing on Ability to Pay and Treating Similarly Situated Taxpayers Similarly

From the broadest perspective, a well-designed tax structure[145] should raise adequate revenues to meet the needs of the community subject to the tax[146] and spread out the burden of paying the tax in an equitable or fair manner.[147] Traditional tax policy uses two distinct principles—vertical eq-

---

143.   Of the fifty-four counties showing low levels of commercial and industrial development, none showed gross retail sales even close to $1 billion (while almost all of the thirteen counties showing significant levels of commercial and industrial development showed gross retail sales more, sometimes substantially more, than $1 billion). *See* CTR. FOR BUS. & ECON. RESEARCH, THE UNIVERSITY OF ALABAMA, ECONOMIC ABSTRACT OF ALABAMA 2000 at 401-23 (2000); Comp. & app. B, *supra* note 46. Only four counties showed gross retail sales exceeding $500 million, while thirty-four counties showed gross retail sales of less than $200 million with twenty-one of those showing gross retail sales of less than $100 million. *Id.*

144.   *See supra* notes 42-49 (discussing sales taxes), 136 (indicating that Alabama's fifty-four rural counties have higher levels of poverty than the other thirteen counties and discussing Alabama's sales tax structure and its disproportionately heavy burden on the poorest Alabamians).

145.   *See* Joseph T. Sneed, *The Criteria of Federal Income Tax Policy*, 17 STAN. L. REV. 567, 568 (1965) (providing seven "pervasive purposes" of a tax structure as supplying adequate revenue, providing a practical and workable system, imposing equal taxes among equals, fostering economic stability, reducing economic inequality, avoiding negatively affecting the economy, and fostering positive harmony in the political order); SLEMROD & BAKIJA, *supra* note 9, at 85-128 (indicating that how taxes affect the economy is a very important aspect of tax policy and evaluating extensively how different tax structures potentially could affect the economy); *id.* at 130-60 (indicating that having a tax system as simple and enforceable as possible is very important, and evaluating extensively the degree to which various tax structures meet this goal).

146.   *See* LIAM MURPHY & THOMAS NAGEL, THE MYTH OF OWNERSHIP: TAXES AND JUSTICE 135 (2002) (arguing that, at a minimum, a tax scheme should provide adequate revenue for public goods, such as defense, law enforcement, and education, and should support a decent standard of living for those the least economically well off); SLEMROD & BAKIJA, *supra* note 9, at 1-2 (indicating all citizens benefit from government sponsored activities paid for by taxes and the alternative of large budget deficits causes undesirable economic consequences); Sneed, *supra* note 145, at 570 ("Revenue is adequate when its quantity is sufficient to accomplish the purpose, or purposes, for which it is raised.").

147.   *See* SLEMROD & BAKIJA, *supra* note 9, at 47-49 (noting the prominence of fairness in tax policy debates and describing violent protests over taxes perceived as unfair); Sneed, *supra* note 145, at 574-86 (discussing in detail the need for equity in the tax structure).

uity and horizontal equity—to evaluate the fairness of tax structures.[148] The first principle, vertical equity, dictates that the tax burdens should reflect the taxpayer's economic well-being, commonly referred to as the taxpayer's ability to pay, which has the effect of imposing different levels of tax burdens on taxpayers with different abilities to pay.[149] Generally, economists and tax policy theorists use income as the yardstick for comparing taxpayers' ability to pay, even when evaluating taxes not based on income, such as sales and property taxes.[150]

A progressive tax structure, which imposes a greater tax burden on those taxpayers with a greater ability to pay, increases both the tax rate on a percentage basis and the total tax liability as the taxpayer's income rises.[151] Steeply progressive income tax structures have more marginal rate brackets that continue to rise to higher levels as the taxpayer's income climbs towards the highest levels.[152] Mildly progressive income tax structures have fewer marginal rate brackets—even as few as two—with lower rates applying at lower income levels.[153] A flat or proportional income tax structure imposes the same percentage of tax on each taxpayer regardless of income level.[154] Although this model places less emphasis on ability to pay than do progressive structures, credible flat tax structures factor in the ability to pay principle by building in exemptions shielding a minimum level of income from the tax in order to avoid unfairly burdening taxpayers that have little or no ability to pay and, from an actual dollar amount perspective, by imposing a greater tax liability on higher income taxpayers.[155]

The major difference between progressive and credible flat income tax structures focuses on the comparative tax burdens borne by taxpayers in the middle and higher income ranges. Depending on the degree of progressiveness, progressive income tax structures always impose a higher burden, sometimes a substantially higher burden, on those taxpayers at the highest income levels, which has the effect of lowering the burden borne

---

148.   SLEMROD & BAKIJA, *supra* note 9, at 49-50.

149.   *Id.* (defining vertical equity generally); *id.* at 52-54 (defining aspects of vertical equity as including the ability to pay principle, which requires tax liability to reflect the taxpayer's economic well-being, and also the benefit principle, which states that tax liability should reflect the benefits the taxpayer receives from the government).

150.   *See* STAFF OF THE J. COMM. ON TAX'N, 99TH CONG., TAX REFORM PROPOSALS: RATE STRUCTURE AND OTHER INDIVIDUAL INCOME TAX ISSUES 2 (Comm. Print 1985) (noting that income, meaning the financial ability to purchase goods and services not needed to earn the income, has been traditionally accepted as a valid measure of the ability to pay taxes).

151.   *See* SLEMROD & BAKIJA, *supra* note 9, at 5.

152.   *Id.* at 31.

153.   *Id.* (defining progressive income tax structure and stating that a tax structure is more progressive than another if its average tax rate rises more rapidly as income rises and noting that the issue of vertical equity explores whether a tax structure should be progressive, and if so, how progressive it should be).

154.   *Id.* at 54.

155.   *Id.*

by taxpayers at the middle and lower-middle income levels.[156] However, when compared to progressive taxes, flat income tax structures always shift the tax burden away from higher income taxpayers, allowing the greatest tax savings to occur at the highest income levels, which has the effect of increasing the tax burden borne by taxpayers at the middle and lower-middle income levels.[157] The question of whether the federal income tax structure should be steeply progressive, mildly progressive, or flat is one of the most controversial issues debated in tax policy circles.[158]

Finally, regressive tax structures impose taxes as a percentage of income that is inversely proportional to income.[159] Regressive tax structures allow taxpayers at higher income levels, those with the greatest ability to pay, to bear the lightest burden, in that the percentage of their income needed to pay the tax liability shrinks to smaller percentages as their income climbs to higher levels.[160] At the same time, low-income taxpayers must bear greater tax burdens because the percentage of their income needed to pay the tax liability grows as their income falls, which ultimately imposes the highest proportional burden on the poorest taxpayers, those least able to pay.[161] Also, flat or proportional taxes that fail to provide a sufficient level of exemptions needed to shield an adequate level of

---

156. *See* SLEMROD & BAKIJA, *supra* note 9, at 5.

157. *See id.* at 10 (discussing proposals to replace the current progressive federal income tax with a flat tax structure as resulting in a dramatic shift of the tax burden away from wealthy taxpayers to middle class and poor taxpayers with one particular proposal potentially increasing the tax liability of taxpayers with incomes below $200,000 by 11.8%, while decreasing the tax liability for taxpayers with income above $200,000 by 28.3%); *id.* at 162-65 (discussing how, in theory, flat tax rates can result in lower burdens at the lower income ranges, but because of political pressure to keep the rate low, the exemption level will not be set high enough, thus undermining the relief at lower income levels; in any event, flat taxes inevitably increase the burden at the middle income ranges and allow for large tax cuts among the highest incomes); *id.* at 222-23 (discussing a Treasury analysis of three different flat tax proposals with all three plans shifting tax liability away from upper income taxpayers, especially those in the top 1%, and increasing the tax liability of all other taxpayers).

158. The literature debating whether the tax structure should be progressive (and if so, how progressive) or flat is literally endless. Two classic sources that seriously question the wisdom of imposing progressive taxes are ADAM SMITH, THE WEALTH OF NATIONS 777 (Edwin Cannan ed., Random House, Inc. 1937) (1776) [hereinafter A. SMITH] (stating that if they follow the maxim of equality and desire, and a soundly imposed and administered tax structure, "[t]he subjects of every state ought to contribute towards the support of the government, as nearly as possible, in proportion to their respective abilities; that is, in proportion to the revenue which they respectively enjoy under the protection of the state") and Walter J. Blum & Harry Kalven, Jr., *The Uneasy Case for Progressive Taxation*, 19 U. CHI. L. REV. 417 (1952). Two classic sources that generally support a progressive tax structure are HENRY C. SIMONS, PERSONAL INCOME TAXATION 19, 205-06 (1938) (recognizing that the debate concerning progression involves a trade off between loss of production and greater income distribution and then concluding that income taxes should be progressive), and Sneed, *supra* note 145, at 582 ("[S]ome progression is presumptively desirable."). An examination as to whether progressive tax structures are more equitable than flat or proportional tax structures is beyond the scope of this Article.

159. SLEMROD & BAKIJA, *supra* note 9, at 50.

160. *See id.*

161. *Id.* (defining a regressive tax structure as one that takes a smaller percentage of income in tax liability from taxpayers with higher incomes).

income from tax will have a regressive effect by increasing the actual proportion of tax liability borne by low-income taxpayers relative to their
income.[162] Although the question as to which of the two tax structures—
progressive or flat—comes the closest to meeting an ideal definition of
fairness cannot be answered by solely resorting to quantitative economic
analysis, and therefore must ultimately be answered using ethically based
value judgments with a philosophical or theological foundation,[163] regressive tax structures or flat taxes with a regressive effect cannot be reasonably defended under any legitimate ethical model.[164]

Horizontal equity dictates that similarly situated taxpayers should be
treated similarly, meaning that taxpayers within the same ability to pay
range should bear equivalent tax burdens.[165] Horizontal equity issues arise
when tax preferences, such as deductions for expenses that are personal in
nature, shift the tax burden, from a global perspective, in a manner that
lightens the burden for the taxpayers enjoying the tax preference, while
increasing the burden on other taxpayers in the same, or even in a lower,
ability to pay range.[166] Tax preferences that vary the tax burden among
similarly situated taxpayers violate horizontal equity unless the particular
tax preference more accurately measures the taxpayer's true ability to pay

---

162.   *See id.* at 54 (providing an example of a hypothetical regressive tax imposing a 25% income
tax on the first $20,000 of income and a 10% flat rate on all income above that level).

163.   *See* MURPHY & NAGEL, *supra* note 146, at 12 (stating that "tax policy must take account of
political morality, or justice," which means that economic theory can only provide information concerning the likely effects of the possible tax options but cannot be the sole criteria for making the
choice); SLEMROD & BAKIJA, *supra* note 9, at 50-51 (indicating that the study of economics or the
theory of political economy cannot yield the answer regarding fairness and that "[f]airness in taxation,
like fairness in just about anything, is an ethical issue that involves value judgments," which should
allow a panel of philosophers or theologians to offer their views on the ethics of tax progressiveness
along with the opinions of economists).

164.   *See* A. SMITH, *supra* note 158 (arguing that the maxim of equality, focusing on paying taxes in
proportion to one's abilities, presumably would deem a regressive tax structure inequitable); Blum &
Kalven, *supra* note 158, at 420, 506-07 (conceding the need for minimum exemptions to ensure people
are not taxed below the subsistence level); Michael J. Graetz, *To Praise the Estate Tax, Not to Bury It*,
93 YALE L.J. 259, 274 (1983) (noting that "the case for regressive taxation is surely wrong"); Nancy
C. Staudt, *The Hidden Costs of the Progressivity Debate*, 50 VAND. L. REV. 919, 921 & n.10 (1997)
(citing numerous sources finding that theorists on both sides of the debate over progressive taxes have
come to a consensus agreeing that poor individuals, those living at or below subsistence levels of
income, should not have to incur tax costs).

165.   SLEMROD & BAKIJA, *supra* note 9, at 74 (defining horizontal equity as the principle that tax
liability should be the same for taxpayers with the same economic well-being); *id.* at 137 (defining
horizontal equity as "the equal treatment of people with equal ability to pay"); *see* MURPHY & NAGEL,
supra note 146, at 164 (positing horizontal equity more broadly as being concerned with tax discrimination in general and noting that questions can arise as to the propriety of tax preferences (such as the
distinction between homeowners and renters, savers and spenders, single and married, young and old,
those with children and those without, and the sighted and the blind) separate from ability to pay
issues).

166.   MURPHY & NAGEL, *supra* note 146, at 164 (noting that tax preferences result in higher taxes
for those not enjoying the preference); SLEMROD & BAKIJA, *supra* note 9, at 73-74, 181 (discussing
tax preferences creating privileges to one group of taxpayers as effectively penalizing all other taxpayers by driving up the rates).

or creates important benefits (beyond the immediate taxpayer) that are best achieved through the tax structure.[167] Although the answer to whether tax preferences raising horizontal equity issues are fair cannot be solely derived through quantitative economic analysis, and therefore must be derived by also using ethically based philosophical or theological models, tax preferences that violate horizontal equity by shifting the tax burden to taxpayers in a lower ability to pay range cannot be defended under any legitimate ethical model because of their hidden regressive effects.[168]

Income taxes structurally based on the yardstick measuring ability to pay are the easiest to evaluate under the principles of vertical and horizontal equity.[169] Sales taxes also can be readily evaluated under these principles. Under the principle of vertical equity, sales taxes generally have a regressive effect, because the sales tax rate applies to the purchase price of a transaction without regard to the taxpayer's ability to pay, which requires low-income purchasers to pay a greater portion of their available income towards the sales tax than higher income purchasers.[170] Moreover, this regressive effect intensifies as the sales tax rate climbs to higher levels.[171] Sales tax structures can also raise horizontal equity issues if certain transactions or taxpayers enjoy preferential treatment through lower rates or exemptions that cannot be justified as making the overall sales tax structure more reflective of the purchaser's true ability to pay or by otherwise serving some important government objective.[172]

Unlike income and sales taxes, property taxes, which broadly represent a tax on the privilege of owning property, are much more difficult to evaluate under the principles of vertical and horizontal equity. Because property taxes are based on the assessed value of property, which for

---

167. SLEMROD & BAKIJA, *supra* note 9, at 75-76, 181-82.

168. *See* sources cited *supra* note 165 (indicating that tax structures that are regressive or have regressive effects are unethical); *see also* SLEMROD & BAKIJA, *supra* note 9, at 74-75 (discussing hypothetical tax preferences that not only violate horizontal equity but also cannot be defended due to their totally arbitrary nature).

169. *See supra* note 150 and accompanying text (discussing income as a measure of ability to pay).

170. SLEMROD & BAKIJA, *supra* note 9, at 171-72.

171. MADDOX & FUQUAY, *supra* note 11, at 364 (identifying sales taxes as regressive because low-income persons, whose expenditures on items subject to the sales tax constitute a large portion of their incomes, will always bear a heavier burden for the tax); SLEMROD & BAKIJA, *supra* note 9, at 50 (identifying a tax that takes a smaller percentage of income from those with higher incomes as regressive); *id.* at 9-10 (discussing proposals to replace the current progressive federal income tax and indicating that a federal retail sales tax would shift a greater portion of the tax burden onto low-income taxpayers because this structure could not build in an exemption for a minimum level of income); *id.* at 196 (identifying the retail sales tax as completely "impersonal" because the rate "is not adjusted to account for any characteristic of the consumer, such as income, marital status, number of dependents, or personal tastes"); Bryce, *supra* note 1, at 545 (noting that the sales tax is, by its nature, regressive).

172. *See supra* notes 163-66 and accompanying text; *see also* SLEMROD & BAKIJA, *supra* note 9, at 196 (discussing ways to ease the burden of sales taxes on poor taxpayers—giving exemptions for basic necessities such as food and medicine, allowing poor and elderly taxpayers to apply for refunds, and charging different rates on different items—and noting that these distinctions would not create horizontal inequity because they would help the sales tax better correlate to a taxpayer's ability to pay).

many taxpayers represents a large capital investment that may or may not correlate closely with their income in a given year, designing the property tax burden to reflect an acceptable relationship to the taxpayer's ability to pay will be difficult. This task is further complicated because many types of property, such as commercial property and other real property used for timber and agriculture, often produce substantial profits for the owner (although there is often a substantial variation in the level of profits from year-to-year), while other types of property, including personal residences, produce no profits until the owner sells the property.[173] Property tax structures that use the valuation process to tax some types of property more lightly than others raise horizontal equity issues, unless the preferential treatment of the favored type of property more accurately measures ability to pay or serves some other important governmental goal.[174] Despite these difficulties, property taxes can be structured within acceptable boundaries of fairness by using the principles of vertical and horizontal equity as guides. A well-administered property tax structure should require a reasonable percentage of the property's fair market value to be subject to the tax in order to ensure that owners of higher valued, especially income producing, property, who enjoy a greater ability to pay, bear their share of the overall tax. However, at the same time the property tax structure should allow appropriate exemptions in order to avoid overtaxing lower valued property, especially property producing little or no income.[175]

B. Judeo-Christian Ethical Principles Forbid the Economic Oppression of Poor Persons and Require That Such Persons Enjoy at Least a Minimum Opportunity to Improve Their Economic Circumstances

Developing moral principles of Judeo-Christian ethics that can be used to evaluate any social structure, including economic and tax structures, under an ethical model involves properly interpreting and applying the Bible, the most important source of these principles. Because the Bible is an ancient text, written in an ancient language, addressing real persons facing a variety of circumstances over two thousand years ago in a cultural setting vastly different from the United States in the twenty-first century, proper interpretation and application of the Bible, a process that scholars

---

173.   *See* EDGAR K. BROWNING & WILLIAM R. JOHNSON, AM. ENTER. INST. FOR PUB. POLICY RESEARCH, THE DISTRIBUTION OF THE TAX BURDEN 33 (1979) (identifying property taxes as being imposed on the assessed value of real property and the taxing of property as essentially a tax on capital with the same effect as taxing income generated by the property).

174.   *See supra* notes 163-66 and accompanying text.

175.   *See* MADDOX & FUQUAY, *supra* note 11, at 373-74 (recognizing that sometimes the value of the taxpayer's property does not correlate exactly with the taxpayer's ability to pay property tax, which makes the job of designing a property tax structure based on ability to pay more complex than designing a comparable income tax structure, but noting that property taxes rest on the assumption that the value of a person's property can be a valid measure of the taxpayer's ability to pay).

call "hermeneutics," requires discovering what the text meant to the original audience and articulating the broad ethical principles that the biblical text established for that audience.[176] If the "specific life situations" of the first audience receiving the biblical text mirror the "specific life situations" of the contemporary audience, then clearly the broad ethical principles of the biblical text apply to the contemporary audience in the same manner as they applied to the first audience.[177] However, even if the "specific life situations" of the original and contemporary audiences do not mirror one another due to vast cultural differences between the two, the broad ethical principles can still be applied to the contemporary audience as long as the contemporary situation is "genuinely comparable," meaning the contemporary problem must be analogous to the situation originally addressed in the text.[178]

The process of discovering the Judeo-Christian ethical principles addressing the relationships between human beings and their societal structures must start with the creation account in the book of Genesis, in which God is the only supreme being and the sole creator of all life.[179] From a

---

176.   See GORDON D. FEE & DOUGLAS STUART, HOW TO READ THE BIBLE FOR ALL ITS WORTH 17-19 (2d ed. 1993). The discovery of what the text meant to the first audience, a process scholars of the Bible call biblical exegesis, is of absolute critical importance because a biblical text cannot be properly applied to a contemporary situation in a way inconsistent with its original meaning. *Id.* at 19-21, 25-26. At a minimum, sound biblical exegesis must involve not only a study of the literary genre of the particular book but also must examine the historical and cultural context. *Id.* at 21-25. For example, the Prophetic books, written roughly from the eighth through the fifth centuries B.C., attribute the proliferation of idolatry and social injustice in both the Northern and Southern Kingdoms of ancient Israel as due to violations of the Mosaic law, which deprived most Israelites of their ancestral land and left them vulnerable to exploitation by the wealthy few. *See* Bernhard Lang, *The Social Organization of Peasant Poverty in Biblical Israel*, 24 J. FOR STUD. OLD TESTAMENT 47 (1982) (describing oppressive social conditions suffered by the poor in the ancient Near East and relating the historical conditions of "rent capitalism"); 2 THE MINOR PROPHETS 637 (Thomas Edward McComiskey ed., 1993) (describing the economic and social ideal of ancient Israel as a nation where everyone owned enough land to maintain their own families, and describing the violation of land tenure and other social aspects of the Mosaic law that turned ancient Israel away from the ideal and into a nation of debt, slaves, sharecroppers, and hired workers). During the earthly ministry of Jesus Christ and the ministry of Paul, rampant social injustice was the norm in Roman-occupied first century Palestine, differing substantially from the norm of the democratically governed United States. *See* WILLIAM L. LANE, THE GOSPEL OF MARK 416 (1974) (discussing the impact of Roman occupation on the social background of Jewish communities in first century Galilee in that great estates of land were owned by a few with a vast number of dispossessed peasants who worked the land as tenant farmers); CHRISTOPHER J.H. WRIGHT, KNOWING JESUS THROUGH THE OLD TESTAMENT 225-66 (1992) [hereinafter WRIGHT, KNOWING JESUS] & CRAIG L. BLOMBERG, NEITHER POVERTY NOR RICHES 90-91 (D.A. Carson ed., 1999) (describing the economic hardships of the many Jewish families dispossessed of their ancestral lands as growing worse in first century Palestine due to the Roman occupation, and the start of the Zealot movement that attacked both the Romans and the aristocratic Jews that accommodated the Romans).

177.   FEE & STUART, *supra* note 176, at 65.

178.   *Id.* at 67-76.

179.   PAUL R. HOUSE, OLD TESTAMENT THEOLOGY 60 (1998) (noting that all scholars recognize the monotheistic portrayal of God as the sole creator in the creation account of *Genesis* as uniquely distinguishing Israel from other ancient Near East cultures, whose creation accounts reflected their worship of multiple gods).

divine perspective, no person or group of persons, regardless of their station in life, stands at a lesser level of importance than other persons because all persons were created in God's image.[180] The commandments "[l]ove the Lord your God with all your heart and with all your soul and with all your strength"[181] and "love your neighbor as yourself,"[182] inseparably link a proper relationship with God to proper relationships with all other human beings.[183] Because all humans are the image of God, all persons have an enormous responsibility from an ethical standpoint as "God's representatives on earth"[184] to be accountable "for the life of his fellow man"[185] and to act as his "brother's keeper."[186] The moral principle equating the unjust treatment of fellow human beings to a wrong committed against God grows out of the biblical account of creation and is further developed throughout the Old Testament.[187]

---

180.   *Genesis* 1:27 ("So God created man in his own image, in the image of God he created him; male and female he created them."); *see* KENNETH A. MATHEWS, THE NEW AMERICAN COMMENTARY: GENESIS 1-11:26 (2001) (positing that humans enjoy a distinction from all other life "[s]ince all human life is created in the image of God, there is no person or class of humans lesser than others").

181.   *Deuteronomy* 6:5.

182.   *Leviticus* 19:18.

183.   *See* HOUSE, *supra* note 179, at 142 (positing that commitment to God requires people to reflect his holiness in all aspects of human relationships and business practices; the call to holiness "is no mere private piety, nor even simply a fervent participation in public worship, but a total way of life, involving every aspect of personal, family and social commitment; God's holiness imposes a complete pattern of moral and social behavior upon the people whom he has chosen, so that his holiness makes their responsive holiness an inescapable demand"); MARK F. ROOKER, THE NEW AMERICAN COMMENTARY: LEVITICUS 231 (2000) (stating that holiness must permeate all aspects of life and so is especially demonstrated in relationships among the community).

184.   HOUSE, *supra* note 179, at 61; *see also* ALLEN P. ROSS, CREATION AND BLESSING: A GUIDE TO THE STUDY AND EXPOSITION OF GENESIS 112-13 (1998) (analyzing the Hebrew text and interpreting creation in the "image" of God as empowering human beings with "ethical and moral sensitivities" reflecting the spiritual nature of God).

185.   *Genesis* 9:5-6; *see also* MATHEWS, *supra* note 180, at 402-04 (discussing the Hebrew text of *Genesis* 9:5-6 as requiring an accounting for human life, meaning human life must be treated with special caution).

186.   *Genesis* 4:9; *see also* MATHEWS, *supra* note 180, at 272 (discussing *Genesis* 4:9 and noting that Cain's treatment of his brother Abel is intrinsically related to his relationship with God); ROSS, *supra* note 184, at 159 (discussing *Genesis* 4:9 and stating that "[i]f a nation or family is to survive, the people must be responsible for the well-being of one another").

187.   CHRISTOPHER J.H. WRIGHT, WALKING IN THE WAYS OF THE LORD: THE ETHICAL AUTHORITY OF THE OLD TESTAMENT 16-17 (1995) [hereinafter WRIGHT, WALKING] (noting that all ethical concerns with a biblical basis begin with creation theology); *see also* JOHN N. OSWALT, THE BOOK OF ISAIAH: CHAPTERS 1-39 at 99 (R.K. Harrison ed., 1986) [hereinafter OSWALT I] (stating that injustice and oppression defy the doctrine of creation); *id.* at 6 (noting that the Prophets identified the people's apostasy as tantamount to their "forgetting God" and linked the peoples' service to other gods as equal to "the abuse of those weaker than oneself"); *id.* at 106 (referring specifically to Isaiah, Jeremiah, and Ezekiel as linking idolatry and social injustice); CHRISTOPHER J.H. WRIGHT, AN EYE FOR AN EYE: THE PLACE OF OLD TESTAMENT ETHICS TODAY 30 (1983) [hereinafter WRIGHT, OLD TESTAMENT ETHICS] (attributing the moral decline and disobedience of the people of ancient Israel to their having "forgotten God"); GARY V. SMITH, AMOS 131-32 (1989) [hereinafter G. SMITH] (discussing God's deliverance of the Israelites from Egypt and the Israelites subsequent violations of the Mosaic law, including treating the poor unjustly, as a failure to "honor God in their lives" meaning they "profane[d] the holy name of God" and failed to show gratitude to God for delivering them from

The entire Old Testament thematically expresses special concern for vulnerable and powerless persons in the community, who in ancient Near East culture were the widows, orphans, aliens, and poor people.[188] Recognizing that "[t]here will always be poor people in the land,"[189] and that poor people are created in the image of God to the same degree as persons enjoying more fortunate economic circumstances,[190] the Old Testament, using both general terms[191] and specific examples,[192] creates a broad ethical principle forbidding the economic oppression of poor persons[193] and

---

slavery); KENNETH L. BARKER & WAYLON BAILEY, THE NEW AMERICAN COMMENTARY: MICAH, NAHUM, HABAKKUK AND ZEPHANIAH 40 (E. Ray Clendenen et al. eds., 1999) (describing Micah's general condemnations of the society worshiping money as their God and the poor being their sacrificial victims).

188.   BREVARD S. CHILDS, THE BOOK OF EXODUS 478-79 (1974) (noting "a particularly intense concern for the poor" in the Old Testament); JOHN I. DURHAM, WORLD BIBLICAL COMMENTARY: EXODUS 329 (Bruce M. Metzger et al. eds., 1987) (noting that the poor are a special concern of Yahweh and that Israelites were to remember the poor are Yahweh's people); EUGENE H. MERRILL, THE NEW AMERICAN COMMENTARY: DEUTERONOMY 323 (E. Ray Clendenen et al. eds., 1994) (describing, in the cultural context of ancient Near East society, the alien as being barred from many privileges and the orphan and widow as being especially vulnerable because they lacked family and tribal affiliation).

189.   *Deuteronomy* 15:11; *see also* MERRILL, *supra* note 188, at 244 (discussing the tension between the ideal world with no poverty and the actual world where poverty will always exist as expressing what could be enjoyed if God's purposes prevailed, as opposed to what happens when God's purposes do not always prevail); CHRISTOPHER J. WRIGHT, NEW INTERNATIONAL BIBLICAL COMMENTARY: DEUTERONOMY 191-92 (1996) [hereinafter WRIGHT, DEUTERONOMY] (discussing the Hebrew text of *Deuteronomy* 15:7-11 and the English translation "the poor and needy" and noting that the second person singular possessive referring to the poor as "yours" and "among you" actually supports a translation of "your poor and needy," which indicates that poor people are not just abstract figures but belong to the community).

190.   MERRILL, *supra* note 188, at 322 (stating that viewing the poor as inferior is slander because they were also created in the image of God).

191.   *Exodus* 22:21-22, 23:9 & *Leviticus* 19:13, 33 (generally forbidding oppression).

192.   The specific Old Testament laws based on the broad moral principle forbidding oppression addressed concrete situations that, given the culture and economic structures of the ancient world, had oppressive effects. *See Deuteronomy* 24:12-13, 17 & *Exodus* 22:26-27 (forbidding the keeping of a cloak as a pledge for a loan); PETER C. CRAIGIE, THE BOOK OF DEUTERONOMY 308 (1976) (describing the cloak in ancient Israel as an outer garment by day and a blanket at night, and for very poor people, it would be the only significant possession they could offer as a pledge); *Deuteronomy* 24:6 (forbidding taking a pair of millstones as security for a debt); WRIGHT, DEUTERONOMY, *supra* note 189, at 256 (describing millstones as essential equipment of a family farm for making bread); *Deuteronomy* 23:19, *Exodus* 22:25, & *Leviticus* 25:37 (forbidding the charging of interest for lending money or the selling of food at a profit); ROOKER, *supra* note 183, at 308 (noting that the prohibitions against interest and selling food at a profit prevented further and complete economic devastation of those falling on hard times); WRIGHT, DEUTERONOMY, *supra* note 189, at 251 (discussing the prohibition against interest in the context of ancient Israel as a mechanism to ensure those who suffered great need would not be further exploited by others taking advantage of the difficult times); *Deuteronomy* 24:14-15 & *Leviticus* 19:13 (forbidding holding back payment of wages overnight); MERRILL, *supra* note 188, at 322 (describing the serious economic plight of ancient workers and their pattern of living "hand to mouth" or "day to day"); *Leviticus* 19:35-36 (forbidding dishonest scales and measurements); ROOKER, *supra* note 183, at 263 (noting that "[h]onest business practices are . . . a common biblical theme" and that the priests were probably responsible for ensuring integrity in measurements).

193.   *See* sources cited *supra* note 177 and accompanying text (discussing the process of biblical interpretation as first discovering what the text meant to the original audience including the broad ethical principles communicated to the first audience from that text); sources cited *supra* notes 191-92 (discussing biblical texts generally forbidding oppression and specific examples of economic oppres-

strongly condemns those who violate this ethical principle.[194] Although the ancient world's examples of economic oppression sometimes differ from contemporary examples, the "specific life situation"—the tendency to take advantage of poor people—has not changed. Therefore, the Judeo-Christian ethical principle forbidding the economic oppression of poor people applies to contemporary audiences in the same manner it applied to the original audience.[195]

The Old Testament builds on and further expands the ethical principle forbidding the economic oppression of the poor by also requiring that poor

---

sion explicitly forbidden); *see also* FEE & STUART, *supra* note 176, at 155 (discussing the specific Old Testament laws as examples intended "as a reliable *guide* with general applicability—not a technical description of *all* possible conditions one could imagine"); WRIGHT, DEUTERONOMY, *supra* note 189, at 82-83 (discussing John Calvin's interpretation of the commandment prohibiting theft as invoking specific Old Testament laws dealing with, for example, wages as well as accurate weights and measures, which set examples broadly forbidding economic exploitation and injustice as well as all forms of unjust gain at the expense of others).

194.   *See Amos* 2:7 ("They trample on the heads of the poor as upon the dust of the ground and deny justice to the oppressed."); BILLY K. SMITH & FRANK S. PAGE, THE NEW AMERICAN COMMENTARY: AMOS, OBADIAH, JONAH 62-63 (1995) (discussing translation difficulties in the Hebrew text of *Amos* 2:7 and noting the general thrust of the accusation to the rich is that they step on the poor and treat them like dirt); G. SMITH, *supra* note 188, at 120-21 (interpreting the oppression of the poor described in *Amos* 2:7 as occurring outside a legal proceeding where "[t]he powerful push them around, control their life, determine how they will live and deprive them of their rights"); *Amos* 2:8 ("They lie down beside every altar on garments taken in pledge."); SMITH & PAGE, *supra* at 64 (stating *Amos* 2:8 discusses the violation of the Mosaic law for keeping garments past nightfall); G. SMITH, *supra* note 187, at 13 (stating the principle emphasis in *Amos* 2:8 is exploitation); *Amos* 8:4-6 ("Hear this, you who trample the needy and do away with the poor of the land . . . buying the poor with silver and the needy for a pair of sandals."); G. SMITH, *supra* note 187, (interpreting *Amos* 8:6 as accusing the wealthy and powerful of driving the poor into bankruptcy and slavery through heavy loans and taxes); *Micah* 2:1 ("Woe to those who plan iniquity, to those who plot evil on their beds! At morning's light they carry it out because it is in their power to do it."); BARKER & BAILEY, *supra* note 187, at 63 (discussing the iniquity in *Micah* 2:1 as "refer[ring] to abuse of power in illegal and unethical machinations, resulting in social injustice" and discussing how "the wealthy oppressors" had the power "because they controlled the power structures of their society, believing that 'might makes right'"); *Isaiah* 10:1-2 ("Woe to those who make unjust laws, to those who issue oppressive decrees, to deprive the poor of their rights and withhold justice from the oppressed of my people, making widows their prey and robbing the fatherless."); OSWALT I, *supra* note 187, at 259 (interpreting *Isaiah* 10:1-2 as describing oppression where the poor are deprived of their rights resulting in the society reaching "the lowest limits of cynicism and self-serving").

195.   *See* sources cited *supra* notes 177-78 and accompanying text (discussing the importance of discovering the meaning and the broad ethical principles of the biblical text to the first audience and the ability to apply the broad ethical principles to the contemporary audience if the "specific life situations" of the ancient and contemporary situations are the same); *supra* notes 191-92 (discussing biblical texts generally forbidding oppression and giving specific examples of economic oppression explicitly forbidden); *see also* BARKER & BAILEY, *supra* note 187, at 36-37, RAYMOND BROWN, THE MESSAGE OF DEUTERONOMY (1993), & ROOKER, *supra* note 183, at 257 (stating that Old Testament laws should be applied to contemporary society according to their general principles, implying that the protection of the poor from economic oppression would be an important general principle); FEE & STUART, *supra* note 176, at 150-63 (noting that the Old Testament law serves as inspired work providing standards and examples which provide principles that apply contemporarily on what it means to be loyal to God); MERRILL, *supra* note 188, at 201 (noting that obeying God requires care and concern for other people, especially people who are economically and socially disadvantaged); WRIGHT, DEUTERONOMY, *supra* note 189, at 195 (stating Israel as the light to the nations has broad "paradigmatic relevance to all cultures and societies").

persons enjoy a minimum opportunity to meet their basic needs and improve their economic circumstances,[196] and strongly condemns those violating this ethical principle.[197] In addition to generally requiring that they be treated justly[198] and generously,[199] the Old Testament mandates that

---

196. *See* WRIGHT, DEUTERONOMY, *supra* note 189, at 260-61 (discussing the Hebrew text of *Deuteronomy* 24:17 and concluding that "justice" is much broader than legal proceedings and encompasses "rights" generally, which, when read in the context of the entire passage, means having a right to opportunities to be able to self-sufficiently provide for themselves); *id.* at 257 (discussing the purpose behind *Deuteronomy* as establishing through enforceable legislation a minimum level of human dignity and empowerment to have discretion over what the people own, giving them an opportunity for self-improvement); WRIGHT, OLD TESTAMENT ETHICS, *supra* note 187, at 77 (noting that the land tenure system of ancient Israel did not ensure everyone the same economic potential but sought to ensure "that every family should have *enough* for economic viability"); DOUGLAS STUART, WORLD BIBLICAL COMMENTARY: HOSEA-JONAH 317 (1987) (analyzing the Hebrew text interpreting the oppression of the poor described in *Amos* 2:7 as also describing the wealthy and powerful as "hindering access or progress" of the poorer members of the community).

197. *See Amos* 2:6 ("They sell the righteous for silver, and the needy for a pair of sandals."); G. SMITH, *supra* note 187, at 227 (interpreting Amos' condemnation of selling the poor for a pair of sandals in *Amos* 2:6 as violations of laws forbidding the charging of interest and requiring the return of land in the year of Jubilee; ignoring these laws resulted in peasant farmers being gradually driven from their land and forced to pay a large portion of their grain in rent to the wealthy who now own the land); *Amos* 5:11 ("You trample on the poor and force him to give you grain."); SMITH & PAGE, *supra* note 194, at 103 (discussing how the wealthy trampled on the poor by taking the fruit of their labor in the form of the greatest share of grain the land produced); STUART, *supra* note 196, at 288 (noting the theme of oppression of the poor throughout *Amos* refers to violations of the law including failing to honor land inheritance rights and failing to observe the Year of the Jubilee; *Micah* 2:2 ("They covet fields and seize them, and houses, and take them. They defraud a man of his home, a fellow man of his inheritance."); BARKER & BAILEY, *supra* note 187, at 64 (discussing *Micah* 2:2 which refers to violations of the Mosaic land tenure laws resulting in "land barons . . . cheating others out of their homes and landed property"); *Micah* 2:9 ("You drive the women of my people from their pleasant homes. You take away my blessing from their children forever."); BARKER & BAILEY, *supra* note 187, at 67-68 (noting *Micah* 2:9 may refer to widows and orphans being denied their inheritance rights in violation of land tenure laws leaving them without property, money, or security); *Isaiah* 5:8 ("Woe to you who add house to house and join field to field till no space is left and you live alone in the land."); OSWALT I, *supra* note 187, at 158 (adding house to house in *Isaiah* 5:8 involved immorally dispossessing people and reducing them to servitude on what was their own land); *see also* CHRISTOPHER J.H. WRIGHT, GOD'S PEOPLE IN GOD'S LAND 65 (1990) [hereinafter WRIGHT, LAND] (describing generally the attack by the Prophets on practices that destroyed large numbers of small family land holdings as being theologically motivated).

198. *Deuteronomy* 24:17 ("Do not deprive the alien or fatherless of justice . . . ."); WRIGHT, DEUTERONOMY, *supra* note 189, at 260 (stating the Hebrew word for justice is broader than courtroom justice, because it refers to a person's rights in general); *Amos* 5:7 (warning those "who turn justice into bitterness and cast righteousness to the ground"); SMITH & PAGE, *supra* note 194, at 100 (characterizing the indictment in *Amos* 5:7 as denying the poor not just justice in the courts for legal matters, but more broadly justice from a divine standard as to how society should be ordered); *Amos* 5:10 (warning those that "hate the one who reproves in court and despise him who tells the truth"); G. SMITH, *supra* note 187, at 226 (discussing *Amos* 5:10 and justice at the court as referring to justice at the gate of an ancient city, covering all aspects of the community's life, revealing "a concerted effort to control and manipulate the legal process to the advantage of special interests instead of justice," giving advantage over the poor, contrary to God's justice); *Amos* 5:14 ("Seek good, not evil, that you may live."); SMITH & PAGE, *supra* note 194, at 106 (interpreting seeking good in *Amos* 5:14 as justice for the poor, and evil as the denial of justice for the poor, with the larger message being "one who truly seeks the Lord also seeks the welfare of the poor"); *Isaiah* 1:17 ("Seek justice, encourage the oppressed."); OSWALT I, *supra* note 187, at 99 (stating justice is valuing persons as God does, consistent with God's character).

199. *Deuteronomy* 15:7-11 & *Leviticus* 25:35, 39-40 (requiring generosity and opportunities to

others leave behind food for poor persons to harvest.[200] Primarily based on the commandment to observe the Sabbath, the Old Testament also creates an infrastructure providing those facing the harshest economic circumstances, which in the ancient Near East world meant indentured servants and those heavily in debt or possessing no land, with an opportunity to achieve economic self-sufficiency.[201] These provisions required servants to be released every seven years,[202] debts to be forgiven every seven years,[203] certain redemption rights of land sold outside the ancestral family to be honored,[204] and also mandated that all land ultimately be returned to the original ancestral owner every fifty years.[205]

---

work to be extended to poor people).

200.   *Deuteronomy* 24:19-21 & *Leviticus* 19:9-10 (requiring farmers to leave part of the harvest behind for the poor); CRAIGIE, *supra* note 192, at 311 (discussing the laws requiring gleaning allowing the poor not only basic food, but an opportunity to secure the food through their own efforts rather than simply begging); R.K. HARRISON, LEVITICUS 197 (1980) (characterizing the practice of gleaning as fostering a sense of community among the Israelites); JOHN E. HARTLEY, WORLD BIBLICAL COMMENTARY: LEVITICUS 1-27 at 314 (1992) (characterizing the gleaning laws as allowing the poor to maintain their dignity by working for their own needs); MERRILL, *supra* note 188, at 324 & ROOKER, *supra* note 183, at 255-56 (describing gleaning as preserving human dignity by allowing the recipient to work); *see also Deuteronomy* 14:28-29 (requiring tithes of food to meet the basic needs of others who cannot provide for themselves); *Exodus* 23:10-11 (requiring land to lay fallow every seventh year so that the poor in the community may claim whatever grows that year).

201.   *See* sources cited *infra* notes 203-06 and accompanying text (discussing the specific provisions mandating the release of servants and debt every seven years, granting certain redemption rights if ancestral land was sold outside the family, and finally stating that the ultimate right of all families to be returned their ancestral land every fifty years acts as a safety net, allowing even the poorest Israelites a minimum opportunity to restore their economic self-sufficiency and limiting how low economically the societal structure allowed people to descend).

202.   *Deuteronomy* 15:12-14, *Exodus* 21:2, & *Leviticus* 25:40-41 (requiring servants to be set free every seven years with generous provisions); WRIGHT, DEUTERONOMY, *supra* note 189, at 192-93 (discussing the requirement that the freed servant be supplied generously as necessary so that the servant has a real chance to attain economic self-sufficiency thus providing substance to his freedom); *see also* ROOKER, *supra* note 183, at 309 (discussing the ancient presumption that a person reduced to servitude presumably had already sold his land and was now forced to sell himself).

203.   *Deuteronomy* 15:1-3 (requiring all debts to be cancelled every seven years); *see also* BROWN, *supra* note 188, at 165 (discussing debt in the ancient world and how one bad harvest could force many families into debt); BARUCH A. LEVINE, THE JPS TORAH COMMENTARY: LEVITICUS 169 (1989) (discussing debt in the context of ancient society being a function of the land; once a person had no land to secure a loan they were forced to sell themselves or their children).

204.   *Leviticus* 25:14-16, 25-28 (providing for redemption rights to buy back family ancestral land with the price being based on the number of years since the Year of the Jubilee); *see also* ROOKER, *supra* note 183, at 306 (stating that because of these redemptions rights and the Year of Jubilee, land sales in ancient Israel were more like leases).

205.   *Leviticus* 25:8-13 (requiring that after seven Sabbaths, in the fiftieth year, all land must be returned to the original ancestral family clan); *see* HARRISON, *supra* note 200, at 228-29 & HARTLEY, *supra* note 200, at 427-28 (summarizing scholarly positions on the origins and practical observance of the Year of the Jubilee); HARTLEY, *supra* note 200, at 436, 443 (discussing the laws related to the price of buying and selling property in conjunction with the Year of the Jubilee as producing a perpetual right to land for all families allowing them to lease the land to others in difficult times until the next Jubilee); HARRISON, *supra* note 200, at 224 (noting that the Year of the Jubilee prevented the accumulation of vast estates); ROOKER, *supra* note 183, at 303-04 (describing the Year of the Jubilee and noting it involved carrying out personal holiness "on the social plane on behalf of the disadvantaged" and it was "a protection for the weak; for the rich to dominate over the weak would be a violation of God's covenant"); WRIGHT, OLD TESTAMENT ETHICS, *supra* note 187, at 83 (noting that

Due to vast cultural differences and the passage of over two thousand years resulting in change of "the specific life situations," the definitions of what is necessary to achieve economic self-sufficiency in the ancient and contemporary economic structures do not mirror one another exactly.[206] Because economic well-being in ancient Israel revolved around ownership of sufficient land, while economic self-sufficiency in contemporary economic structures requires an adequate education and marketable skills, the specific provisions of the Old Testament relating to harvesting practices, the release of servants and debt, and land tenure rights do not seem to apply contemporarily.[207] However, the ancient indicator of poverty, owning no land (which led to individuals and families being hopelessly in debt and forced into servitude), is "genuinely comparable" to the contemporary problem of poor people having an inadequate education and little or no marketable skills and thus being unable to break out of the cycle of poverty.[208] Consequently, the Judeo-Christian ethical principle mandating that poor persons enjoy at least a minimum opportunity to improve their economic circumstances applies to contemporary audiences but today calls for action which will at least ensure that poor children enjoy a minimum opportunity to achieve an adequate education, because that is "genuinely comparable" to the biblical texts responding to the ancient indicator of

---

Jubilee was designed to put limits and safeguards on the worst effects of the Fall, such as people falling into poverty); WRIGHT, LAND, *supra* note 197, 177-79 (arguing that Jubilee was intended to periodically restore the economic viability of small family land units as part of the theological identity of ancient Israel).

206. *See* WRIGHT, WALKING, *supra* note 187, at 149-55 (discussing ancient Israel's tribally based society, which placed a heavy emphasis on the extended family and was geared toward the social health and economic viability of the lowest units, in contrast to the complex economic structures of modern society); WRIGHT, OLD TESTAMENT ETHICS, *supra* note 187, at 37-38 (discussing the kinship structures of ancient Israel and noting that "Israelite society was more broadly 'egalitarian' rather than 'hierarchical'").

207. FEE & STUART, *supra* note 178, at 156-58 (identifying the law of the Old Testament related to release of servants and others like it as "casuistic law," meaning law which does not literally apply to contemporary Christians but provides an example of God's character, his demand for fairness, and his ideals, which can be applied broadly); ROOKER, *supra* note 183, at 74 (stating Old Testament civil laws "should not be brought over wholesale as applicable to the governing of the contemporary state"); WRIGHT, OLD TESTAMENT ETHICS, *supra* note 187, at 43 (discussing the contemporary application of the Old Testament in general and noting that "[w]e cannot simply transpose the social laws of an ancient people into the modern world and try to make them work as written").

208. *See* sources cited *supra* note 178 and accompanying text (discussing both the problem of applying the moral principles behind biblical texts when the "specific life situations" of the ancient and contemporary worlds do not mirror each other and the ability to apply the broad moral principles to contemporary problems that are "genuinely comparable" to the underlying problem addressed by the text); sources cited *supra* notes 200-03 and accompanying text (discussing general provisions and specific examples of biblical texts revolving around land ownership and the ability to be freed from servitude and crippling debt as providing all Israelites a minimum opportunity for economic self-improvement); sources cited *supra* notes 102-06 and accompanying text (discussing the importance of an adequate education as necessary to develop marketable skills needed for economic self-sufficiency in the contemporary economic marketplace and the role of adequate funding for the public schools towards achieving that goal).

poverty by mandating certain harvesting practices and the release of servants and debts, as well as establishing land tenure rights.[209]

In addition to establishing broad ethical principles, the Old Testament
imposes on persons empowered with political or spiritual authority—the
priests, prophets, kings, and judges of ancient Israel[210]—a substantially
greater moral obligation to maintain the general well-being of the entire
community, especially a duty to protect the poor from economic oppression and to ensure that they enjoy at least a minimum opportunity to improve their economic circumstances.[211] In addition to lavishly praising

---

209.   *See* sources cited at *supra* notes 195-96 (citing numerous commentators stating that the general
moral principles of the Old Testament law should apply contemporarily, and indicating that care and
concern for poor people are among these moral principles); HARRISON, *supra* note 200, at 229 (discussing the contemporary application of the Old Testament's land laws to today's church and noting
that "the tenor of the laws pursued a middle course between the extremes of unrestricted capitalism
and rampant communism"); ROOKER, *supra* note 183, at 312 (discussing the application of the principles behind the Year of the Jubilee to the church today, and noting that it forbids the accumulation of
vast amounts of property by a wealthy few but respects the basic right to ownership of private property); WRIGHT, WALKING, *supra* note 187, at 31-32 (discussing contemporary application of the
principles of the Year of Jubilee requiring every family to have enough property, which will not nec-
essarily be equal amounts, to preserve economic viability); *id.* at 197-208 (discussing the application
of the Year of the Jubilee using the biblical hermeneutics and concluding Jubilee "could also support
ethical challenge for justice to the oppressed in contemporary history"); WRIGHT, DEUTERONOMY,
supra note 189, at 83 (noting that John Calvin "implied a corresponding affirmative—to seek the good
of the neighbor by generosity and kindness" in his interpretation of the commandment prohibiting theft
and that this interpretation has the same "broad relevance to matters of material property and economic institutions, policies, and practice" as the commandment prohibiting murder does when applied
to the difficult questions involving human life); *id.* at 261 (applying principles of biblical hermeneutics
to the Old Testament law and finding that these principles broadly require the poorest and weakest in
the community to have access to opportunities they need to provide for themselves, which "may include financial resources, but could also include access to education, legal assistance, investment in
job opportunities, etc.; [s]uch things should not be leftovers or handouts, but a matter of rights and
responsibilities in a caring society"); WRIGHT, LAND, *supra* note 197, at 178-79 (discussing moral
principles established by the Jubilee as requiring (not by just relying on good will and sympathy) steps
(without directly endorsing a particular political course of action) "to halt the relentless economic
forces in society whereby the rich get richer and the poor get poorer" so that the poor have an opportunity to restore themselves to economic viability).
210.   *See* BARKER & BAILEY, *supra* note 187, at 80-81 (identifying and briefly discussing ancient
Israel's leaders and their responsibilities); *Ezekiel* 22:25-29 (containing a stinging indictment accusing
the leaders of vast social injustices and distinguishing among ancient Israel's classes of leaders);
DANIEL I. BLOCK, THE BOOK OF EZEKIEL, CHAPTERS 1-24 at 724-26 (1997) [hereinafter BLOCK I]
(discussing the imagery in *Ezekiel* 22:25-29, the roles of the different classes of ancient Israel's leaders, and their failure to uphold their responsibilities).
211.   *See* sources cited *supra* notes 189-203 and accompanying text (outlining general principles and
specific provisions of the Old Testament law regarding the just treatment of the poor and needy);
Deuteronomy 1:15-17 (stating that God appointed leaders from the leading men of the tribe to "judge
fairly . . . both small and great alike"); *Deuteronomy* 16:18-20 (commanding the people to appoint
judges to judge people fairly without perverting justice, showing partiality, or accepting a bribe;
judges are commanded to "[f]ollow justice and justice alone"); *Deuteronomy* 17:15-20 (stating kings
are not to amass huge amounts of wealth); WRIGHT, DEUTERONOMY, *supra* note 189, at 26, 209 &
MERRILL, *supra* note 188, at 70, 266 (elaborating on the integrity required of all tribal leaders and
kings, for the Law with God behind it has authority over even those who administer the Old Testament
law; *see also* *Proverbs* 31:2-9 (advising the king that he should "[s]peak up for those who cannot
speak for themselves, for the rights of all who are destitute . . . defend the rights of the poor and
needy"); *Jeremiah* 22:2-4 ("Hear the word of the LORD, O king of Judah, you who sit on David's

leaders that served the entire community, especially the poorest and neediest members, in a manner consistent with the character of God,[212] the Prophetic Books of the Old Testament contain harsh criticisms of, and judgment against, leaders that made decisions promoting expediency rather than justice and who exercised their authority in order to secure the greatest financial benefits for themselves.[213] In addition to criticizing unjust leaders in general terms, the Prophetic Books metaphorically describe many of ancient Israel's leaders as cannibals, rebels, thieves, and drunkards.[214] Although the source of authority of ancient Israel's leaders (being

---

throne . . . . Do what is just and right. Rescue from the hand of his oppressor the one who has been robbed."); F.B. HUEY, THE NEW AMERICAN COMMENTARY: JEREMIAH, LAMENTATIONS 203-04 (1993) (discussing *Jeremiah* 22:2-4 as a reminder to rulers of their responsibilities to protect the weak and defenseless).

212.   *Jeremiah* 22:15-16 ("He did what was right and just, so all went well with him. He defended the cause of the poor and needy, and so all went well."); HUEY, *supra* note 211, at 206 (stating that *Jeremiah* 22:15-16 refers to King Josiah who was truly a king in God's eyes and how generally this passage "is a remarkable and profound statement of what it means to know God"); *Psalm* 72 (describing a good and just king as one who will "defend the afflicted among the people and save the children of the needy . . . rescue them from oppression and violence").

213.   *Jeremiah* 21:12-13 ("Administer justice every morning; rescue from the hand of his oppressor the one who has been robbed, or my wrath will break out and burn like fire because of the evil you have done—burn with no one to quench it."); HUEY, *supra* note 211, at 201 (discussing the imagery of fire as God's judgment to rulers abusing their power); *Jeremiah* 22:13-17 ("Woe to him who builds his palace by unrighteousness, his upper rooms by injustice, making his countrymen work for nothing, not paying them for their labor . . . your eyes and your heart are set only on dishonest gain . . . oppression and extortion."); HUEY, *supra* note 211, at 206-07 (indictment against Jehoiakim, an unrighteous king building a palace on the backs of other people); *Ezekiel* 34:2-5 ("Woe to the shepherds of Israel who only take care of themselves! Should not shepherds take care of the flock? You eat the curds, clothe yourselves with the wool and slaughter the choice animals, but you do not take care of the flock. You have not strengthened the weak or healed the sick or bound up the injured. You have not brought back the strays or searched for the lost. You have ruled them harshly and brutally. So they were scattered because there was no shepherd, and when they were scattered they became food for all the wild animals."); DANIEL I. BLOCK, THE BOOK OF EZEKIEL, CHAPTERS 25-48 at 279-85 (1998) [hereinafter BLOCK II] (describing the shepherd and sheep as metaphorically representing Israel's leaders and her people thus illustrating the disastrous effects of bad leadership and concluding that ultimately the responsibility of the well-being of the community falls on the shoulders of the leaders); *Micah* 3:11 ("Her leaders judge for a bribe, her priests teach for a price, and her prophets tell fortunes for money."); BARKER & BAILEY, *supra* note 187, at 77-81 (discussing the financial motivation of all three classes of ancient Israel's corrupt leaders referred to in *Micah* 3:11); *Amos* 6:1 ("Woe to you who are complacent in Zion, and to you who feel secure on Mount Samaria, you notable men of the foremost nation, to whom the people of Israel come!"); G. SMITH, *supra* note 187, at 117 (interpreting the intended audience in *Amos* 6:1 to be the leaders of ancient Israel who have achieved notoriety and status in government and society).

214.   *Micah* 3:1-3 ("Listen, you leaders of Jacob, you rulers of the house of Israel. Should you not know justice, you who hate good and love evil; who tear the skin from my people and the flesh from their bones; who eat my people's flesh, strip off their skin and break their bones in pieces; who chop them up like meat for the pan, like flesh for the pot?"); BARKER & BAILEY, *supra* note 187, at 75-76 (discussing the vivid imagery of ancient Israel's leaders treating the people like animals to be slaughtered and eaten as illustrating the wickedness of allowing unjust and oppressive practices to occur under their watch, or even worse, with the leader's direct participation); *Isaiah* 1:23 ("Your rulers are rebels, companions of thieves; they all love bribes and chase after gifts."); OSWALT I, *supra* note 187, at 105-06 (describing the irony of those who are supposed to keep order being rebels and linking ancient Israel's idolatry with their leadership becoming trash); *Isaiah* 5:22-23 ("Woe to those who are heroes at drinking wine and champions at mixing drinks, who acquit the guilty for a bribe, but deny

largely monarchy based) differs substantially from that of those serving contemporary governments or churches in the democratic United States, the "specific life situation"—leaders with power over the lives of others— has not changed. Therefore, the general moral principle demands a greater responsibility for the welfare of the community, especially for the poorest members, from contemporary leaders and ministers, as it did from ancient Israel's leaders.[215]

Although the New Testament abolished many of the Old Testament's laws for Christians,[216] the Old Testament's moral principles still apply, as affirmed and re-established under the teachings of Jesus Christ.[217] Jesus himself declared that he had come to fulfill the Law and the Prophets of the Old Testament[218] and considered the scriptures, which set forth the

---

justice to the innocent."); OSWALT I, *supra* note 187, at 165 (depicting ancient Israel's leaders as irresponsibly drinking and making decisions based on who pays the highest price without caring or being able to even tell the difference between the guilty and the innocent).

215.	*See* sources cited *supra* note 177 and accompanying text (discussing the importance of discovering the meaning and broad ethical principles of the biblical text as understood by the first audience, and discussing the importance of applying these broad ethical principles to contemporary circumstances where the "specific life situations" of the ancient and contemporary circumstances are the same); *see also* JOHN N. OSWALT, THE BOOK OF ISAIAH, CHAPTERS 40-66 at 336-37 (1998) [hereinafter OSWALT II] (discussing the theological implications of leadership from *Isaiah* that are applicable to contemporary leaders as including the requirements of self-denial, self-sacrifice, innocence, faithfulness, and holy love, to rule justly); BLOCK I, *supra* note 210, at 714 (discussing the theological implications from *Ezekiel* applicable to contemporary leaders as "community leaders bear special responsibility for the maintenance of justice and the welfare of its citizenry; [t]he call to leadership is primarily a call to responsibility, not privilege").

216.	*Mark* 7:1-8 & *Matthew* 15:1-3 (telling of Jesus's refusal to conform to ceremonial rituals of cleansing); *Matthew* 15:11-20 (telling of Jesus's declaration that food cannot make people unclean, rather evil thoughts and other evil deeds make people unclean); *Mark* 7:14-23 (telling of Jesus's declaration that all food is clean); *Matthew* 12:1-14 (telling of the Pharisees' questioning Jesus allowing his disciples to pick grain on the Sabbath and Jesus's healing a man with a withered hand on the Sabbath, and Jesus responding with the quote from the Prophet Hosea "I desire mercy, not sacrifice," declaring "the Son of Man is Lord of the Sabbath," and "it is lawful to do good on the Sabbath"); *see generally Hebrews* (explaining that Jesus Christ served as the great high priest who sacrificed his own blood in his death to atone for all sins of those who accept him as their personal savior, rendering unnecessary the need to make regular animal sacrifices); ROOKER, *supra* note 183, at 58-63 & FRANK THIELMAN, THE LAW AND THE NEW TESTAMENT 111-34 (1999) [hereinafter THIELMAN, LAW] (discussing Jesus's fulfillment of the law of sacrifice).

217.	BLOMBERG, *supra* note 176, at 39 (discussing the general relevance of the Old Testament to Christians and stating "[n]o command issued to Old Testament followers of Yahweh necessarily carries over into the Christian era unchanged, but every command reflects principles at some level that are binding on Christians"); *see* FEE & STUART, *supra* note 176, at 131-34 (discussing important hermeneutical principles for contemporarily interpreting the teachings of Jesus as including an understanding that "the basic theological framework of the entire New Testament is eschatological," meaning concerned with the end, but the earthly ministry, death, and resurrection of Jesus did "not come to usher in the 'final' end, but the 'beginning' of the end;" under this framework, for Christians, all ethical behavior based on the teachings of Jesus reflects a commitment to the ethics of his kingdom, which will not be fully realized until "the end," but still has "implications for the present," and still must be "worked out in our own lives and world in this present age").

218.	*Matthew* 5:17 ("Do not think that I have come to abolish the Law or the Prophets; I have not come to abolish them but to fulfill them."); CRAIG S. KEENER, A COMMENTARY ON THE GOSPEL OF MATTHEW 177 (1999) (stating that the language of Jesus clearly affirms his commitment to the Mosaic law and fulfillment through obedience); THIELMAN, LAW, *supra* note 216, at 48 (stating that to fulfill

teachings of Moses and the Prophets, to be sufficient guidance for those seeking salvation.[219] Paul, undoubtedly reflecting on the teachings of Jesus, considered the Old Testament in general to be God-breathed—useful for teaching, rebuking, correcting, and training in righteousness.[220] An important moral concern of the Old Testament. affirmed in the New Testament, addresses the plight of the poor and needy.[221] Jesus himself, in-

---

the law, Jesus focused on the law's fundamental principles and required the results of those principles in his teachings); *id.* at 181 (noting that Mosaic law is still valid for Christians because it provides structure theologically for the gospel and "constitutes a rich repository of specific ethical material"); DARRELL L. BOCK, LUKE: 1:1-9:50 at 39 (1994) [hereinafter BOCK I] ("[T]he law is reaffirmed in ways that parallel the O[ld] T[estament] prophets."); WRIGHT, KNOWING JESUS, *supra* note 176, at 186-87 (saying the words of Moses to Israel shaped the values, priorities, and convictions of Jesus's life); *id.* at 219 (stating that Jesus's fulfillment of the law clarified its scale of values and sense of priorities); WRIGHT, DEUTERONOMY, *supra* note 189, at 11, 57 (discussing how the teachings and revelation of God in Jesus cannot be separated from the God and mission of Israel, thus not allowing Christians to abandon the Hebrew scriptures of the Old Testament); HARTLEY, *supra* note 200, at 325 (stating Jesus affirms the principles of the holiness code of *Leviticus* 19); HARRISON, *supra* note 200, at 32-33 (discussing generally the importance of Levitical law in the teachings of Jesus Christ); ROOKER, *supra* note 183, at 68 (discussing Jesus's fulfillment of the law as providing a true interpretation, and not detracting from or denying the law); LANE, *supra* note 176, at 432-33 (discussing the Mosaic law origins of the two great commandments); *id.* at 70 (discussing how moral law associated with the Ten Commandments as well as other ethical principles of the Old Testament have permanent validity to Christians); BARKER & BAILEY, *supra* note 187, at 115 (stating that Christians have the law placed on their hearts, and justice, mercy, and faithfulness are the most important aspects of the law).

219.   *See Luke* 16:19-31 (relating the parable of a rich man who is tormented in Hades for his indifference towards the poor and needy, pleading with Abraham to allow him to warn his still living brothers to repent and change their lives so that they may avoid his fate, being told: "They have Moses and the Prophets; let them listen to them . . . . If they do not listen to Moses and the Prophets, they will not be convinced even if someone rises from the dead"); DARRELL L. BOCK, LUKE: 9:51-24:53 at 1360, 1375, 1378 (1996) [hereinafter BOCK II] (discussing how the Mosaic law and the Prophets of the Old Testament provided ample guidance to the rich man as to how he should have treated the poor during his earthly life, illustrating how the foundations of the teachings of Jesus concerning how human beings are to treat each other essentially comes from the Old Testament).

220.   *See* 2 *Timothy* 3:16-17; GORDON D. FEE, NEW INTERNATIONAL BIBLICAL COMMENTARY: 1 AND 2 TIMOTHY, TITUS 279-80 (1988) (discussing all scripture as being of divine origin).

221.   *See Luke* 1:46-55 (giving Mary's prayer before the birth of Jesus, in which she reflects on God's past work and anticipates that God, on a massive scale through the work of the Messiah, will lift up the humble and fill the hungry with good things); BOCK I, *supra* note 218, at 153, 157 (discussing how Mary's Magnificat considers God's specific action to the community on behalf of God fearers, for God will lift the humble and fill the hungry with good things while sending the rich away empty); *id.* at 158 (cautioning against over spiritualizing this material and its warnings against excessive wealth and notes that this material cannot support a manifesto for political action without recognizing the basic need to turn to God); *see also* 1 *Samuel* 2:1-10 (giving Hannah's prayer following the birth of Samuel, which uses similar imagery of the Lord "rais[ing] the poor from the dust and lift[ing] the needy from the ash heap"). A classic example of Jesus affirming the Old Testament's requirements to help those in need can be found in the Parable of the Good Samaritan, *Luke* 10:30-37, where a Samaritan (a race of persons hated by many Jews in first century Palestine) provided extraordinary assistance to a victim of robbery and assault. *See* THIELMAN, LAW, *supra* note 216, at 148 (noting that in the parable of the Good Samaritan, Jesus requires more of disciples than the law would require); BOCK II, *supra* note 219, at 1035 (interpreting the Parable of the Good Samaritan as showing how a positive response to our fellow human beings is a necessary outgrowth of love for God, and that becoming a neighbor requires a sensitive response to the needs of others); TIMOTHY GEORGE, THE NEW AMERICAN COMMENTARY: GALATIANS 383 (E. Ray Clendenen et al. eds., 1994) (discussing generally Jesus's parable of the good Samaritan and noting that "[o]ur neighbors include the loveless, the least, the unlikely").

voking themes of the creation account equating a person's treatment of their fellow human beings as reflecting their relationship with God, identified himself as among "the least of these" and stated that the failure to serve "the least of these" is the same as failing to serve him.[222] By identifying the love of God and the love of neighbors as the two greatest commandments, Jesus not only explicitly reaffirmed the Old Testament's moral principles concerning the treatment of the poor and needy, but arguably clarified or even strengthened these principles.[223]

In addition to generally affirming the moral principles of the Old Testament, the New Testament explicitly forbids the economic oppression of the poor, weak, and vulnerable members of society. These passages include specific instructions to tax collectors and soldiers seeking baptism and repentance to avoid extorting money.[224] Jesus himself scathingly criticized certain hypocritical religious leaders for "devour[ing] widows' houses," meaning they were economically oppressing widows, who were arguably the most vulnerable and least powerful segment of ancient Near

---

222.   *Matthew* 25:31-46 (explaining when Jesus comes again the "sheep" will be blessed with eternal life because they fed and clothed the needy, took in the stranger, looked after the sick, and visited those in prison, which in effect amounted to doing those things for Jesus personally, while the "goats" will be cursed to eternal punishment because they failed to help those in need, which in effect amounted to failing to help Jesus personally for Jesus declared "I tell you the truth, whatever you did not do for one of the least of these, you did not do for me"); *see* WRIGHT, KNOWING JESUS, *supra* note 176, at 198-99 (identifying creation theology behind Jesus's identification with "the least of these" and emphasizing that true believers must show gratitude to God through generosity to others).

223.   *Matthew* 22:37-40, 7:12, *Mark* 12:29 & *Luke* 6:31 (articulating directly or by example the two great commandments, loving God and loving neighbors); *see* LANE, *supra* note 176, at 432 (discussing the Mosaic law origins of the two great commandments); BOCK I, *supra* note 218, at 595-96 (discussing the "Golden Rule" as being rooted in the Old Testament command of *Leviticus* 19:18 to love your neighbor as yourself, and as commanding more than just avoiding treating others unfairly, but requiring positive action "to give the same sensitive consideration to others"); KEENER, *supra* note 218, at 475 (stating that love for God requires active service on behalf of neighbors); WRIGHT, KNOWING JESUS, *supra* note 176, at 190 (noting that Jesus's two greatest commandments sum up "the essence of the Old Testament"); *id.* at 200-01 (discussing Jesus's command to love your neighbor as yourself as not being a new revolutionary idea but essentially coming from the ethical community standards of the Holiness Code of *Leviticus*); HARTLEY, *supra* note 200, at 318 (explaining that Jesus elevated the commandment to love your neighbor and extended the concept of neighbor to include all human beings, especially those in need); *see Philippians* 2:3-4 ("Do nothing out of selfish ambition or vain conceit, but in humility consider others better than yourselves. Each of you should look not only to your own interests, but also to the interests of others."); *Galatians* 5:14 ("The entire law is summed up in a single command: 'Love your neighbor as yourself.'"); *Romans* 13:9-10 ("[A]nd whatever other commandment[s] there may be, are summed up in this one rule: Love your neighbor as yourself. Love does no harm to its neighbor. Therefore love is the fulfillment of the Law."); THIELMAN, LAW, *supra* note 216, at 9 (summarizing Paul's beliefs, expressed in *Galatians* and *Romans*, that Christians are bound by a set of ethical standards that Paul refers to as "the law of Christ," which is "analogous to the Mosaic law and incorporat[es] some of its precepts, but based on Jesus's ethical teaching"); *id.* at 72 (stating that in fulfilling the Mosaic law, Jesus created something new by elevating the principles of the Mosaic law "to the highest level of importance").

224.   *Luke* 3:12-14; *see* BOCK I, *supra* note 218, at 312-14 (discussing the response to the tax collectors and soldiers as requiring them to conduct themselves fairly without taking advantage of their authority unfairly through fraud, bribery, kickbacks, or extortion to gain an unfair monetary advantage over those with less power).

East society.[225] Based on the teachings of Jesus, and invoking the moral themes of the Old Testament, the Epistle of James harshly criticizes wealthy individuals for hoarding wealth and economically oppressing poor workers by failing to pay wages.[226]

Finally, the New Testament explicitly continues the moral principles of the Old Testament requiring that the basic needs of poor persons be met, and that such persons enjoy at least a minimum opportunity to improve their economic circumstances.[227] In addition to issuing specific instructions to share economic resources with those in need, especially those who cannot reciprocate,[228] the New Testament also warns those enjoying an abundance of wealth to avoid the temptation of putting their trust and loyalty in money and possessions rather than God,[229] and makes extraordi-

---

225. *Luke* 20:47; *Mark* 12:40; *see* BOCK II, *supra* note 219, at 1643 (discussing the factual connotations of devouring the houses of widows, given the ancient culture and context, and concluding that this involves taking from a group the most in need and leaving them economically devastated).

226. *James* 5:1-6 ("Now listen, you rich people, weep and wail because of the misery that is coming upon you. Your wealth has rotted, and moths have eaten your clothes. Your gold and silver are corroded. Their corrosion will testify against you and eat your flesh like fire. You have hoarded wealth in the last days. Look! The wages you failed to pay the workman who mowed your fields are crying out against you. The cries of the harvesters have reached the ears of the Lord Almighty. You have lived on earth in luxury and self-indulgence. You have fattened yourselves in the day of slaughter. You have condemned and murdered innocent men, who were not opposing you."); DOUGLAS J. MOO, THE LETTER OF JAMES 210-12 (2000) (explaining that the rich attacked in *James* 5:1-6 were wealthy landowners misusing their wealth by exploiting those forced to work on the land for them, and noting that this carries a serious question to Christians with wealth today); *id.* at 214 ("People who hoard wealth are . . . depriving others of their very life."); *id.* at 219 (noting that the murder of innocent men means that hoarding wealth and exploiting others cheats the poor of their land and deprives them of their gainful employment, resulting in the poor starving to death); *see also Deuteronomy* 24:14-15, *Leviticus* 19:13 & *Malachi* 3:5 (forbidding or criticizing oppression, specifically referring to the failure to pay wages).

227. *See* WRIGHT, WALKING, *supra* note 187, at 111, 114 (noting that the laws of ancient Israel collectively intended to be a paradigm relevant beyond its historical borders with universal application to Christians and their communities); WRIGHT, KNOWING JESUS, *supra* note 176, at 197-98 (discussing the parable of the unmerciful servant in *Matthew* 18:23-35 (where a servant who enjoyed the benefit of having his large debt cancelled refused to cancel a smaller debt owed to him by another) as having a strong parallel with the requirement of *Deuteronomy* 15:7-16 (servants are to be released after seven years and sent away with ample provisions) because both require mercy, even in the form of economic assistance and opportunities, to be extended to others because God has extended mercy).

228. *Luke* 3:11 ("John answered, '[t]he man with two tunics should share with him who has none, and the one who has food should do the same.'"); BOCK I, *supra* note 218, at 309-10 (discussing how John's call for repentance involving meeting the needs of others by sharing clothes and food reflected the concerns of the Old Testament prophets); *Luke* 14:13-14 ("But when you give a banquet, invite the poor, the crippled, the lame, the blind, and you will be blessed. Although they cannot repay you, you will be repaid at the resurrection of the righteous."); BOCK II, *supra* note 212, at 1265-67 (discussing table fellowship in the context of ancient Jewish society and how *Luke* illustrates that humility, openness, and service to the needs of others are major facets to the ethics of Jesus); *Luke* 6:32-34 (telling of Jesus using negative examples to illustrate that a disciple's love and assistance must be towards those who will not return it back); BOCK I, *supra* note 218, at 601 ("Jesus is saying that the 'I'll scratch your back, if you scratch mine' approach to meeting needs is not an example of a disciple's love."); *see also* 1 *John* 3:16-17 ("This is how we know what love is: Jesus Christ laid down his life for us. And we ought to lay down our lives for our brothers. If anyone has material possessions and sees his brother in need but has no pity on him, how can the love of God be in him?").

229. *Luke* 16:13; *Matthew* 6:24 ("No one can serve two masters. Either he will hate the one and

narily costly demands on certain wealthy individuals[230] and communities[231] for the purpose of meeting the needs of the poor. Moreover, in his declaration that he has come "to preach good news to the poor" and "release the oppressed," Jesus himself, invoking Old Testament scripture and moral principles, elevated the specific instructions concerning the poor and needy as necessitating broader changes to societal structures.[232] Although

---

love the other, or he will be devoted to the one and despise the other. You cannot serve both God and Money."); BOCK II, *supra* note 219, at 1336 (discussing that even though the ethics of Jesus do not forbid the making of money per se, ultimately God must always take priority over money; therefore, for some believers "[t]here might even be a time when a choice for God is a choice not to have money or not quite so much money," and noting that "[i]n this context, money is a litmus test about greater issues and responsibilities, and it is clear that one should choose to serve God"); KEENER, *supra* note 218, at 233-34 (discussing the love of money as idolatry, and noting that materialism is the greatest threat to western Christianity); 1 *Timothy* 6:10 ("For the love of money is a root of all kinds of evil."); FEE, *supra* note 220, at 145-46 (discussing the love of money, not money per se, as a desire that can cause one to forget God); *Matthew* 6:19-21 ("Do not store up for yourselves treasures on earth, where moth and rust destroy, and where thieves break in and steal. But store up for yourselves treasures in heaven, where moth and rust do not destroy, and where thieves do not break in and steal. For where your treasure is, there your heart will be also."); KEENER, *supra* note 218, at 230-32 (discussing Jesus's teachings on wealth and his prohibition of storing up wealth as requiring people to value basic needs of others over personal accumulation of possessions beyond basic needs); *Luke* 12:16-21 (giving the parable of a rich fool where the rich man builds a larger barn to store excess possessions only to have them do him no good when he dies that very evening); BOCK II, *supra* note 219, at 1154 (discussing the parable of the rich fool as not condemning planning and wealth in the abstract but condemning the person who directs all the benefits of wealth toward themselves); *see also* BLOMBERG, *supra* note 176, at 245 (discussing general applications of the Bible's teachings on wealth and possessions, noting that "[t]here are certain extremes of wealth and poverty which are in and of themselves intolerable," and while no exact definition defines those extremes in all circumstances, once the extreme of wealth has been reached "such a surplus prevents others from having a better opportunity for a reasonably decent standard of living").

230.   *See Luke* 18:18-25; *Matthew* 19:16-22 (telling the story of the ruler with many possessions that asked what he must do to inherit eternal life, and Jesus answered "[S]ell your possessions and give to the poor, and you will have treasure in heaven. Then come follow me."); BOCK II, *supra* note 219, at 1473, 1482-83 (discussing the radical nature of Jesus's request, and stating that the key to understanding is in the response of the ruler rather than the request of Jesus); THIELMAN, LAW, *supra* note 216, at 59 (discussing Matthew's account of Jesus's request of the rich ruler to give all his wealth to the poor and follow Jesus as an example of Jesus requiring true disciples to do more than follow the technical requirements of the Mosaic law because the rich ruler stated that he had kept the law his entire life); *Luke* 19:5-10 (declaring that salvation had come to a wealthy tax collector who gave half his possessions to the poor and vowed to repay anyone cheated by him four times the amount); BOCK II, *supra* note 219, at 1513-14, 1520-21 (discussing the response of the tax collector who changed his use of money from taking advantage of people to instead serving people, which shows he had genuine faith in God).

231.   *Acts* 2:44-45, 4:32-35 (describing the common sharing of resources among members of the early church with no needy among them); JOHN R.W. STOTT, THE MESSAGE OF ACTS 84-85, 107 (1990) (noting that although the sale of possessions was voluntary, these versus challenge Christians to be more sharing and caring); *see generally* 2 *Corinthians* 8:9, 12-15 (referring to the generosity of the Macedonians, Paul urges the Corinthians to generously give to the poor, and likens Christians to ancient Israelites in the wilderness during the Exodus where none had too little and none had too much at the expense of others); S. McKnight, *Collection For the Saints, in* DICTIONARY OF PAUL AND HIS LETTERS 143-46 (Gerald F. Hawthorne et al. eds., 1993) (discussing Paul's campaign for collecting resources for the poor and reviewing the historical context, purpose, and results of such collection).

232.   *See Luke* 4:16-21 ("He went to Nazareth, where he had been brought up, and on the Sabbath day he went into the synagogue, as was his custom. And he stood up to read. The scroll of the prophet Isaiah was handed to him. Unrolling it, he found the place where it is written: 'The Spirit of the Lord is on me, because he has anointed me to preach good news to the poor. He has sent me to proclaim

the degree of societal change required by the teachings of Jesus is the subject of an intense debate,[233] at the very least this passage, along with the other moral teachings of Jesus, calls for societal structures that provide the poor, vulnerable, and powerless persons within the society a minimum opportunity to improve their economic circumstances.[234] A community that operates in a manner consistent with the moral principles of Judeo-Christian ethics must foster the minimum well-being of everyone in the community and cannot be based solely on an economy driven by money and power that only guards the well-being of those with power enjoying access to sufficient money and material possessions.[235]

---

freedom for the prisoners and recovery of sight for the blind, to release the oppressed, to proclaim the year of the Lord's favor.'"); BOCK I, *supra* note 218, at 405-06 (discussing Old Testament overtones of the reference to Isaiah's servant song quoted by Jesus and its thematic relationship with the prophetic rebuke in *Isaiah* 58 of a nation for failing to promote justice for those in need); *id.* at 400-01 (interpreting the message of *Luke* 4:16-21 as confronting and changing the hearts of individuals within society's structures so that those individuals can impact societal structures in order to elevate the community to be in line with God's values of providing for the minimum well-being of all members of the community, especially the poor and oppressed); BLOMBERG, *supra* note 176, at 45 (noting that principles underlying the Jubilee apply to Christians and "these challenge all major, modern economic models"); *see also* WRIGHT, OLD TESTAMENT ETHICS, *supra* note 187, at 115-16 (noting that Christian social ethics must "pay more serious attention to the institutions and conventions of our society than we are accustomed to in the insulation of our 'religious' concerns," which entails more than just offering criticism of and moral visions concerning evil and injustice; the work is not done without weaving the ethical "insight into the fabric of society").

233.   *See* BOCK I, *supra* note 218, at 400-01 (discussing both extremes of the interpretations of Jesus's message, especially in the context of *Luke* 4:16-30, as requiring everything from full scale social revolution (the liberation theology interpretation) to little more than individual piety). A complete examination of all these interpretations and their implications is beyond the scope of this Article.

234.   *Id.* (rejecting both extremes of interpretation of Jesus's teachings, the liberation theology interpretation and the interpretation that over emphasizes the spiritual message to the point of ignoring the societal implications on how the redeemed community is to approach other people and social structures, and stating that the Gospel of Jesus Christ has societal implications concerning how the redeemed community treats humans and uses social structures, and requires the church to reflect "[c]ompassion, concern, love, truth, and service" as Jesus did); HARTLEY, *supra* note 200, at 447-48 (noting that the purpose behind the Year of the Jubilee was central to the goals of Jesus's teaching, and finding that a contemporary application of these teachings does not allow for ownership of property to reach a level where the rich have huge tracts that displace the poor); WRIGHT, WALKING, *supra* note 187, at 209-10 (discussing the teachings of Jesus invoking themes of the Jubilee without directly referring to it); WRIGHT, KNOWING JESUS, *supra* note 176, at 228-29 (noting Jesus's call to preach the good news to the poor invoked images of the Jubilee to characterize the demands of the kingdom of God); *id.* at 230-31 (noting that Jesus required his followers to work for community standards that "change the social conditions that crushed the life out of people by indebtedness"). This Article makes no substantive determination whether the moral principles of Judeo-Christian ethics, particularly as affirmed and re-established under the teachings of Jesus Christ, require a greater level of care for the poor than providing a minimum opportunity to improve their economic circumstances. Because Alabama's tax structure and the corresponding negative effects on the funding of Alabama's public schools fail to reach even this minimum standard, a full discussion of possible broader implications mandated by these moral principles is beyond the scope of this Article.

235.   *See* BOCK I, *supra* note 218, at 33, 37 (discussing the accountability of the community to God in their service and ethical treatment of those both within and without the community); *id.* at 410 (discussing the tendency of some in ministry to stress the individual response to such an extent that they miss the "elements of ministry, which reach out to a full range of people's needs"); WRIGHT, WALKING, *supra* note 187, at 165-67 (stating the principles behind the structures of ancient Israel's social life were a major part of God's revelation, which illustrates that God's demands on the entire

C. Alabama's Tax Structure Fails to Meet Any Reasonable
Definition of Fairness and Violates the Moral Principles
of Judeo-Christian Ethics, Therefore, All Alabamians
Have a Moral Obligation to Support Tax Reform

Alabama's income, sales, and property tax structures, individually and in concert, are not only extremely unfair to the poorest and neediest Alabamians under any legitimate ethical model, they also violate the moral principles of Judeo-Christian ethics. By regressively imposing the greatest tax burdens on those least able to pay, Alabama's income and sales tax structures fail to factor in any level of ability to pay under traditional vertical equity theory, and therefore are unfair under any reasonable ethical model for evaluating tax policy.[236] By taxing poor people working at wage levels well below the poverty line, the income tax system takes from poor people a portion of their scarce resources that even the federal government deems too low to fairly tax.[237] Moreover, by reducing the tax burden on higher income taxpayers, Alabama's allowance of a full deduction for federal taxes paid further aggravates the regressive effects of the income tax structure by creating a need to collect more revenue from low-income individuals and families.[238] In addition, Alabama's high sales tax rates and heavy reliance on sales taxes for revenues force the poorest Alabamians to pay a greater portion (compared to those at higher income levels) of their scarce resources in sales tax every time they make a consumer purchase,

---

social system at the community level remain applicable to Christians and their communities); *id.* at 210 (stating contemporary application of Jubilee as interpreted by Jesus requires "broadly equitable distribution of the resources of the earth, especially land, and a curb on the tendency to accumulation with its inevitable oppression and alienation"); ROOKER, *supra* note 183, at 264-65 (stating that the general principles of the ethics of the holiness code of *Leviticus* 19 are directly applicable to Christians individually and collectively as a community, and that "[i]t is their demonstration of ethics and holiness that characterizes their corporate identity"); BLOCK I, *supra* note 210, at 714 (discussing Ezekiel's orations criticizing how the ancient societal structures treated the poor and needy, and noting that "[n]othing has changed in the N[ew] T[estament]").

236.   *See supra* notes 159-64 and accompanying text (discussing regressive tax structures and tax structures with regressive effects as imposing the greatest tax burdens on those least able to pay, and stating virtually all reasonable ethical positions of sound tax policy uniformly deem these structures unfair).

237.   *See supra* notes 17-29 and accompanying text (discussing regressive features of Alabama's income tax and the imposition of an income tax at income levels well below the poverty line).

238.   *See supra* notes 39-41 and accompanying text (discussing the deduction for federal taxes paid in Alabama's income tax structure); CITIZENS FOR TAX JUSTICE, *supra* note 40, at 3 (noting that of the five very regressive tax states that do have a broad-based personal income tax, two—Alabama and Louisiana—allow a deduction for federal taxes paid). The existence of the deduction for federal taxes paid, which benefits only those taxpayers incurring federal income tax liability, violates horizontal equity because the deduction fails to accurately measure ability to pay and serves no legitimate public policy purpose. Moreover, by allowing the tax savings from the deduction to increase proportionally as the taxpayer's income rises, the deduction for federal taxes paid has the effect of shifting the overall income tax burden to taxpayers with less ability to pay; *supra* notes 165-68 and accompanying text (discussing the standards for horizontal equity and the potential for inequitable tax benefits to shift the tax burden to those with less ability to pay).

even for the most basic needs such as food, clothing, and certain medicines.[239] Although the specific details of Alabama's income and sales tax structures differ from the ancient examples of economic oppression addressed by the Old and New Testaments, the Judeo-Christian moral principle forbidding the economic oppression of poor persons contemporarily applies, and under this principle, Alabama's income and sales tax structures are grossly unethical.[240]

Although the property tax structure does not raise ability to pay issues to the degree of the income and sales tax structures (because the poorest and neediest Alabamians tend to own no property of significant fair market value), Alabama's property tax structure still raises significant ethical issues under traditional tax policy analysis. The different assessment ratios applied to the four classes of property raise horizontal equity concerns, and the extremely low assessment ratio for timber property (which results in that class of property bearing by far the lightest property tax burden—less than two percent of Alabama's total property taxes) conclusively violates horizontal equity.[241] Therefore, the property tax structure is unfair under any reasonable ethical model for evaluating tax policy. Because timber acres constitute a highly important source of wealth and income in the state—covering approximately seventy-one percent of Alabama's landmass—the corresponding *de minimis* property taxes levied on this type of property when compared to other classes of property cannot possibly be justified as a more accurate measurement of ability to pay, or by any other legitimate policy reason, and therefore only fosters the self-serving interests of powerful lobby groups.[242]

Finally, by generating inadequate revenues and thus rendering the state and the local governments unable to adequately fund the public schools, Alabama's tax structure violates the Judeo-Christian moral principle requiring that the poorest and most vulnerable persons of the population enjoy at least a minimum opportunity to improve their economic cir-

---

239.   *See supra* notes 44-49 and accompanying text (discussing the high level of Alabama's sales tax rates and their regressive effects).

240.   *See supra* notes 189-95, 217-26 and accompanying text (discussing the development of the Judeo-Christian moral principle forbidding the economic oppression of poor persons and its relevance to evaluating contemporary economic structures).

241.   *See supra* notes 64-89 and accompanying text (documenting Alabama's property tax structure as setting up four different classes of property with different assessment ratios for each class, and providing additional opportunities for timber and agriculture to enjoy an even lower assessment ratio than other Class III property); *supra* notes 165-68 (discussing the principles of horizontal equity as requiring that similarly situated taxpayers be treated the same, unless disparate treatment results in a more accurate measurement of ability to pay or serves some other very important governmental policy goal).

242.   *Id.*; *see also supra* notes 77-81, 90-101 and accompanying text (discussing the *de minimis* property taxes contributed by timber acres and the dominance of timber over both Alabama's landmass and economy).

cumstances.[243] Although no specific provision or example in the biblical text addresses the need to educate children, nevertheless this Judeo-Christian moral principle requires that children from low-income families, the most vulnerable and powerless segment of the population—the cultural equivalent of the widows, orphans, aliens and poor people of the ancient world—enjoy at least a minimum opportunity to achieve an adequate education.[244] Although the opportunity to achieve an adequate education does not culturally mirror the "specific life situations" explicitly discussed in the biblical texts, the objective behind these texts—to provide all persons, regardless of how low their station in life, a minimum opportunity to achieve better economic circumstances—is still contemporarily relevant.[245]

---

243.   *See supra* notes 50-63 and accompanying text (documenting Alabama's extremely low property tax revenues, the lowest in the nation, as being largely responsible for Alabama's inadequate total revenues, which are also the lowest in the nation in terms of revenue per person); *supra* notes 102-26 (discussing the inadequate funding of Alabama's public schools and the negative effects suffered especially by low-income children); *supra* notes 127-44 (documenting that the inadequate funding of Alabama's public schools is largely due to the property tax structure, especially the features that allow only a *de minimis* portion of the value of timber acres to be subject to the property tax millage rates).

244.   In making the argument that the moral principles of Judeo-Christian ethics contemporarily require a minimum level of adequate funding for public education in order to offer low-income children a minimum opportunity to improve their economic situation, this Article recognizes the inherent difficulties in defining exactly what constitutes a minimum opportunity when you compare Alabama as a community with other communities, especially from a worldwide perspective. Because some third-world countries cannot even meet the minimum food needs of their impoverished children, and certainly offer their children no opportunity to achieve any level of an education, it can be very tempting to compare the worst of Alabama's schools to what exists in those countries and conclude that the moral principle of Judeo-Christian ethics requiring that poor persons enjoy a minimum opportunity to improve their economic circumstances has been satisfied. This conclusion is flawed for several reasons. First, the fact that the treatment of children in third-world countries fails abysmally to meet the moral demands of Judeo-Christian ethics in no way supports an argument that Alabama's standards meet these moral demands simply because the situation in Alabama is not as desperate. Although all determinations whether a minimum level of any moral standard has been met will involve subjective judgments, given the standards of the United States regarding education as reflected by the national spending per student grades, the empirical evidence of this Article soundly supports the assertion that most of Alabama's schools fail to meet a minimum level of adequate funding. Moreover, because the situation in Alabama is literally "in the backyard" of all Alabamians, and the changes needed in Alabama's tax structure to bring Alabama's revenues and public school funding up to a minimum level can be accomplished far more easily than addressing the complex economic structures producing the tragic circumstances in third-world nations, Alabamians have simply no excuse for ignoring the problems close to home because the problems far from home are worse. Finally, supporting tax reform in Alabama does not preclude a positive and loving response towards mitigating the situation in developing nations. Because third-world problems are of international scope, the proper response from most citizens must come, for example, in the form of responsibly voting for candidates seeking political office at the national level, increasing contributions to charitable organizations dedicated to addressing third-world poverty, and finally, boycotting the products produced by corporations whose business practices contribute to the complex economic structures perpetuating the desperate poverty in the third-world. *See* WRIGHT, OLD TESTAMENT ETHICS, *supra* note 187, at 120 (urging Christians to make "moral arguments with persuasive force and practical relevance," and to especially direct such debate at specific issues with limited objectives that are achievable).

245.   *See* sources cited *supra* notes 206-09 and accompanying text (discussing the contemporary relevance of the moral principle of Old Testament law requiring that the poorest and most vulnerable segment of society enjoy a minimum opportunity to improve their economic circumstances); sources cited *supra* notes 217-35 and accompanying text (discussing specific support in the New Testament affirming the moral principles of the Old Testament); *see also* WRIGHT, WALKING, *supra* note 187, at

Moreover, because sufficient funding of public schools, as a necessary ingredient towards building an adequate school system,[246] is "genuinely comparable" to the "specific life situations" of the biblical texts, this Judeo-Christian moral principle contemporarily applies and requires that public schools receive at least a minimum level of adequate funding in order to offer low-income children a chance to break out of the cycle of poverty by achieving an adequate education.[247]

Although the ethical problems caused by Alabama's inadequate tax revenues could be partially mitigated by requiring higher income taxpayers to bear their fair share of the income tax,[248] Alabama's property tax structure, especially the features requiring only a *de minimis* portion of the value of timber acres to be subject to the millage rates, is responsible for the inadequate funding of Alabama's public schools.[249] Because in many areas across the state (often the same areas with a significant portion of the

---

114-16, 144-45 (outlining an approach to biblical hermeneutics for applying the moral principles of Old Testament law to contemporary situations: first define the functions behind the institutions of ancient Israel, the broad objectives of the law in the ancient context, and the moral principles developed from these objectives; then identify analogous contemporary situations where those broad objectives are relevant in the contemporary world; and finally, apply the moral principles developed from these broad objectives to the contemporary situation); BLOMBERG, *supra* note 176, at 84 (discussing the relevance of the biblical teachings on wealth and possessions to contemporary society, and stating that "[t]he key to evaluating any individual church or nation in terms of its use of material possessions (personally, collectively or institutionally) is how well it takes care of the poor and powerless in its midst, that is, its cultural equivalents to the fatherless, widow and alien").

246.   *See* sources cited *supra* note 102 (discussing extensively the role of funding as a tool to build quality education systems, presenting both sides of the debate concerning the effect of increased funding on the quality of the education offered, and concluding that at least a minimum level of adequate funding is absolutely necessary to help low-income students perform at an acceptable level).

247.   *See* sources cited *supra* notes 195-96, 206-09 and accompanying text (discussing application of the Old Testament's moral principles to contemporary society); WRIGHT, DEUTERONOMY, *supra* note 189, at 261 (applying principles of biblical hermeneutics to the Old Testament law and finding that these principles broadly require the poorest and weakest in the community to have access to opportunities they need to provide for themselves, which "may include financial resources, but could also include access to education, legal assistance, investment in job opportunities, etc.; [s]uch things should not be leftovers or handouts, but a matter of rights and responsibilities in a caring society"); OSWALT II, *supra* note 215, at 282 ("The creation of a stable environment where children can mature and become productive persons is a direct concomitant of having listened to the instruction of God about the nature of human life."); BROWN, *supra* note 195, at 145-46 (noting that children and their welfare are a special concern of the Old Testament); WRIGHT, LAND, *supra* note 197, at 97-99 (discussing the importance of the land tenure laws of the Old Testament in the context of guarding the welfare of children); *see also* sources cited *supra* notes 217-35 (discussing the New Testament's affirmation of the Old Testament's moral principles); *Luke* 18:15-17 (showing special concern for children as worthy of the kingdom); BOCK II, *supra* note 219, at 1472 (summarizing the message of *Luke* 18:15-17 as indicating that "[p]eople of any size count," and that a mission of a true disciple of Christ must not only be "to the powerful, but also to the dependent").

248.   *See supra* note 17 (noting Alabama's revenues collected from the income are among the lowest per capita in the United States); *supra* notes 30-44 (discussing features of the income tax, including its flat rates, lack of limits on the use of exemptions, and full deduction for federal taxes paid, which allow high income taxpayers to substantially reduce their tax burden).

249.   *See* sources cited *supra* notes 127-44 (documenting that the inadequate funding of Alabama's public schools is largely due to the property tax structure, especially the features that favor timber acres).

population below the poverty line) timber acres represent the most important, and in some cases the only, source of valuable property available to
tax, the low ten percent assessment ratio and the current use formula work
together to prevent even millage rates exceeding the state's average from
producing sufficient property tax revenues, thus crippling these areas from
raising sufficient revenues from fair property taxes.[250] The failure of owners of timber acres to pay even close to their fair share in property taxes
denies the poorest areas of the state the ability to fairly tax the only valuable wealth within their borders, leaving the vast number of low-income
children living in those areas with no opportunity to achieve an adequate
education.[251]

In addition to being the most responsible for the inadequately funded
schools, the inadequate revenues raised from property taxes, especially
timber acres, force local governments to raise sales tax rates to intolerably
oppressive levels.[252] By greatly favoring the wealthiest landowners and
high-income Alabamians, the regressive income and sales tax structures
combined with the oppressive effects caused by the failure of Alabama's
property tax structure to raise adequate revenues perpetuates a permanent
underclass of poor Alabamians, and metaphorically, at the broadest ethical
level, corresponds to the societal structures condemned by the Old Testament prophets and Jesus Christ as inconsistent with God's character.[253]

Because Alabama's tax structure creates a fundamentally unjust social
structure under any reasonable ethical model, all Alabamians should support tax reform efforts designed to both eliminate the harsh economic tax
burdens imposed on the poorest Alabamians and to raise enough additional
revenues to meet minimum needs, which includes bringing the funding of

---

250. *See supra* notes 67-72 (discussing Alabama's four classes of property with timber and agriculture enjoying the lowest Class III assessment ratio (10%) of the property's value); *supra* note 137
(identifying areas with inadequately funded schools despite having millage rates exceeding the state
average); *supra* note 136 (discussing poverty figures in areas with inadequately funded schools).

251. *See id.*; *supra* note 102 (discussing the importance of a minimum level of adequate funding for
low-income children to have a chance of achieving an adequate education); *supra* notes 107-28 (discussing the inadequate level of funding for most of Alabama's public schools); *supra* notes 132-44
(discussing the inability of most areas to raise adequate property tax revenues due to limitations built
into the property tax structure).

252. *See supra* notes 46-49, 142 and accompanying text (discussing the high sales tax rates created
by local governments substantially raising the state's 4% rate as being fueled by inadequate revenues
raised from property taxes).

253. *See supra* notes 192-95, 224-35 and accompanying text; *see also* OSWALT II, *supra* note 215,
at 523-24 (warning that covering up the oppression of the weak with lies, or pretending that the oppression really does not exist, leads to totally corrupted hearts which prevent the truth from being
recognized, and that without a standard of integrity higher than individual self-interest, "justice will
always fall prey to devouring self-interest," and "life quickly falls to the lowest common denominator
of self-seeking"); HUEY, *supra* note 211, at 446 (stating that a contemporary application of the *Lamentations*, which describes the misery of ancient Israel after they ignored the Prophets and suffered
military defeat and exile, warns that the "wickedness of any people will eventually result in the disin-
tegration of that society"); WRIGHT, DEUTERONOMY, *supra* note 189, at 192 (noting that the ethics of
biblical principles forbid marginalizing the poor and victimizing the underclass).

all of Alabama's public schools up to a minimally adequate level. Because Alabama's tax structure also violates the moral principles of Judeo-Christian ethics, Alabamians practicing Christianity or Judaism, by virtue of their knowledge, acceptance, love, and worship[254] of the one true God, have an even more compelling affirmative moral duty to support these tax reform efforts as part of their response in gratitude to God.[255] Because all qualified Alabamians have a constitutionally guaranteed right to vote in public elections, at a bare minimum this moral duty encompasses an af-

---

254.   Both the Old Testament and the New Testament state that mere worship and adherence to religious ritual cannot alone indicate the authentic practice of religion. *See* ROOKER, *supra* note 183, at 252 ("[E]very statement about the moral nature of God in the Bible carries the implied demand that the believer exhibit this same quality in daily living. It is thus not possible to divorce ethics and theology, since human morality is justified by the nature of God."); GEORGE, *supra* note 221, at 150 ("Theology and ethics can never be divorced in an ultimate sense."); MERRILL, *supra* note 188, at 201 (discussing the covenant relationship with God as having both horizontal and vertical elements—loving and serving God comes with societal obligations to love and serve your neighbor); BROWN, *supra* note 195, at 152 (stating the worship of God can only be genuine if it comes with compassion and love towards the people God loves); G. SMITH, *supra* note 187, at 252 ("God requires just and righteous living as a prerequisite of worship. If their social and legal relationships to each other, and especially to the poor and weak, are not consistent with the responsibilities outlined in the law of God, they can hardly expect God's approval."); *see also Amos* 5:21-24 ("I hate, I despise your religious feasts; I cannot stand your assemblies. Even though you bring me burnt offerings and grain offerings, I will not accept them. Though you bring choice fellowship offerings, I will have no regard for them. Away with the noise of your songs! I will not listen to the music of your harps. But let justice roll on like a river, righteousness like a never-failing stream!"); SMITH & PAGE, *supra* note 194, at 111-13 (describing *Amos* 5:21-24 as a strong condemnation of hollow worship that applies to worship today, stating "Religious activity is no substitute for national or personal righteousness. It may even sometimes be a hindrance."); *id.* at 106 ("Seeking God and seeking good represent the two dimensions of true religion, not rituals and forms but relationships with God and other persons . . . [t]he implication of the larger message . . . is that one who truly seeks the Lord also seeks the welfare of the poor."); *Micah* 6:8 ("He has showed you, O man, what is good. And what does the LORD require of you? To act justly and to love mercy and to walk humbly with your God."); BARKER & BAILEY, *supra* note 187, at 121-23 (discussing extensively *Micah* 6:8 as a summary of true religion and analyzing the Hebrew text interpreting "to walk humbly" as to live carefully the way God wants you to live); *see also Matthew* 21:13; HUEY, *supra* note 211, at 106 (interpreting *Jeremiah* 7:9-11, referring to the temple becoming a "den of robbers," and quoted by Jesus in *Matthew* 21:13, as characterizing the temple as a refuge, much like a cave for robbers, where people may engage in worship in an attempt to purge themselves from wicked behavior); *James* 1:22 ("Do not merely listen to the word, and so deceive yourselves. Do what it says."); *James* 2:26 ("As the body without the spirit is dead, so faith without deeds is dead."); MOO, *supra* note 226, at 38, 89-90, 141 (describing the theology of *James* as focusing on the determination of whether a person's faith is genuine, and does not espouse salvation by works); THOMAS R. SCHREINER, ROMANS 66-67 (1998) (discussing the overall theology of justification by faith in *Romans* as stated in *Romans* 1:17 as "both forensic and transformative," meaning "[t]hose whom God has vindicated he also changes"); GEORGE, *supra* note 221, at 222-23 (discussing John Calvin's interpretation of *James* as opposing a false faith, as opposed to espousing a works salvation, and noting that true faith results in the person "living out of the word").

255.   ROOKER, *supra* note 183, at 57, 67; WRIGHT, DEUTERONOMY, *supra* note 189, at 61-63, 95, 98; WRIGHT, OLD TESTAMENT ETHICS, *supra* note 187, at 21; WRIGHT, WALKING, *supra* note 187, at 133 (stating all moral activity can only be a response in gratitude to God); OSWALT II, *supra* note 215, at 455, 509, 559 (interpreting the general message of Isaiah as calling for righteous living and obedience as a response to salvation); *see also* GEORGE, *supra* note 221, at 37 (discussing the tension of Christians living in the present age in light of the eschatological message of the New Testament and noting that "we are not to opt out of our present responsibilities but rather give ourselves fully to the work of the Lord").

firmative obligation to vote responsibly for candidates seeking election to Alabama's House of Representatives and Senate, as well as to the office of Governor—to vote for candidates who will actively work towards quickly mitigating the harsh injustices perpetuated by the current tax structure.[256]

The moral principles of Judeo-Christian ethics impose greater moral responsibilities, beyond merely exercising their right to vote, on Alabamians with substantially more knowledge and privileges than the average Alabamian.[257] Examples of such persons include Alabamians enjoying the fortunate circumstances of having a high level of education, being a member of a profession (such as the legal profession) with access to power structures, having an abundance of material wealth compared to most Alabamians, or being a respected member of their local community for any reason. The moral principles of Judeo-Christian ethics urge these Alabamians to use their special gifts and circumstances to help educate the community as to the moral imperatives mandating tax reform and to help combat the negative effects of those who distort the facts regarding the tax structure and its consequences purely for selfish reasons.[258] In a democratic state government where each person's vote counts equally, the numerous poor and uneducated Alabamians who vote in favor of increasing sales tax rates, who fail to vote at all, or who vote for candidates that are indifferent towards or opposed to efforts reducing or eliminating the harsh injustices perpetuated by the current tax structure, are victims of their own lack of knowledge. Alabamians who selfishly take advantage of the poor's lack of knowledge in order to maintain the status quo (such as those Alabamians perpetuating false or misleading advertisements or engaging in other abusive tactics to thwart others seeking to communicate the truth) are directly violating the Judeo-Christian moral principle forbidding the economic oppression of the poor and powerless.[259]

---

256. *See supra* note 7 (discussing free exercise of religion and freedom of speech); *see also* SCHRIENER, *supra* note 254, at 687-88 (discussing the command of *Romans* 13:1-7 to submit to governing authorities as not precluding political activity, especially lawful political activity, geared towards correcting unjust features of government); FRANK THIELMAN, THE NIV APPLICATION COMMENTARY: PHILIPPIANS 106 (1995) (noting that government in Western democratic societies differs substantially from the government faced by the early church, and stating that modern Christians in democratic societies should work for more just policies in government as part of loving your neighbor as yourself); BROWN, *supra* note 195, at 66-67 (cautioning Christians to avoid becoming so busy with church activities that they ignore other social and political opportunities in serving God).

257. *Luke* 12:48 ("From everyone who has been given much, much will be demanded; and from the one who has been entrusted with much, much more will be asked."); BOCK II, *supra* note 219, at 1184-86 (discussing *Luke* 12:47-48 in the context of judgment and punishment of the unfaithful servant, with greater punishments for servants with more knowledge, and the principle "the more one knows, the more responsible one becomes, so that more will be asked of one when evaluated"); *see also* J.A. MOTYER, THE MESSAGE OF AMOS 17-18 (1974) (discussing the general message of *Amos* regrading judgment as requiring more "from those to whom more has been given").

258. *See supra* note 257.

259. *See supra* notes 191, 224-26 (discussing the biblical texts and the general moral principle of Judeo-Christian ethics forbidding the economic oppression of poor people), especially note 192 (for-

The moral principles of Judeo-Christian ethics impose on Alabama's political leaders who practice Christianity or Judaism an even greater responsibility for securing and maintaining the minimum well-being of the entire community, especially the poor and needy.[260] Because Alabama's tax structure inflicts extreme injustice on low-income Alabamians and their children—the poorest, weakest, and most vulnerable segment of the population—these ethical principles, which treat leadership as a call to responsibly do what is just, not merely politically expedient, require Alabama's leaders to work to the highest degree to reverse these unjust effects. Because Alabama's political leaders hold the power over the lawmaking process, the moral principles of Judeo-Christian ethics hold them directly responsible for perpetuating the unjust tax structure that continues to oppress and keep the poorest Alabamians in a permanent underclass, while denying to all Alabamians the benefits of a well-run government. Failure to work for tax reform because of fear of not being re-elected, or worse, to protect personal economic interests by maintaining the status quo, amounts to an abuse of the leadership position, and metaphorically, at the broadest ethical level, corresponds to the conduct of ancient Israel's kings and judges condemned by the Old Testament prophets more than two thousand years ago.[261]

Finally, Alabama's religious leaders, those called into the ministry to preach and teach God's word and serve as God's special representatives on earth to defend the cause of the poor and needy, bear the greatest responsibility for educating the community as to the oppressive and unjust effects of Alabama's current tax structure and the need for tax reform to correct these injustices. The moral principles of Judeo-Christian ethics command religious leaders to preach and teach the word of God, even if the most influential and powerful members of the society, those capable of making life difficult, do not agree with the message. The moral principles of Judeo-Christian ethics hold religious leaders, the preachers and teachers

---

bidding the economic oppression of poor people also generally forbids the use of dishonest techniques to accomplish this economic oppression). In contemporary society the use of false or misleading advertisements or other means to trick poor people into voting for proposals or candidates that will continue or worsen the economic oppression that Alabama's tax system inflicts upon them is "genuinely comparable" to the biblical text specifically forbidding the use of dishonest scales and measurements because of the analogous economically oppressive effects, therefore, the general moral principle of Judeo-Christian ethics forbidding the use of dishonest techniques as a tool to economically oppress poor people applies to these contemporary practices. *See generally supra* notes 176-78.

260.   All but a tiny handful of Alabama's elected political leaders with direct access to the legislative process practice Christianity. *See* Comp. & app. A, *supra* note 5.

261.   *See supra* notes 210-15 and accompanying text; *see also* BLOCK I, *supra* note 210, at 714 (stating under *Ezekiel*'s broad theological message that "community leaders bear special responsibility for the maintenance of justice and the welfare of its citizenry; [t]he call to leadership is primarily a call to responsibility, not privilege; [t]he Lord will rise up against those who use the office for personal advantage, especially those who run roughshod over the rights of the most vulnerable people").

of God's word, to the highest level of accountability.[262] As spiritual leaders in a community made up of a vast number of people professing to be among the People of God,[263] Alabama's religious leaders must assume a greater role in the efforts to achieve fair and just tax reform. In addition to educating members of their congregations and visibly supporting efforts to achieve fair and just tax reform, Alabama's religious leaders have an affirmative responsibility to speak up and rebuke those who are using fraudulent and manipulative means to maintain the status quo in order to selfishly protect their own interests at the expense of the greater community. Failure to accept this responsibility due to fear of those embedded in Alabama's power structures, or due to the desire to protect personal economic interests by maintaining the status quo, amounts to an abuse of the calling to proclaim God's word with courage and clarity, whatever the personal cost may be. Metaphorically, that failure, at the broadest ethical level, corresponds to the conduct of ancient Israel's priests and the religious leaders of first century Palestine condemned by the Old Testament prophets and by Jesus Christ more than two thousand years ago.[264]

CONCLUSION

The empirical research of this Article documenting the oppressive consequences that Alabama's income, sales, and property tax structures foist upon the poorest Alabamians and their children, paints a disgraceful picture. Alabama's income, sales, and property tax structures work together from two different angles to keep the poorest Alabamians as a permanent underclass. At the front end, the income and sales tax structures take an unacceptably large portion of the scarce resources these Alabam-

---

262.   BLOCK I, *supra* note 210, at 714.

263.   *See supra* note 4 (stating that 93% of Alabamians claim to be Christians).

264.   *See generally supra* notes 210-15, 225 and accompanying text; *see also* OSWALT II, *supra* note 215, at 325 (interpreting the broad theological message of Isaiah as indicating that God's true prophets often stand outside the mainstream, professing a message not often well received because they confront godless behavior with a call for change, rather than making it easy for persons to manipulate God; and quoting John Calvin as saying "whoever faithfully administers the Word will be exposed to a contest with the world"); *id.* at 496 (noting that it is possible to desire God's ways and forsake God's justice, citing as a clear example the Pharisees, the religious leaders harshly criticized by Jesus who would meet the tithing laws to the letter and at the same time put a widow out on the street); *see also James* 3:1 ("Not many of you should presume to be teachers, my brothers, because you know that we who teach will be judged more strictly."). Further, the second *Timothy* states:

> In the presence of God and of Christ Jesus, who will judge the living and the dead, and in view of his appearing and his kingdom, I give you this charge: Preach the Word; be prepared in season and out of season; correct, rebuke and encourage—with great patience and careful instruction. For the time will come when men will not put up with sound doctrine. Instead, to suit their own desires, they will gather around them a great number of teachers to say what their itching ears want to hear. They will turn their ears away from the truth and turn aside to myths. But you, keep your head in all situations, endure hardship, do the work of an evangelist, discharge all the duties of your ministry.

2 *Timothy* 4:1-5.

ians must have to meet basic needs and try to improve their lives. At the back end, the property tax structure leaves the state and the local areas perpetually revenue-starved and unable to adequately fund public schools, which in turn denies the children of the poorest Alabamians any reasonable opportunity to break out of this cycle of poverty and economic oppression. These effects are not only grossly unfair under all reasonable ethical models, but they also violate the moral principles of Judeo-Christian ethics that forbid the economic oppression of poor persons and require that such persons enjoy at least a minimum opportunity to improve their economic circumstances. The principles of Judeo-Christian ethics impose affirmative moral obligations on all persons practicing Christianity or Judaism to work towards reforming this unjust tax structure. Persons enjoying greater talents, gifts, opportunities, and resources that can be effectively channeled towards this goal have a greater moral responsibility; those elected to serve in Alabama's House of Representatives, Senate and the Office of the Governor have an even greater responsibility; and those serving in a leadership capacity for a church, synagogue, or other religious organization have the greatest moral responsibility to work towards reforming this unjust tax structure.

Although the details spelling out exactly what must be done to sufficiently reform Alabama's tax structure to reach a minimum level of fairness are beyond the scope of this Article, the moral principles of Judeo-Christian ethics provide general guidance as to the steps that must be taken. First, Alabama's leaders must ascertain the minimum standards of basic health, education, and welfare that the moral principles of Judeo-Christian ethics require all Alabamians to have and determine the cost to heed God's charge to meet these standards.[265] The tax structure then must be reformed to raise adequate revenues to meet this cost based on ability to pay, which must involve removing the unfair heavy tax burden that the

---

265. A detailed discussion of the minimum funding needs for all of Alabama's vital programs is beyond the scope of this Article. However, given the empirical evidence showing that: (1) Alabama's revenues are the lowest per capita in the nation, (2) close to 90% of Alabama's public schools are inadequately funded, and (3) anecdotal evidence documenting a significant number of other serious budget crises, it is unreasonable to pretend that a minimum level of adequate revenues can be raised under a tax reform proposal that is revenue neutral. *See supra* notes 60, 126. The moral requirement that a legitimate tax reform proposal must be revenue positive represents the first of three major "elephants in the room" that few people in leadership positions are willing to acknowledge. Although a legitimate tax reform proposal should carefully address how the revenues are spent and contain reasonable accountability measures, arguments that Alabama's chronic shortage of revenues can be addressed solely by cutting back on wasteful and inefficient spending ignores both the large degree that Alabama's revenues fall short of minimum adequacy and the fact that no proof exists that Alabama's spending patterns show a higher degree of waste or inefficiency than the spending patterns of other states. Arguments that Alabama's budget difficulties can be addressed by eliminating the earmarking of funds ignores the fact that the practice of earmarking, which is very inefficient, is a defense mechanism used by government actors to protect funding levels when the total revenues available to meet the state's budget are inadequate. Until Alabama raises adequate revenues to meet at least minimum needs, it is nearly impossible to eliminate the motives for keeping earmarking alive.

current tax structure imposes on the poorest Alabamians. In order to accomplish the twin goals of removing the unfair tax burden imposed on the poorest Alabamians and raising adequate revenues to meet the minimum needs of the entire state, the reformed tax structure must require Alabamians at higher income levels, those owning property of significant value, to pay higher taxes.[266]

The moral principles of Judeo-Christian ethics also shed some light on the general changes that must be made to the three most important parts of Alabama's tax system: the income, sales, and property tax structures.[267] At a minimum, the income tax structure must be reformed to raise the exemptions to a sufficient level so that individuals and families below the poverty line do not pay any income taxes.[268] Concurrently, the income tax burden

---

266.   The moral requirement that Alabamians enjoying the fortunate circumstances of having a greater ability to pay taxes, especially those with the greatest ability to pay, must pay more taxes represents the second of three major "elephants in the room" that few people in leadership positions are willing to acknowledge. Instead, many political leaders avoid the issue by stating that they are against new taxes. This statement is at best unhelpful because it effectively treats all taxpayers the same when, in fact, enormous variations exist in the levels of income and wealth enjoyed by different Alabamians. *See supra* note 136. This statement also implies that the current tax structure is fair and adequate when the evidence indisputably indicates the tax structure is neither fair nor adequate. *See supra* Parts I.A-B; *see also supra* note 1. The hard truth is, even in a revenue neutral posture, it is impossible to remove the unfair heavy tax burdens on the poorest Alabamians without requiring wealthier Alabamians to pay more taxes. More bluntly, under the moral principles of Judeo-Christian ethics Alabamians of wealth and privilege are not paying their fair minimum share of Alabama's tax burden and because of that the poorest Alabamians are suffering the brunt of their windfall. A tax reform effort meeting the moral principles of Judeo-Christian ethics would reduce the tax burden for many Alabamians at and below the poverty line as well as many others at the lower ranges of the middle class, while increasing the tax burden for Alabamians at the highest levels of income and wealth, in proportion to their abilities to pay. Statements that represent tax reform efforts in Alabama as attempts to create a steeply progressive tax structure while raising a generous level of revenues, comparable to states with the highest revenues per capita nationwide, are fraudulent because the tax reform efforts in Alabama, including the arguments made in this Article, have urged that the tax structure be reformed to achieve a minimum level of fairness while raising only enough revenues to meet minimum needs. *See supra* notes 102, 157, 234.

267.   *See supra* note 9 (stating that income, sales and property tax structures are the three most important sources of revenue for state and local governments generally). This Article acknowledges that a legitimate tax reform effort would also take a hard look at all the components of Alabama's tax structure and reform many of them, including the business tax structure. However, many have argued that a minimum level of fairness and needed revenue can be achieved by focusing solely on reforming the business tax structure. These statements ignore the fact that business taxes are not traditionally an important component of state and local finance. Although tax reform in Alabama probably should include reform of the business tax structure, it is unreasonable to assume that focusing on big business, while ignoring the inequities of the income, sales, and property tax structures, can bring about the minimum level of tax reform required by the moral principles of Judeo-Christian ethics. It has also been suggested that revenues raised from a lottery can save Alabama from its revenue crisis. This assumption is false because it ignores that the revenues from a lottery cannot possibly meet the level of funding needed to meet Alabama's minimum needs. Moreover, because it is well known that a lottery is in substance a regressive tax burdening the poor, despite its voluntary nature, a lottery proposal violates the moral principle of Judeo-Christian ethics forbidding the economic oppression of the poor. This Article also acknowledges that many Christians interpret biblical principles as forbidding gambling generally but, because the research of this Article did not focus on biblical principles addressing gambling, this Article takes no position on that issue.

268.   Representative John D. Knight (D. Montgomery) has made numerous efforts over the last few

on taxpayers with a greater ability to pay must be increased, in an equitable fashion, to both cover the net revenue loss that will occur from removing truly poor persons from the income tax roles and to also generate additional positive revenues in order to partially address Alabama's woefully inadequate revenues. A legitimate proposal to reform the income tax structure should also remove the elements that favor the highest income taxpayers (including phasing out the right to claim exemptions at very high income levels and eliminating certain deductions, such as the deduction for federal income taxes paid), and could consider adopting a mildly progressive rate schedule, thereby requiring those taxpayers with a greater ability to pay to bear a greater proportional income tax burden.[269]

Because sales taxes, especially those at high rates without appropriate exemptions, always disproportionately burden the poor, at a minimum the reform of Alabama's sales tax structure should include a limit on how high sales tax rates can climb and adopt appropriate exemptions for food, clothing, medicine, and other basic needs.[270] However, because Alabama relies heavily on sales taxes for more than fifty percent of its tax revenues and, at the same time, collects the lowest per capita property tax and overall revenues in the United States,[271] reforming the sales tax structure fairly and raising Alabama's overall per capita revenues to an adequate level cannot be accomplished without also reforming the property tax structure. This reform of the property tax structure must involve increasing the portion of the true fair market value of all property subject to the millage rates, which will require owners of all classes of property, especially owners of property with significant fair market value, to pay more property taxes.[272] In addition, a well-designed proposal to reform the property tax

sessions to reform the income tax structure in a manner that reduces the economic oppression suffered by the poor. *See* H.B. 583, 2002 Leg., Reg. Sess. (Ala. 2002); H.B. 586, 2002 Leg., Reg. Sess. (Ala. 2002); H.B. 11, 2001 Leg., 4th Spec. Sess. (Ala. 2001); H.B. 12, 2001 Leg., 4th Spec. Sess. (Ala. 2001); H.B. 40, 2001 Leg., 1st Spec. Sess. (Ala. 2001); H.B. 41, 2001 Leg., 1st Spec. Sess. (Ala. 2001).

269. The debate as to the fairness of progressive tax structures versus flat tax structures that have no regressive effect is very controversial among tax policy theorists. *See supra* note 158. An evaluation of whether the moral principles of Judeo-Christian ethics can be invoked to affirmatively support proposals that create a progressive rate structure is beyond the scope of this Article.

270. *See supra* note 172 (discussing ways to ease the burden of sales taxes on poor people); *see also supra* note 47 (discussing significant caps on how high sales tax rates in Georgia, North Carolina, and South Carolina can be raised by local governments). Although reductions in sales tax rates and the establishment of exemptions for basic necessities will also benefit Alabamians with a greater ability to pay, if those changes were part of an overall tax reform package that included increases of income and property taxes for taxpayers with a greater ability to pay, then the benefit from a cut in sales taxes could be more than offset by tax increases in other areas.

271. *See supra* notes 43, 50-63 and accompanying text.

272. The need for comprehensive tax reform to include an overhaul of the property tax structure in a manner that produces more property tax revenues, as a necessary ingredient towards eliminating the regressive features of Alabama's current tax structure and bringing Alabama's overall revenues up to an adequate level, represents the third of the three major "elephants in the room" that few people in leadership positions are willing to acknowledge. Proper reform of Alabama's property tax structure

structure should carefully provide for sufficient exemptions to avoid over-taxing lower valued property where owners' ability to pay is an issue.

In addition to requiring all classes of property to pay more property tax in general, genuine tax reform in accordance with moral principles of Judeo-Christian ethics also requires owners of timber property to pay a substantially greater proportional share of the total property taxes than they do under the current structure. This reform can only be accomplished by increasing the portion of the value of timber acres subject to the millage rates to the level needed to ensure that owners of timber acres bear a fair proportional share of the total property taxes.[273] In addition, a well-designed proposal should carefully provide for exemptions in order to avoid overtaxing small farmers and other landowners where ability to pay is truly an issue. Allowing owners of timber acres, who as a group dominate Alabama's economy and landmass, to continue to pay less than two percent of the property taxes, averaging less than one dollar per acre,[274] is both patently unfair under any reasonable ethical model and also consti-

---

consistent with the moral principles of Judeo-Christian ethics must first determine the portion of Alabama's total revenues that property taxes should raise in order to remove the heavy tax burden imposed on the poorest Alabamians and raise the minimum level of adequate revenues. Because Alabama's property taxes currently contribute as little as approximately 5% (and possibly as much as 13%) of Alabama's total revenues which is significantly out of balance with the national average showing property taxes contributing approximately 25% of state and local revenues generally, reform of the property tax structure must increase the portion that property taxes contribute to Alabama's total state and local revenues. *See supra* notes 9, 55. Except for the empirical evidence proving that timber property must proportionally pay a greater share of Alabama's property taxes, the details spelling out exactly what portion of Alabama's total revenues property taxes should bear and how to fairly apportion the property tax burden across different classes of property is beyond the scope of this Article. *See supra* notes 92-101 and accompanying text. A legitimate property tax reform effort should take into account the individual circumstances related to business cycles of the owners of the different classes of property, other tax burdens such as income and severance taxes borne by the owners of different classes of property, and should also consider expanding the property tax base to include the value of intangible property, such as securities.

273.   *See supra* notes 101 (noting that the precise degree of additional property taxes needed to bring the share borne by owners of timber acres up to a fair level is beyond the scope of this Article), 173-75 and accompanying text (discussing the issues involved in designing a fair property tax structure). This Article acknowledges that significant differences exist between the business of harvesting timber acres (which will not produce profits every year) and other commercial businesses (which, assuming business is going well, normally do produce profits every year), and that these differences should be accounted for in any reform proposal creating a fair property tax structure that appropriately factors in the property owner's ability to pay. This Article also recognizes that property owners harvesting timber bear other taxes, for example severance taxes. Although a legitimate property tax reform proposal that fairly apportions the burden for the property tax revenues among the different classes of property must take into account the relative differences in the business cycles for producing profits as well as all other taxes that owners of that class of property bear, the legitimate need to factor in these considerations in no way justifies the *de minimis* share or amount of property taxes currently paid by owners of timber property. Business and commercial property, which proportionally pay well over 50% of Alabama's property taxes, also bear other taxes, such as income and business taxes. The owners of personal residences, which proportionally contribute well over 25% of Alabama's property taxes, also bear other taxes, such as income and sales taxes, and realize no profits until their house is sold, while many owners of timber property who are not in the business of harvesting trees receive a periodic income stream from other, non-farm sources, such as hunting leases.

274.   *See supra* notes 90-101 and accompanying text.

tutes the most troubling violation of Judeo-Christian moral principles because children from low-income families—the most vulnerable and powerless segment of Alabama's population—suffer the brunt of that windfall by
being denied a minimum opportunity to secure an adequate education.

The State of Alabama stands at the crossroads of a new century. It
currently has in place a tax structure—one of many unfortunate vestiges of
the 1901 Constitution—that not only economically oppresses the poorest
and most vulnerable Alabamians, but also denies the children of these
families a minimum opportunity to seek a better life. The tax structure,
with all its unjust effects, is morally wrong, not only under any reasonable
ethical model for evaluating tax policy, but more persuasively because it
violates the moral principles of Judeo-Christian ethics. The vast majority
of Alabamians practice Christianity or Judaism and hold these ethical principles near to their hearts, and, as individuals, Alabamians tend to be very
compassionate and caring towards their less fortunate neighbors. Unfortunately, many Alabamians, especially those that the tax structure harms the
most, have been manipulated into believing falsehoods perpetuated by a
few special interest groups. These falsehoods spread myths that Alabama's
current tax structure is fair and have stood as a barrier keeping that oppressive tax structure in place.

The vast number of Alabamians practicing Christianity, more than
ninety percent of the population, know that when Jesus came into this
world He taught us to treat each other fairly and to love each other
through our actions—not with mere lip service to the love that Christ ex-
emplifies. Despite the clear teachings of Jesus, many Alabamians that do
not pay their fair share of Alabama's tax burden are guilty of tactics that
have selfishly thwarted efforts to change the deplorable aspects of the current tax structure. Many more Alabamians, busy and preoccupied with
other matters, are guilty of allowing inertia to lull them into complacently
accepting the current unjust tax structure without seriously questioning its
effects on their less fortunate neighbors. However, under Christian principles the degree of each individual Christian's guilt does not matter. By
dying on the cross Jesus bore the penalty for all this guilt—indeed for the
sins of the entire world, offering all people salvation by grace and allowing Christians to start over with a new ledger sheet. As Christians living in
Alabama today, we have a moral obligation to start over and get the tax
structure right.[275] All Alabamians of goodwill, including Christian and
Jewish adherents and practitioners of other faiths and philosophies, have a
unique opportunity to confront those manipulating the truth and to demand
a fair and just tax structure for all Alabamians, especially the poorest Ala-

---

275. Professor Hamill gratefully acknowledges her colleague and friend Bob McCurley for sharing
these ideas, which came from a sermon prepared by his daughter Leah McCurley, a student at the
Candler School of Theology, Emory University.

bamians, who lack the power, knowledge, and resources to effectively speak up for themselves. This movement must begin with the leaders of the churches, synagogues, and other religious organizations insisting that all Alabamians within their congregations, especially those elected to political office or otherwise enjoying special abilities or resources, rise up and demand that the old way end, which will pave the way for the reforms needed to give birth to a new community that offers the poorest and most vulnerable citizens minimum safety nets and opportunities to improve their lives.[276] Only then can real spiritual renewal take place, allowing Alabama to become the light to the nation and the world that it was meant to be.

PRAYER

Heavenly Father, I thank You for all the blessings I have received, especially a loving home while growing up, a loving husband and two children, and an excellent education.

I thank You for the opportunity to serve the State of Alabama and I pray for guidance as I continue in that fiduciary role.

I ask for Your forgiveness for my transgressions, especially for taking seven years to see and understand the widespread injustices suffered by the vast majority of Alabamians and their children, the very people I have a fiduciary responsibility to serve.

I offer this scholarship as my best work, in Your name and glory, representing my honest interpretation of Your word, in response to You.

I pray that You will soften the hearts of my fellow Alabamians; give them eyes to see, ears to hear, and the ability to understand and guide them towards the path of justice.

I pray that You will be with the political leaders of our state; show them the way to justice, give them courage and perseverance to do what is right and resist being tempted by expediency, and provide them the strength to face the inevitable opposition they will encounter.

I especially pray that You will be with the religious leaders of our state; guide them towards leading a true spiritual renewal of our state so that Alabama may reflect Your character and serve as a light to other states and the world.

I make this prayer in Jesus' name, Amen.

---

276.   Because virtually every political leader at the highest levels in Alabama's recent history (except for former Governor Albert Brewer) has failed to acknowledge and confront the need for complete and total tax reform, a certain amount of courage is necessary for anyone who publicly endorses the need for tax reform. For those choosing the high road of publicly supporting tax reform, the Old Testament prophets, who in their day were treated like outcasts for opposing evils that broadly compare to the evils perpetuated by Alabama's current tax structure, offer a comforting example that helps one find the courage to boldly "confront evils in a world where evil is normalized." *See* HUEY, *supra* note 211, at 36.

APPENDIX A*
RELIGIOUS AFFILIATIONS OF MEMBERS OF ALABAMA'S
SENATE AND HOUSE OF REPRESENTATIVES (INCLUDING
GOVERNOR AND LIEUTENANT GOVERNOR)

Christian Denomination Identified by the Person	Senate and House Members Identifying with a Particular Denomination	Percent of Total Alabama Senate and House Members
Baptist (including all Baptist variations)	66	46%
Methodist (including AME and CME)	34	24%
Church of Christ	10	7%
Presbyterian	10	7%
Catholic	5	4%
Episcopal	3	2%
Other Protestant Denominations	8	6%
Total Senate and House Members with Christian Affiliations	136	96%
Unknown	6	4%
Total	**142**	**100%**

   * See www.legislature.state.al.us, for a biography of each member of Alabama's Senate and House of Representatives (including Governor and Lieutenant Governor).

APPENDIX B*
RANGE OF ALABAMA'S SALES TAX

Appendix B breaks down the sales tax range in each Alabama county. The counties are grouped in their geographic region as designated in this Article.

Northeast Alabama Counties	Lowest Sales Tax Rate	Highest Sales Tax Rate	1998 Gross Retail Sales
Blount	6.00%	8.00%	$183,858,000
Calhoun	5.00%	9.00%	$979,669,000
Cherokee	6.50%	8.50%	$113,414,000
Clay	6.00%	8.00%	$46,388,000
Cleburne	5.00%	8.00%	$48,988,000
Cullman	8.00%	11.00%	$562,055,000
DeKalb	5.00%	9.00%	$343,219,000
Etowah	5.00%	8.00%	$788,665,000
Jackson	6.00%	9.00%	$315,725,000
Jefferson	5.00%	9.00%	$7,394,319,000
Marshall	5.00%	9.00%	$771,250,000
Randolph	4.00%	7.00%	$91,090,000
Shelby	5.00%	8.00%	$1,047,594,000
St. Clair	6.00%	10.00%	$293,065,000
Talladega	5.00%	8.00%	$505,665,000

Northwest Alabama Counties	Lowest Sales Tax Rate	Highest Sales Tax Rate	1998 Gross Retail Sales
Colbert	5.00%	8.50%	$529,990,000
Franklin	5.00%	8.00%	$149,803,000
Lauderdale	6.00%	9.50%	$779,050,000
Lawrence	7.00%	8.00%	$121,647,000
Limestone	6.00%	8.00%	$367,926,000
Madison	4.50%	8.00%	$2,285,979,000
Morgan	7.00%	10.00%	$930,682,000

Lower Alabama Counties	Lowest Sales Tax Rate	Highest Sales Tax Rate	1998 Gross Retail Sales
Baldwin	6.00%	9.00%	$1,104,610,000
Coffee	5.00%	8.00%	$373,392,000
Conecuh	6.00%	8.00%	$46,682,000
Covington	6.00%	8.00%	$280,714,000
Dale	6.00%	9.00%	$208,709,000
Escambia	5.00%	8.00%	$259,587,000
Geneva	5.00%	8.00%	$113,308,000
Henry	6.00%	8.00%	$64,331,000
Houston	5.00%	8.00%	$1,243,393,000
Mobile	5.00%	10.00%	$3,232,860,000
Monroe	6.00%	7.50%	$155,033,000

West Alabama Counties	Lowest Sales Tax Rate	Highest Sales Tax Rate	1998 Gross Retail Sales
Bibb	7.00%	10.00%	$85,117,000
Choctaw	6.00%	9.00%	$51,917,000
Clarke	5.00%	9.00%	$165,510,000
Fayette	6.00%	9.00%	$95,766,000
Greene	7.00%	9.00%	$19,812,000
Hale	6.00%	8.00%	$42,680,000
Lamar	6.00%	9.00%	$56,500,000
Marengo	5.00%	8.00%	$132,851,000
Marion	6.00%	9.00%	$160,060,000
Perry	6.00%	9.00%	$26,983,000
Pickens	7.00%	8.00%	$51,379,000
Sumter	7.00%	9.00%	$53,835,000
Tuscaloosa	7.00%	9.00%	$1,493,851,000
Walker	6.00%	8.00%	$598,580,000
Washington	4.00%	8.00%	$32,771,000
Winston	6.00%	8.00%	$155,826,000

Alabama Black Belt Counties	Lowest Sales Tax Rate	Highest Sales Tax Rate	1998 Gross Retail Sales
Autauga	6.00%	9.00%	$253,448,000
Barbour	5.00%	8.00%	$159,494,000
Bullock	6.50%	8.50%	$26,059,000
Butler	5.00%	8.00%	$118,926,000
Chambers	5.00%	8.00%	$163,834,000
Chilton	6.00%	9.00%	$223,492,000
Coosa	5.00%	8.00%	$20,829,000
Crenshaw	7.00%	9.00%	$61,455,000
Dallas	5.00%	9.00%	$297,814,000
Elmore	5.00%	8.50%	$290,396,000
Lee	7.00%	9.50%	$750,853,000
Lowndes	7.00%	9.50%	$34,737,000
Macon	6.00%	9.00%	$55,386,000
Montgomery	6.50%	9.00%	$2,430,824,000
Pike	5.00%	7.00%	$211,140,000
Russell	6.50%	9.50%	$246,783,000
Tallapoosa	5.00%	8.50%	$254,999,000
Wilcox	7.50%	9.50%	$38,388,000

* *See* CTR. FOR BUS & ECON. RESEARCH, THE UNIV. OF ALA., ECONOMIC ABSTRACT OF ALABAMA 400-23 (2000). 1 ALA. ST. TAX. REP. (CCH) ¶ 60-120 (2001).

APPENDIX C
PROPERTY TAX REVENUES ASSESSED BY CLASS OF PROPERTY, TOTAL LANDMASS, AND TOTAL TIMBER LANDMASS

Note that Tables may differ slightly due to rounding. Data are from compilation of property tax assessments and Hartsell & Brown. For more information see notes 90 and 95, supra.

Table 1: Black Belt Counties

TOTAL REVENUE BY CLASS OF PROPERTY

	TOTALS	CLASS 1		CLASS 2		CLASS 3 OTHER		CLASS 3 CURRENT USE		CLASS 4	
STATE OF ALABAMA	$1,562,939,115	$140,800,053	9%	$865,776,203	56%	$459,623,645	29%	$22,040,594	2%	$74,698,619	4%
TOTAL FOR ALL BLACK BELT COUNTIES	$209,047,550	$19,300,233	9%	$105,566,633	51%	$66,091,426	31%	$5,949,812	3%	$12,139,445	6%
BLACK BELT COUNTIES											
Autauga	7,228,714	$653,366	9%	$3,706,678	51%	$2,057,822	29%	$165,227	2%	$645,620	9%
Barbour	5,560,345	$468,893	8%	$2,670,837	48%	$1,547,030	29%	$518,182	9%	$355,402	6%
Bullock	2,463,882	$354,140	14%	$872,569	36%	$744,695	31%	$340,859	14%	$151,618	6%
Butler	4,740,469	$479,788	10%	$2,241,062	48%	$1,531,040	32%	$197,933	4%	$290,645	6%
Chambers	8,983,228	$480,323	5%	$5,309,484	59%	$2,381,557	27%	$221,066	2%	$590,797	7%
Chilton	10,139,576	$2,425,643	24%	$2,734,046	27%	$3,498,626	34%	$465,512	5%	$1,015,748	10%
Coosa	2,299,896	$473,945	21%	$691,059	30%	$881,876	38%	$119,115	5%	$133,900	6%
Crenshaw	2,788,093	$265,205	10%	$1,002,961	36%	$901,548	32%	$343,822	12%	$274,556	10%
Dallas	11,907,141	$1,383,302	12%	$6,391,043	54%	$2,767,582	24%	$647,709	5%	$717,504	6%
Elmore	10,934,752	$1,352,341	12%	$4,527,149	42%	$4,072,984	37%	$146,011	1%	$836,266	8%
Lee	34,673,703	$3,054,881	9%	$19,388,313	56%	$10,022,148	29%	$375,102	1%	$1,833,258	5%
Lowndes	2,612,671	$529,607	20%	$607,970	24%	$960,211	37%	$272,429	10%	$242,453	9%
Macon	9,245,746	$508,019	5%	$1,716,192	19%	$6,134,815	66%	$417,709	5%	$469,010	5%
Montgomery	61,419,072	$4,359,418	7%	$35,296,051	57%	$18,426,208	30%	$491,901	1%	$2,845,493	5%
Pike	6,312,521	$416,524	7%	$3,367,752	53%	$1,770,812	28%	$324,854	5%	$432,578	7%
Russell	12,462,628	$909,467	7%	$7,025,760	56%	$3,569,526	29%	$331,567	3%	$626,307	5%
Tallapoosa	12,700,973	$931,242	7%	$6,937,777	55%	$4,071,359	32%	$269,623	2%	$490,971	4%
Wilcox	2,574,157	$254,129	10%	$1,079,930	42%	$751,587	29%	$301,191	12%	$187,319	7%

TOTAL LANDMASS AND TOTAL TIMBER LANDMASS

	TOTAL ACRES	TOTAL TIMBER	TIMBER %	AVG $ PER ACRE OF CLASS 3	PRIVATE CORPORATE	PRIVATE INDIVIDUAL	PRIVATE TIMBER	PRIVATE TIMBER %	TIMBER INDUSTRY ACRES	TIMBER INDUSTRY %	NAT'L FOREST	MISC. FEDERAL	STATE	COUNTY/ MUNI.	TOTAL GOV'T	GOV'T TIMBER %
STATE OF ALABAMA	32,480,200	22,925,600	71%	$0.96	2,560,200	15,396,000	17,956,200	78%	3,740,400	16%	604,400	262,700	240,900	122,000	1,230,000	5%
TOTAL FOR ALL BLACK BELT COUNTIES	8,118,300	6,063,800	75%	$0.98	302,800	4,432,400	4,735,200	78%	1,188,200	20%	35,500	35,100	45,200	24,800	140,600	2%
BLACK BELT COUNTIES																
Autauga	381,400	283,000	74%	$0.58	11,400	161,300	172,700	61%	105,300	37%	0	0	5,000	0	5,000	2%
Barbour	566,400	450,600	80%	$1.15	0	349,800	349,800	78%	76,200	17%	0	10,700	13,800	0	24,500	5%
Bullock	400,000	316,500	79%	$1.08	0	264,900	264,900	84%	51,600	16%	0	0	0	0	0	0%
Butler	497,200	417,300	84%	$0.47	13,600	227,300	240,900	58%	172,200	41%	0	0	0	4,200	4,200	1%
Chambers	382,300	319,200	83%	$0.69	36,100	216,600	252,700	79%	65,000	20%	0	1,500	0	0	1,500	0%
Chilton	444,200	324,900	73%	$1.43	4,400	237,400	241,800	74%	60,300	19%	22,800	0	0	0	22,800	7%
Coosa	417,600	356,000	85%	$0.33	33,600	222,400	256,000	72%	100,000	28%	0	0	0	0	0	0%
Crenshaw	390,200	321,700	82%	$1.07	24,000	247,000	271,000	84%	47,500	15%	0	0	3,100	0	3,100	1%
Dallas	627,700	421,700	67%	$1.54	30,700	316,100	346,800	82%	72,700	17%	2,100	0	0	0	2,100	0%
Elmore	397,800	271,700	68%	$0.54	10,200	225,100	235,300	87%	30,500	11%	0	0	6,000	0	6,000	2%
Lee	389,600	273,600	70%	$1.37	0	228,000	228,000	83%	39,700	15%	0	0	0	5,900	5,900	2%
Lowndes	459,500	306,300	67%	$0.89	0	190,800	190,800	62%	109,600	36%	0	0	0	5,800	5,800	2%
Macon	390,800	307,300	79%	$1.36	0	278,700	278,700	91%	18,100	6%	10,600	0	0	0	10,600	3%
Montgomery	505,500	250,600	50%	$1.96	18,800	201,600	220,400	88%	18,000	7%	0	0	6,300	6,100	12,400	5%
Pike	429,500	286,000	67%	$1.14	10,300	258,100	268,400	94%	17,600	6%	0	0	0	0	0	0%
Russell	410,300	309,400	75%	$1.07	12,000	217,300	229,300	74%	59,300	19%	0	18,000	0	2,800	20,800	7%
Tallapoosa	459,500	379,600	83%	$0.71	60,200	234,100	294,300	78%	79,800	21%	0	0	5,600	0	5,600	1%
Wilcox	568,800	468,400	82%	$0.64	37,500	355,900	393,400	84%	64,800	14%	0	4,900	5,400	0	10,300	2%

Table 2: Northeast Alabama Counties

TOTAL REVENUE BY CLASS OF PROPERTY

	TOTALS	CLASS 1		CLASS 2		CLASS 3 OTHER		CLASS 3 CURRENT USE		CLASS 4	
STATE OF ALABAMA	$1,562,939,115	$140,800,053	9%	$865,776,203	56%	$459,623,645	29%	$22,040,594	2%	$74,698,619	4%
TOTAL FOR ALL NORTHEAST COUNTIES	$719,271,400	$65,625,332	9%	$411,966,029	57%	$212,160,582	29%	$4,291,396	1%	$25,228,060	4%
NORTHEAST COUNTIES											
Blount	$8,730,561	$622,738	7%	$3,042,167	35%	$4,006,711	46%	$141,462	2%	$917,482	10%
Calhoun	$24,623,493	$2,382,390	10%	$13,323,680	54%	$6,888,950	28%	$189,055	1%	$1,839,417	7%
Cherokee**	*$4,935,733	$473,746	10%	$1,108,776	22%	*$2,756,378	56%	*$169,287	3%	$427,546	9%
Clay	$2,805,742	$285,498	10%	$1,191,862	42%	$922,499	33%	$194,948	7%	$210,934	8%
Cleburne	$3,708,134	$601,297	16%	$1,516,332	41%	$1,188,094	32%	$159,705	4%	$242,705	7%
Cullman	$16,250,795	$705,549	4%	$8,674,095	53%	$5,597,572	35%	$174,794	1%	$1,098,784	7%
Dekalb	$12,205,193	$800,761	7%	$6,057,060	50%	$3,905,754	32%	$391,995	3%	$1,049,622	8%
Etowah	$26,122,738	$2,324,658	9%	$14,424,254	55%	$7,402,937	28%	$143,216	1%	$1,827,672	7%
Jackson	$12,161,354	$804,627	7%	$5,719,339	47%	$4,495,383	37%	$226,798	2%	$915,206	7%
Jefferson	$392,876,561	$44,951,692	11%	$209,965,077	53%	$125,180,299	32%	$1,116,645	1%	$11,662,847	3%
Marshall	$20,014,321	$780,486	4%	$10,342,179	52%	$7,243,999	36%	$146,700	1%	$1,500,956	7%
Randolph	$5,882,121	$1,658,714	28%	$1,811,443	31%	$1,949,356	33%	$101,927	2%	$360,680	6%
Shelby	$77,293,598	$5,918,126	8%	$38,241,271	49%	$31,367,931	41%	$613,875	1%	$1,152,394	1%
St. Clair	$13,101,505	$1,745,566	13%	$5,094,330	39%	$4,954,304	38%	$260,069	2%	$1,047,235	8%
Talladega	$98,559,564	$1,569,484	2%	$91,454,164	92%	$4,300,415	4%	$260,920	1%	$974,580	1%

** For Cherokee County, see Compilation of Property Tax Assessments, *supra* note 90, for an explanation of the process for estimating the total revenue assessed for Class 3 Other and Class 3 Current Use property.

TOTAL LANDMASS AND TOTAL TIMBER LANDMASS

	TOTAL ACRES	TOTAL TIMBER	TIMBER %	AVG $ PER ACRE OF CLASS 3	PRIVATE CORPORATE	PRIVATE INDIVIDUAL	PRIVATE TIMBER ACRES	PRIVATE TIMBER %	TIMBER INDUSTRY ACRES	TIMBER INDUSTRY %	NAT'L FOREST	MISC. FED.	STATE	COUNTY/ MUNI.	TOTAL GOV'T	GOV'T TIMBER %
STATE OF ALABAMA	32,480,200	22,925,600	71%	$0.96	2,560,200	15,396,000	17,956,200	78%	3,740,400	16%	604,400	262,700	240,900	122,000	1,230,000	5%
TOTAL FOR ALL NORTHEAST COUNTIES	6,740,400	4,367,900	65%	$0.98	467,800	2,931,500	3,399,300	78%	565,600	13%	212,700	73,700	73,700	43,300	403,400	9%
NORTHEAST COUNTIES																
Blount	413,200	236,300	57%	$0.60	25,300	194,300	219,600	93%	12,000	5%	0	0	0	4,700	4,700	2%
Calhoun	389,400	252,900	65%	$0.75	6,400	128,400	134,800	53%	48,000	19%	20,500	38,400	11,200	0	70,100	28%
Cherokee**	354,000	230,300	65%	$0.74	6,000	163,100	169,100	73%	57,500	25%	2,300	0	0	1,500	3,800	2%
Clay	387,300	311,900	81%	$0.63	38,800	172,500	211,300	68%	44,400	14%	56,200	0	0	0	56,200	18%
Cleburne	358,500	304,400	85%	$0.52	24,600	120,300	144,900	48%	64,600	21%	88,700	0	6,200	0	94,900	31%
Cullman	472,600	229,600	49%	$0.76	39,300	177,700	217,000	95%	12,600	5%	0	0	0	0	0	0%
Dekalb	497,900	235,400	47%	$1.67	6,100	211,000	217,100	92%	12,200	5%	0	0	6,100	0	6,100	3%
Etowah	342,300	231,000	67%	$0.62	0	224,800	224,800	97%	0	0%	0	0	0	6,200	6,200	3%
Jackson	690,400	450,700	65%	$0.50	34,000	342,300	376,300	83%	37,400	8%	0	22,900	14,200	0	37,100	8%
Jefferson	712,100	439,400	62%	$2.54	234,100	179,500	413,600	94%	0	0%	0	0	4,300	21,500	25,800	6%
Marshall	363,000	177,400	49%	$0.83	0	163,800	163,800	92%	0	0%	0	5,800	3,600	4,300	13,700	8%
Randolph	371,900	289,500	78%	$0.35	12,600	259,200	271,800	94%	12,600	4%	0	0	0	5,100	5,100	2%
Shelby	508,700	351,200	69%	$1.75	18,400	184,600	203,000	58%	135,400	39%	0	0	12,900	0	12,900	4%
St. Clair	405,800	302,400	75%	$0.86	15,600	209,500	225,100	74%	72,100	24%	0	0	5,200	0	5,200	2%
Talladega	473,300	325,500	69%	$0.80	6,600	200,500	207,100	64%	56,800	17%	45,000	6,600	10,000	0	61,600	19%

** For Cherokee County, see Compilation of Property Tax Assessments, *supra* note 90, for an explanation of the process for estimating the total revenue assessed for Class 3 Other and Class 3 Current Use property.

Table 3: Northwest Alabama Counties

TOTAL REVENUE BY CLASS OF PROPERTY

	TOTALS	CLASS 1		CLASS 2		CLASS 3 OTHER		CLASS 3 CURRENT USE		CLASS 4	
STATE OF ALABAMA	$1,562,939,115	$140,800,053	9%	$865,776,203	56%	$459,623,645	29%	$22,040,594	2%	$74,698,619	4%
TOTAL FOR ALL NORTHWEST COUNTIES	$218,716,582	$8,034,383	3%	$123,734,298	57%	$72,594,212	33%	$2,254,194	1%	$12,099,494	6%
NORTHWEST COUNTIES											
Colbert	$11,186,392	$742,457	7%	$5,204,959	47%	$4,284,001	38%	$201,757	2%	$753,217	6%
Franklin	$6,915,111	$561,936	8%	$3,134,653	45%	$2,428,076	35%	$193,486	3%	$596,959	9%
Lauderdale	$21,582,887	$642,957	3%	$9,819,592	45%	$9,229,357	43%	$420,315	2%	$1,470,665	7%
Lawrence	$6,138,034	$498,089	8%	$2,887,045	47%	$1,894,586	31%	$249,651	4%	$608,662	10%
Limestone	$13,477,783	$400,452	3%	$6,961,564	52%	$4,589,511	34%	$358,092	2%	$1,168,163	9%
Madison	$111,554,145	$3,527,498	3%	$63,714,384	57%	$38,471,849	35%	$457,830	1%	$5,382,583	4%
Morgan	$47,862,236	$1,660,994	3%	$32,012,101	67%	$11,696,832	25%	$373,063	1%	$2,119,245	4%

TOTAL LANDMASS AND TOTAL TIMBER LANDMASS

	TOTAL ACRES	TOTAL TIMBER ACRES	TIMBER %	AVG $ PER ACRE OF CLASS 3	PRIVATE CORPORATE	PRIVATE INDIVIDUAL	PRIVATE TIMBER ACRES	PRIVATE TIMBER %	TIMBER IND. ACRES	TIMBER INDUSTRY %	NAT'L FOREST	MISC. FED.	STATE	COUNTY/ MUNI.	TOTAL GOV'T	GOV'T TIMBER %
STATE OF ALABAMA	32,480,200	22,925,600	71%	$0.96	2,560,200	15,396,000	17,956,200	78%	3,740,400	16%	604,400	262,700	240,900	122,000	1,230,000	5%
TOTAL FOR ALL NORTHWEST COUNTIES	2,911,000	1,382,300	47%	$1.63	47,300	1,097,100	1,144,400	83%	84,200	6%	66,100	71,500	14,800	1,400	153,800	11%
NORTHWEST COUNTIES																
Colbert	380,500	225,500	59%	$0.89	8,000	199,200	207,200	92%	6,100	3%	0	0	12,200	0	12,200	5%
Franklin	406,800	296,500	73%	$0.65	28,500	196,600	225,100	76%	64,800	22%	1,200	5,400	0	0	6,600	2%
Lauderdale	428,500	200,900	47%	$2.09	0	189,000	189,000	94%	12,000	6%	0	0	0	0	0	0%
Lawrence	443,800	194,400	44%	$1.28	5,000	119,400	124,400	64%	1,300	1%	64,900	3,800	0	0	68,700	35%
Limestone	363,600	108,900	30%	$3.29	0	91,700	91,700	84%	0	0%	0	17,200	0	0	17,200	16%
Madison	515,200	180,900	35%	$2.53	5,800	139,300	145,100	80%	0	0%	0	31,800	2,600	1,400	35,800	20%
Morgan	372,600	175,200	47%	$2.13	0	161,900	161,900	92%	0	0%	0	13,300	0	0	13,300	8%

Table 4: Lower Alabama Counties

TOTAL REVENUE BY CLASS OF PROPERTY

	TOTALS	CLASS 1		CLASS 2		CLASS 3 OTHER		CLASS 3 CURRENT USE		CLASS 4	
STATE OF ALABAMA TOTAL FOR ALL	$1,562,939,115	$140,800,053	9%	$865,776,203	56%	$459,623,645	29%	$22,040,594	2%	$74,698,619	4%
LOWER ALABAMA COUNTIES	$295,978,583	$31,812,505	11%	$165,682,486	56%	$75,438,082	25%	$5,401,413	2%	$17,644,096	6%
LOWER ALABAMA COUNTIES											
Baldwin	$74,658,501	$2,731,748	4%	$48,488,981	65%	$20,008,091	27%	$826,076	1%	$2,603,604	3%
Coffee	$9,064,685	$634,223	7%	$3,795,039	42%	$3,722,227	41%	$329,064	4%	$584,131	6%
Conecuh	$3,939,943	$278,487	7%	$1,840,431	47%	$1,057,996	27%	$516,501	13%	$246,527	6%
Covington	$7,234,907	$1,399,552	19%	$3,315,788	46%	$1,565,317	22%	$422,414	6%	$531,835	7%
Dale	$9,414,597	$837,682	9%	$4,633,524	49%	$2,864,956	30%	$279,533	3%	$798,901	7%
Escambia	$7,864,891	$1,112,999	13%	$3,975,402	51%	$1,818,480	23%	$433,250	6%	$524,759	7%
Geneva	$4,217,632	$401,509	10%	$1,498,618	36%	$1,260,055	30%	$616,357	15%	$441,092	9%
Henry	$4,524,840	$379,727	8%	$1,781,203	40%	$1,725,665	38%	$268,495	6%	$369,749	8%
Houston	$27,579,832	$8,389,258	30%	$11,953,976	43%	$5,526,744	21%	$282,680	1%	$1,427,173	5%
Mobile	$127,399,729	$548,047	1%	$81,536,604	64%	$34,618,914	27%	$961,399	1%	$9,734,764	7%
Monroe	$20,079,036	$15,099,273	74%	$2,862,920	13%	$1,269,637	6%	$465,644	6%	$381,561	1%

TOTAL LANDMASS AND TOTAL TIMBER LANDMASS

	TOTAL ACRES	TOTAL TIMBER ACRES	TIMBER %	AVG $ PER ACRE OF CLASS 3 CURRENT USE	PRIVATE CORPORATE	PRIVATE INDIVIDUAL	PRIVATE TIMBER ACRES	PRIVATE TIMBER %	TIMBER IND. ACRES	TIMBER INDUSTRY %	NAT'L FOREST	MISC. FED.	STATE	COUNTY/ MUNI.	TOTAL GOV'T	GOV'T TIMBER %
STATE OF ALABAMA	32,480,200	22,925,600	71%	$0.96	2,560,200	15,396,000	17,956,200	78%	3,740,400	16%	604,400	262,700	240,900	122,000	1,230,000	5%
TOTAL FOR ALL LOWER ALABAMA COUNTIES	6,174,800	4,304,800	70%	$1.25	637,200	2,571,900	3,209,100	75%	870,100	20%	79,800	57,300	56,000	32,500	225,600	5%
LOWER ALABAMA COUNTIES																
Baldwin	1,021,800	671,400	66%	$1.23	82,400	311,500	393,900	59%	253,200	38%	0	6,500	14,000	3,900	24,400	4%
Coffee	434,700	301,900	69%	$1.09	30,700	231,800	262,500	87%	32,500	11%	0	6,800	0	0	6,800	2%
Conecuh	544,600	469,500	86%	$1.10	41,200	254,000	295,200	63%	174,300	37%	0	0	0	0	0	0%
Covington	662,200	505,800	76%	$0.84	106,000	317,600	423,600	84%	30,200	6%	52,100	0	0	0	52,100	10%
Dale	359,100	238,200	66%	$1.17	5,700	187,900	193,600	81%	8,600	4%	0	34,500	0	1,400	35,900	15%
Escambia	606,400	458,800	76%	$0.94	131,300	152,300	283,600	62%	134,000	29%	27,700	0	7,900	5,600	41,200	9%
Geneva	368,900	203,600	55%	$3.03	0	191,200	191,200	94%	6,200	3%	0	0	6,200	0	6,200	3%
Henry	359,600	224,500	62%	$1.20	10,600	187,400	198,000	88%	26,500	12%	0	0	0	0	0	0%
Houston	371,500	166,100	45%	$1.70	12,000	148,800	160,800	97%	0	0%	0	5,300	0	0	5,300	3%
Mobile	789,400	531,800	67%	$1.81	145,400	294,600	440,000	83%	47,500	9%	0	0	22,700	21,600	44,300	8%
Monroe	656,600	533,200	81%	$0.87	71,900	294,800	366,700	69%	157,100	29%	0	4,200	5,200	0	9,400	2%

Table 5: West Alabama Counties

	TOTALS	CLASS 1	%	CLASS 2	%	CLASS 3 OTHER	%	CLASS 3 CURRENT USE	%	CLASS 4	%
						TOTAL REVENUE BY CLASS OF PROPERTY					
STATE OF ALABAMA	$1,682,864,119	$140,800,053	9%	$865,776,203	56%	$459,623,645	29%	$22,040,594	2%	$74,698,619	4%
TOTAL FOR ALL WEST COUNTIES	$119,925,004	$16,027,600	13%	$58,826,757	50%	$33,339,343	28%	$4,143,779	3%	$7,587,524	6%
WEST ALABAMA COUNTIES											
Bibb	$14,261,032	$383,510	14%	$977,881	35%	$955,079	34%	$144,150	5%	$323,937	12%
Choctaw	$14,273,011	$437,719	10%	$2,421,521	57%	$877,856	20%	$300,774	7%	$245,016	6%
Clarke	$12,474,168	$558,737	8%	$3,210,804	45%	$2,521,259	35%	$478,204	7%	$424,582	5%
Fayette	$8,219,555	$345,341	12%	$1,135,366	41%	$1,023,928	37%	$4,422	1%	$287,479	9%
Greene	$8,437,308	$1,359,653	55%	$360,404	15%	$453,089	18%	$204,794	8%	$106,103	4%
Hale	$10,845,398	$513,819	17%	$991,236	34%	$853,969	29%	$295,240	10%	$284,709	10%
Lamar	$12,423,706	$307,848	10%	$1,383,863	46%	$1,001,232	33%	$26,792	1%	$294,554	10%
Marengo	$11,868,212	$802,607	16%	$2,147,908	44%	$1,039,681	21%	$523,945	11%	$377,992	8%
Marion	$11,477,726	$372,480	8%	$2,197,626	49%	$1,372,797	31%	$194,319	4%	$380,059	8%
Perry	$10,754,944	$418,598	17%	$636,056	26%	$924,063	38%	$258,061	10%	$222,017	9%
Pickens	$55,791,799	$587,220	13%	$1,776,900	39%	$1,738,483	39%	$41,957	1%	$357,087	8%
Sumter	$63,086,797	$688,957	18%	$1,472,853	39%	$1,246,683	33%	$226,028	6%	$159,978	8%
Tuscaloosa	$69,264,631	$3,216,642	7%	$28,308,756	60%	$13,076,708	28%	$500,908	1%	$2,392,636	4%
Walker	$26,770,131	$2,793,476	24%	$4,518,203	38%	$3,338,019	28%	$154,621	1%	$992,326	4%
Washington	$14,973,485	$2,786,005	28%	$5,124,340	51%	$1,116,496	12%	$608,444	6%	$337,048	3%
Winston	$5,001,151	$454,988	9%	$2,163,040	43%	$1,800,001	36%	$181,120	4%	$402,001	8%

TOTAL LANDMASS AND TOTAL TIMBER LANDMASS

	TOTAL ACRES	TOTAL TIMBER ACRES	TIMBER %	AVG $ PER ACRE OF CLASS 3 CURRENT USE	PRIVATE CORPORATE	PRIVATE INDIVIDUAL	PRIVATE TIMBER ACRES	PRIVATE TIMBER %	TIMBER IND. ACRES	TIMBER INDUSTRY %	NAT'L FOREST	MISC. FED.	STATE	COUNTY/M UNI.	TOTAL GOV'T	GOV'T TIMBER %
STATE OF ALABAMA	32,480,200	22,925,600	71%	$0.96	2,560,200	15,396,000	17,956,200	78%	3,740,400	16%	604,400	262,700	240,900	122,000	1,230,000	5%
TOTAL FOR ALL WEST COUNTIES	8,535,200	6,806,900	80%	$0.61	1,105,100	4,363,100	5,468,200	80%	1,032,300	15%	210,300	25,100	51,200	20,000	306,600	5%
WEST ALABAMA COUNTIES																
Bibb	398,300	345,500	87%	$0.42	18,100	183,100	201,200	58%	84,500	24%	59,800	0	0	0	59,800	17%
Choctaw	584,700	520,100	89%	$0.58	84,400	341,100	425,500	82%	90,500	17%	0	4,100	0	0	4,100	1%
Clarke	792,600	724,900	91%	$0.66	131,300	496,100	627,400	87%	86,500	12%	0	0	5,500	5,500	11,000	2%
Fayette	401,800	333,600	83%	$0.01	21,600	226,500	248,100	74%	67,600	20%	0	0	17,900	0	17,900	5%
Greene	413,400	284,300	69%	$0.72	53,600	174,800	228,400	80%	37,200	13%	0	14,300	0	4,400	18,700	7%
Hale	412,000	263,100	64%	$1.12	16,800	171,200	188,000	71%	47,000	18%	28,100	0	0	0	28,100	11%
Lamar	387,100	314,600	81%	$0.09	28,800	232,300	261,100	83%	48,400	15%	0	0	5,200	0	5,200	2%
Marengo	625,400	452,400	72%	$1.16	101,000	285,100	386,100	85%	66,300	15%	0	0	0	0	0	0%
Marion	474,500	365,900	77%	$0.53	12,900	266,100	279,000	76%	85,700	23%	0	0	0	1,200	1,200	0%
Perry	460,500	357,000	78%	$0.72	18,500	245,600	264,100	74%	60,500	17%	32,400	0	0	0	32,400	9%
Pickens	564,100	480,700	85%	$0.09	22,500	327,900	350,400	73%	129,900	27%	0	500	0	0	500	0%
Sumter	579,200	430,800	74%	$0.52	123,000	260,300	383,300	89%	35,200	8%	0	6,200	6,200	0	12,400	3%
Tuscaloosa	848,200	659,600	78%	$0.76	114,100	390,000	504,100	76%	128,800	20%	10,500	0	16,100	0	26,600	4%
Walker	508,400	354,000	70%	$0.44	144,700	195,300	340,000	96%	5,000	1%	0	0	0	8,900	8,900	3%
Washington	691,700	610,200	88%	$1.00	148,400	443,900	592,300	97%	17,700	3%	0	0	300	0	300	0%
Winston	393,300	310,100	79%	$0.58	65,400	123,800	189,200	61%	41,500	13%	79,500	0	0	0	79,500	26%

Appendix D
The Funding of Alabama's School Systems

Each of the Tables in this Appendix analyzes the level of funding, and source of funding for each school system in the State of Alabama. Each Table represents the level of adequacy of funding of each of the systems.

Table 1: Schools with minimum adequate funding.

Name of System	Total Spending	Spent Per Student	S.E. Grade	National Grade	Property Tax Millage	State Funding	Local Funding	Other Funding	Federal Funding
State of Alabama	4,703,381,512.80	$5,303	D	D	12.05	56%	27%	8%	9%
Mountain Brook City	33,455,352.27	$7,119	A-	C+	42.3	32%	43%	24%	1%
Homewood City	28,957,060.31	$6,896	B+	C	23.3	37%	59%	1%	3%
Florence City	36,649,371.58	$6,736	B	C	18	39%	32%	21%	8%
Linden City	5,084,271.87	$6,397	C+	C-	8	64%	19%	0%	17%
Hoover City	83,294,954.57	$6,379	C+	C-	22.1	26%	37%	36%	1%
Athens City	22,668,734.47	$6,356	C+	C-	8.5	34%	30%	32%	4%
Tuscaloosa City	68,357,791.66	$6,320	C+	C-	21	43%	29%	21%	7%
Huntsville City	160,784,149.71	$6,278	C+	C-	21	51%	38%	4%	7%
Sheffield City	9,579,124.55	$6,194	C	C-	14	56%	33%	1%	10%
Muscle Shoals City	25,268,018.47	$6,172	C	C-	20	38%	57%	1%	4%
Tuscumbia City	10,912,396.59	$6,113	C	C-	17.5	60%	31%	1%	8%
Decatur City	59,857,884.19	$6,111	C	C-	9.4	48%	45%	1%	6%
Tarrant City	8,795,299.34	$6,101	C	C-	19.4	57%	33%	1%	9%
Auburn City	28,841,867.64	$6,038	C	C-	8	51%	40%	4%	5%
Barbour County	14,424,504.25	$6,035	C	C-	13.5	50%	11%	27%	12%

*Table 2: Schools without minimum adequate funding
with a national grade of "D+."*

Name of System	Total Spending	Spent Per Student	S.E. Grade	National Grade	Property Tax Millage	State Funding	Local Funding	Other Funding	Federal Funding
State of Alabama	4,703,381,512.80	$5,303	D	D	1205%	56%	27%	8%	9%
Jasper City	17,125,299.54	$5,967	C	D+	8	58%	36%	0%	6%
Greene County	12,861,877.94	$5,955	C	D+	3	66%	15%	0%	19%
Pike County	14,997,827.47	$5,926	C	D+	10.2	63%	18%	2%	17%
Vestavia Hills City	37,707,524.42	$5,859	C-	D+	23.3	46%	48%	2%	4%
Lowndes County	18,320,911.47	$5,740	C-	D+	5.5	63%	12%	0%	25%
Walker County	55,642,447.70	$5,739	C-	D+	8	62%	26%	1%	11%
Gadsden City	35,441,044.72	$5,731	C-	D+	16	58%	28%	2%	12%
Anniston City	21,774,820.82	$5,715	C-	D+	13.5	54%	18%	17%	11%
Bessemer City	32,233,405.71	$5,702	C-	D+	13.6	63%	18%	6%	13%
Morgan County	48,828,059.78	$5,702	C-	D+	14.53	52%	33%	9%	6%
Scottsboro City	19,352,361.37	$5,687	C-	D+	7	57%	31%	5%	7%
Colbert County	21,706,553.45	$5,677	C-	D+	15.1	61%	30%	1%	8%
Elba City	6,332,498.09	$5,653	D+	D+	16	66%	23%	0%	11%
Dothan City	56,125,873.38	$5,619	D+	D+	8	61%	25%	2%	12%
Wilcox County	19,751,103.35	$5,605	D+	D+	3	67%	15%	1%	17%
Shelby County	169,444,975.88	$5,549	D+	D+	23.67	39%	32%	26%	3%
Russellville City	20,015,494.47	$5,532	D+	D+	23.6	63%	30%	0%	7%
Talladega City	19,889,744.64	$5,518	D+	D+	10	63%	20%	7%	10%

Table 3: Schools without minimum adequate funding with national grade of "D."

Name of System	Total Spending	Spent Per Student	S.E. Grade	National Grade	Property Tax Millage	State Funding	Local Funding	Other Funding	Federal Funding
State of Alabama	4,703,381,512.80	$5,303	D	D	1205%	56%	27%	8%	9%
Guntersville City	10,995,001.65	$5,491	D+	D	8	59%	35%	0%	6%
Hartselle City	18,535,195.91	$5,479	D+	D	17.1	62%	33%	1%	4%
Sumter County	17,407,410.67	$5,467	D+	D	13.8	65%	17%	1%	17%
Opelika City	27,838,437.75	$5,439	D	D	8	58%	27%	7%	8%
Sylacauga City	14,085,409.05	$5,437	D	D	10	62%	28%	1%	9%
Fort Payne City	14,807,168.01	$5,429	D	D	14.5	68%	24%	1%	7%
Choctaw County	14,912,764.40	$5,427	D	D	6	53%	16%	19%	12%
Jackson County	38,508,359.91	$5,424	D	D	7	62%	29%	0%	9%
Baldwin County	140,968,639.53	$5,417	D	D	12	54%	39%	1%	6%
Jefferson County	335,745,507.77	$5,411	D	D	24.42	45%	24%	26%	5%
Midfield City	9,081,519.30	$5,385	D	D	24.7	70%	19%	0%	11%
Phenix City	31,999,014.61	$5,384	D	D	21.5	59%	27%	1%	13%
Henry County	17,077,124.84	$5,384	D	D	12	62%	18%	11%	9%
Crenshaw County	13,401,834.62	$5,372	D	D	8	69%	18%	1%	12%
Escambia County	31,365,220.20	$5,368	D	D	7	50%	16%	25%	9%
Perry County	17,560,562.97	$5,366	D	D	9	69%	13%	1%	17%
Ozark City	17,792,736.60	$5,360	D	D	9	68%	20%	1%	11%
Franklin County	19,165,067.74	$5,333	D	D	10	65%	26%	1%	8%
Conecuh County	12,603,008.70	$5,319	D	D	9.5	67%	16%	1%	16%
Winston County	21,275,497.46	$5,313	D	D	12	63%	23%	6%	8%

Table 4: Schools falling below the State of Alabama's average spending per student. These school systems spent less than $5303 per student during the 1998-'99 academic year.

Name of System	Total Spending	Spent Per Student	S.E. Grade	National Grade	Property Tax Millage	State Funding	Local Funding	Other Funding	Federal Funding
State of Alabama	4,703,381,512.80	$5,303	D-	D	1205%	56%	27%	8%	9%
Albertville City	$19,081,996.21	$5,289	D	D	8	62%	29%	1%	8%
Pickens County	21,879,132.80	$5,281	D	D	11.2	67%	16%	1%	16%
Alexander City	22,489,318.95	$5,266	D	D	15/7.5*	61%	27%	6%	6%
Coffee County	11,743,244.65	$5,257	D-	D	14	64%	23%	1%	12%
Bullock County	10,770,296.40	$5,253	D-	D	18.5	59%	12%	13%	16%
Birmingham City	241,010,876.35	$5,239	D-	D	21	45%	32%	15%	8%
Enterprise City	30,882,312.73	$5,238	D-	D	9	65%	27%	0%	8%
Monroe County	27,005,982.97	$5,211	D-	D	8.5	70%	20%	0%	10%
Cullman County	61,857,955.65	$5,196	D-	D	6	64%	20%	9%	7%
Selma City	26,441,875.04	$5,190	D-	D	11.5	63%	17%	5%	15%
Clarke County	23,743,156.93	$5,180	D-	D	15.5	57%	16%	17%	10%
Brewton City	8,409,439.70	$5,179	D-	D	7	61%	31%	1%	7%
Oneonta City	6,803,004.42	$5,174	D-	D	16.5	65%	30%	0%	5%
Limestone County	50,160,058.74	$5,171	D-	D	7.5	48%	24%	24%	4%
Russell County	30,407,762.26	$5,171	D-	D	19.5	46%	14%	34%	6%
Marengo County	16,058,460.61	$5,169	D-	D	8	45%	12%	33%	10%
Lawrence County	41,555,063.18	$5,154	D-	D	9	64%	25%	1%	10%
Butler County	29,479,874.13	$5,152	D-	D	12	52%	36%	0%	12%
Lanett City	7,939,821.88	$5,151	D-	D	10.7	67%	21%	0%	12%
Dallas County	28,621,690.70	$5,149	D-	D	11.5	72%	13%	0%	15%
Thomasville City	11,971,697.79	$5,139	D-	D	5	50%	38%	5%	7%
Cleburne County	14,310,870.05	$5,136	D-	D	17	68%	17%	7%	8%
Pell City	22,334,778.86	$5,127	D-	D	13.5	65%	24%	1%	10%
Chambers County	25,193,308.60	$5,124	D-	D	10.7	48%	18%	26%	8%
Washington County	23,022,138.05	$5,117	D-	D	12	61%	23%	7%	9%
Lauderdale County	50,023,990.64	$5,111	D-	D	18	60%	24%	11%	5%
Marshall County	41,734,777.25	$5,108	E-	D	10.375	61%	27%	4%	8%
Opp City	8,852,967.63	$5,106	E-	D	7	63%	22%	7%	8%
Eufaula City	17,983,326.76	$5,086	D-	D	20	62%	28%	1%	9%
Calhoun County	55,207,356.00	$5,072	D-	D	18.79	72%	20%	1%	7%
Macon County	25,672,151.98	$5,072	D-	D	22	59%	15%	13%	13%
Tallapoosa County	18,959,085.41	$5,070	D	D	12	68%	24%	0%	8%
Cherokee County	22,717,338.63	$5,066	D-	D	22	66%	23%	3%	8%

* 15 outside Midway, 7.5 inside Midway

Table 5: Schools without minimum adequate funding with a Southeastern grade of "F" and a national grade of "D" or below.

Name of System	Total Spending	Spent Per Student	S.E. Grade	National Grade	Property Tax Millage	State Funding	Local Funding	Other Funding	Federal Funding
State of Alabama	4,703,381,512.80	$5,303	D	D	12.05	56%	27%	8%	9%
Dale County	15,541,783.64	$5,061	F	D	8.67	68%	23%	1%	8%
Hale County	23,904,215.63	$5,049	F	D	7	66%	16%	5%	13%
Attalla City	10,953,680.15	$5,043	F	D	15	67%	22%	1%	10%
Madison City	105,636,936.47	$5,041	F	D	18.5	58%	28%	9%	5%
Piedmont City	6,425,550.23	$5,041	F	D	20	70%	18%	2%	10%
Lee County	52,766,704.81	$5,041	F	D	11.33	63%	31%	0%	6%
Arab City	15,305,327.32	$5,030	F	D	8	69%	26%	0%	5%
Mobile County	375,041,860.62	$5,029	F	D	17.5	65%	21%	2%	12%
Cullman City	16,503,993.63	$5,028	F	D	7	52%	25%	14%	9%
Montgomery County	185,758,703.54	$5,020	F	D	8	66%	21%	2%	11%
Troy City	12,481,130.51	$5,019	F	D	10.7	60%	28%	1%	11%
Covington County	20,487,596.43	$5,013	F	D	7	66%	20%	3%	11%
Marion County	23,376,394.24	$5,011	F	D	7	71%	22%	0%	7%
Coosa County	10,168,576.33	$5,008	F	D	12	67%	16%	6%	11%
Clay County	14,975,673.53	$5,004	F	D	13.5	73%	19%	0%	8%
Chilton County	35,577,211.89	$5,003	F	D	8	64%	20%	9%	7%
Talladega County	45,606,813.26	$4,985	F	D-	15.11	61%	21%	9%	9%
Tuscaloosa County	99,125,221.53	$4,968	F	D-	13.3	63%	29%	1%	7%
Roanoke City	8,998,407.55	$4,964	F	D-	7	74%	14%	3%	9%
Fayette County	16,048,085.59	$4,937	F	D-	7	71%	20%	1%	8%
Demopolis City	12,354,715.17	$4,920	F	D-	8	67%	22%	0%	11%
Fairfield City	11,455,800.43	$4,904	F	D-	40.5	64%	24%	1%	11%
Daleville City	10,518,188.29	$4,885	F	D-	8	73%	15%	0%	12%
Geneva County	15,269,155.95	$4,863	F	D-	11.4	70%	17%	3%	10%
Etowah County	48,814,005.87	$4,858	F	D-	15.3	71%	22%	1%	6%
Geneva City	8,281,084.96	$4,856	F	D-	11.4	68%	23%	2%	7%
Bibb County	19,635,328.52	$4,853	F	D-	7	72%	15%	0%	13%
Haleyville City	9,344,319.85	$4,829	F	D-	12	65%	27%	0%	8%
Andalusia City	11,720,412.42	$4,822	F	D-	7	47%	43%	3%	7%
Dekalb County	41,595,623.59	$4,819	F	D-	14.5	67%	23%	1%	9%
Lamar County	15,117,630.94	$4,818	F	D-	7	71%	19%	1%	9%
Oxford City	19,366,029.89	$4,809	F	D-	18.5	68%	23%	4%	5%
Houston County	33,037,191.89	$4,799	F	D-	8	63%	26%	2%	9%
Randolph County	12,454,977.50	$4,772	F	D-	9.5	66%	19%	7%	8%
Winfield City	7,405,461.82	$4,763	F	D-	7	42%	17%	33%	8%
Jacksonville City	9,247,920.81	$4,737	F	D-	18.5	71%	19%	1%	9%
Blount County	37,372,386.57	$4,696	F	D-	11.5	69%	22%	2%	7%
Tallassee City	10,851,816.00	$4,682	F	D-	7.5/15/7**	71%	17%	3%	9%
Elmore County	53,214,077.96	$4,627	F	D-	7	66%	20%	7%	7%
Autauga County	53,050,877.60	$4,596	F	D-	7	71%	21%	1%	7%
St. Clair County	34,135,979.34	$4,517	F	D-	13.5	68%	26%	0%	6%
Madison City	30,521,461.22	$4,417	F	F	11	58%	36%	3%	3%

** 7.5 outside Carville, Tallapoosa County, 15 inside Carville, 7 in Elmore County

APPENDIX E

STATISTICS ILLUSTRATING THE IMPACT OF TIMBER
ON ALABAMA'S ECONOMY AND DEPICTING BUSINESS AND
FORESTRY ACTIVITY IN ALABAMA COUNTIES

Table 1: Alabama Forestry and Logging Industry

Relative Statistics on the Forestry & Logging Industry (NAICS Code 113), 2000								
Rank	State	Establish-ments	Rank	State	Employ-ment*	Rank	State	Annual Payroll ($1,000)
1	Oregon	1,041	1	Oregon	8,006	1	Washington	270,038
2	**Alabama**	**941**	2	Washington	7,794	2	Oregon	265,327
3	Washington	894	**3**	**Alabama**	**6,852**	**3**	**Alabama**	**155,009**
4	Georgia	752	4	Georgia	5,855	4	Georgia	146,458
5	North Carolina	722	5	Mississippi	4,571	5	California	141,866
6	Mississippi	673	6	North Carolina	4,120	6	Mississippi	106,156
7	Arkansas	596	7	Louisiana	3,927	7	South Carolina	102,549
8	Louisiana	529	8	South Carolina	3,821	8	North Carolina	98,794
9	Maine	527	9	California	3,439	9	Louisiana	92,987
10	California	507	10	Arkansas	3,363	10	Florida	91,351
10	Virginia	507						

Source: U.S. Dep't of Comm., Census Bureau, County Business Patterns
Database, *at* http://censtats.census.gov/cbpnaic/cbpnaic.shtml (last visited
July 25, 2002).

* Total number of employees for the week that included March 12, 2000. U.S. Dep't of Comm.,
Census Bureau, County Business Patterns Database, *at*
http://censtats.census.gov/cbpnaic/cbpnaic.shtml (last visited July 25, 2002).

Detailed Statistics on the Alabama Logging Industry (NAICS Code 1153) from the 1997 Economic Census				
Establish-ments	Employ-ment	Payroll ($1000)	Value Added by Mfg. ($1000)	Value of Ship-ments ($1000)
1,048 (45 with 20 or more employees)	7,109	$145,407	$437,946	$913,593

Source: U.S. Dep't of Comm., Census Bureau, 1997 Economic Census, Manufacturing Industry Series: Logging, No. EC97M-1133A, tbl. 2d (1999) *at* http://www.census.gov/prod/ec97/97m1133a.pdf (last visited July 25, 2002).

Cash Receipts for Alabama Agricultural and Forestry Commodities, 2000		
Commodity	**Cash Receipts ($1000)******	**% of Total**
Broilers	1,748,100	38.1%
Forestry	**877,732**	**19.1%**
Cattle & Calves	476,300	10.4%
Eggs	259,600	5.7%
Greenhouse & Nursery	230,000	5.0%
Cotton	146,200	3.2%
Catfish	81,600	1.8%
Peanuts	71,600	1.6%
Dairy	49,000	1.1%
Hogs	39,100	0.9%
Total, including unlisted commodities:	4,588,900	100%

Source: ALA. AGRIC. STATISTICS SERV., ALABAMA AGRICULTURAL STATISTICS, Bulletin 43, at 8, 45, 51-52 (2001), *at* http://www.aces.edu/departments/nass/bulletin/2000/pg04.htm (last visited July 26, 2002).

**   Cash receipts are "[s]ales of agricultural commodities at the first point of sale by establishments (farms) from which $1000 or more of agricultural products were or would normally be sold during the year. Cash receipts include sales of commodities regardless of the year produced. They exclude non-monetary transactions such as on-farm use of agricultural commodities." ALA. AGRIC. STATISTICS SERV., Bulletin 43, at 44 (2001), *at* http://www.aces.edu/departments/nass/bulletin/2000/pg04.htm (last visited July 26, 2002).

Private Earnings from Forestry, 2000		
Rank	State	Earnings ($1,000)
1	Oregon	303,132
2	Washington	178,859
3	California	104,543
4	Georgia	95,629
5	**Alabama**	**88,491**
6	Florida	67,943
7	Mississippi	65,953
8	South Carolina	58,698
10	North Carolina	49,184
10	Arkansas	45,211

Source: BUREAU OF ECON. ANALYSIS, REGIONAL ACCOUNTS DATA, ANNUAL STATE PERSONAL INCOME, tbl. SA05, *at* http://www.bea.gov/bea/regional/spi (last modified Apr. 23, 2002) (displaying 2000 data for the United States and comparing code 121—Forestry).

Table 2: Alabama Forestry Support Industry

Relative Statistics on Forestry Support Activities (NAICS Code 1153), 2000								
Rank	State	Busi-nesses	Rank	State	Employed*	Rank	State	Annual Payroll ($1,000)
1	Oregon	211	1	Oregon	3,385	1	Oregon	74,409
2	Washington	128	2	Georgia	1,217	2	**Alabama**	**25,726**
3	Georgia	113	3	Washington	1,130	3	California	25,585
4	California	99	4**	**Alabama**	**1,038**	4	Washington	24,793
5	**Alabama**	**93**	4**	Arkansas	1,000-2,499	5	Georgia	21,833
6	Mississippi	75	4**	New York	1,000-2,499	6	S.Carolina	13,725
7	N. Carolina	70	7	California	707	7	Idaho	11,941
8	S.Carolina	63	8	Idaho	579	8	Mississippi	10,335
9	Florida	54	9	S.Carolina	497	9	Louisiana	7,287
10	Arkansas	53	10	Mississippi	490	10	Florida	6,470

Source: U.S. DEP'T OF COMM., CENSUS BUREAU, COUNTY BUSINESS PATTERNS DATABASE, *at* http://censtats.census.gov/cbpnaic/cbpnaic.shtml (last visited July 25, 2002).

* Total number of employees for the week that included March 12, 2000.

** Because the employment totals for Arkansas and New York are reported as a range, it is not possible to distinguish a precise rank for these states or for Alabama.

Table 3: Alabama Wood Products Industries*

Detailed Statistics on the Alabama Wood Products Industries from the 1997 Economic Census				
	Establishments	Employment	Payroll ($1,000)	Shipment Value ($1,000)**
Wood Products Mfg. (NAICS 321)	487	25,949	625,499	4,381,779
Paper Mfg. (NAICS 322)	89	19,091	966,527	6,287,709
Furniture & Related Prods. Mfg. (NAICS 337)	471	14,789	313,242	1,494,617
Wood Products Industries Total	1047	59,829	1,905,268	12,164,105
Mfg. Total	5,444	352,618	10,187,756	67,970,076
Wood Products Industries' % of Total Mfg	19.2%	17.0%	18.7%	17.9%

Source: U.S. DEP'T OF COMM., CENSUS BUREAU, 1997 ECONOMIC CENSUS: MANUFACTURING, ALABAMA, *at* http://www.census.gov/epcd/ec97/AL000_31.HTM (last visited Feb. 6, 2001).

*   *See supra* note 98 discussing the industries chosen to represent the wood products industries.
**   Value of shipments "[i]ncludes the total sales, shipments receipts, revenue, or business done by establishments within the scope of the economic census." U.S. DEP'T OF COMM., CENSUS BUREAU, 1997 ECONOMIC CENSUS: SALES, SHIPMENTS, RECEIPTS, REVENUE, OR BUSINESS DONE, *at* http://www.census.gov/epdc/ec97brdg/def/ECVALUE.htm (last visited July 26, 2002).

Private Earnings for Alabama from Wood Products Industries, 2000***	
	Private Earnings ($1000)
Lumber & Wood Prods.	1,230,904
Paper & Allied Prods.	1,116,634
Furniture & Fixtures	337,202
Wood Products Industries Total	2,684,740
Manufacturing Total	13,754,534
Wood Products Industries' Percentage of Total Manufacturing	19.5%

*** The Bureau of Economic Analysis uses non-standard industry codes. This Article attempts to use BEA data for codes that most closely correspond to the NAICS codes discussed herein.

Relative Statistics on Wood Products Mfg. (NAICS Code 321), 2000								
Rank	State	Businesses	Rank	State	Number Employed ****	Rank	State	Annual Payroll ($1,000)
1	California	1,271	1	California	41,082	1	California	1,193,878
2	Pennsylvania	1,023	2	Oregon	35,338	2	Oregon	1,145,955
3	N. Carolina	828	3	N. Carolina	33,089	3	N. Carolina	866,899
4	Texas	787	4	Texas	31,391	4	Wisconsin	844,873
5	Ohio	698	5	Wisconsin	29,858	5	Texas	788,408
6	Wisconsin	670	6	Georgia	29,215	6	Georgia	757,922
7	New York	621	7	Pennsyl-vania	26,348	7	Pennsylvania	696,884
8	Michigan	617	8	**Alabama**	**25,336**	8	Washington	692,479
9	Indiana	608	9	Indiana	22,653	9	**Alabama**	**647,637**
9	Tennessee	608	10	Virginia	21,890	10	Indiana	647,406
11	Missouri	567	11	Washing-ton	21,274	11	Minnesota	617,745
11	Virginia	567	12	Ohio	20,827	12	Virginia	585,205
13	Georgia	557	13	Tennessee	20,320	13	Ohio	551,451
14	Oregon	550	14	Mississippi	16,747	14	Tennessee	500,208
15	Washington	545	15	Minnesota	16,571	15	Mississippi	434,734
16	Florida	528	16	Arkansas	16,132	16	Florida	414,114
17	**Alabama**	**460**	17	Florida	15,762	17	Arkansas	410,039

			Relative Statistics on Paper Mfg. (NAICS Code 322), 2000					
Rank	State	Businesses	Rank	State	Employed ****	Rank	State	Ann. Payroll ($1,000)
1	California	555	1	Wisconsin	42,378	1	Wisconsin	1,888,267
2	Ohio	382	2	California	33,881	2	California	1,363,240
3	New York	365	3	Pennsylvania	32,339	3	Pennsylvania	1,315,370
4	Illinois	361	4	Ohio	29,205	4	Georgia	1,161,623
5	Pennsylvania	327	5	Illinois	28,784	5	Ohio	1,161,489
6	Texas	289	6	Georgia	26,600	6	Illinois	1,106,057
7	Wisconsin	256	7	New York	23,209	7	N. Carolina	929,319
8	New Jersey	254	8	Texas	22,102	8	New York	923,612
9	Massachusetts	223	9	N. Carolina	21,918	**9**	**Alabama**	**854,721**
10	Michigan	219	10	Michigan	18,851	10	Texas	825,680
11	Georgia	210	11	Massachusetts	18,088	11	Michigan	800,967
12	N. Carolina	188	12	New Jersey	17,437	12	Massachusetts	735,311
13	Tennessee	172	13	Tennessee	17,293	13	New Jersey	720,196
14	Indiana	170	**14**	**Alabama**	**16,225**	14	Tennessee	712,070
15	Florida	160	15	Minnesota	15,538	15	Washington	705,448
16	Minnesota	133	16	Virginia	14,085	16	Minnesota	699,468
17	Missouri	132	17	S. Carolina	14,039	17	Maine	635,297
18	Virginia	112	18	Washington	13,649	18	Virginia	632,547
19	Washington	106	19	Arkansas	13,130	19	S. Carolina	615,395
20	S. Carolina	101	20	Indiana	12,869	20	Arkansas	565,854
21	Kentucky	90	21	Missouri	12,510	21	Louisiana	513,282
22	Connecticut	89	22	Maine	12,033	22	Florida	479,757
23	**Alabama**	**88**	23	Florida	11,129	23	Indiana	460,996

			Relative Statistics on Furniture & Related Products Mfg. (NAICS Code 337), 2000				
Rank	State	Businesses	Rank	State	Employed ****	Rank	State	Annual Payroll ($1,000)
1	California	2,716	1	North Carolina	78,595	1	North Carolina	1,995,218
2	Florida	1,253	2	California	74,549	2	California	1,986,033
3	New York	1,141	3	Michigan	34,534	3	Michigan	1,473,955
4	North Carolina	1,123	4	Mississippi	32,936	4	Pennsylvania	832,712
5	Texas	1,014	5	Texas	28,004	5	Mississippi	801,527
6	Pennsylvania	825	6	Indiana	27,818	6	Indiana	772,568
7	Illinois	776	7	Pennsylvania	26,960	7	Texas	746,563
8	Ohio	712	8	Tennessee	26,546	8	Ohio	737,485
9	Georgia	623	9	Ohio	25,225	9	New York	675,539
10	Michigan	572	10	Virginia	23,170	10	Tennessee	665,166
11	New Jersey	498	11	New York	22,237	11	Illinois	649,144
11	Wisconsin	498	12	Illinois	21,009	12	Wisconsin	573,869
13	Indiana	479	13	Florida	18,645	13	Virginia	570,335
14	Tennessee	473	14	Wisconsin	18,393	14	Florida	471,533
15	Minnesota	470	15	**Alabama**	**16,122**	15	Minnesota	404,959
16	Virginia	442	16	Georgia	14,496	16	Georgia	381,371
16	Washington	442	17	Minnesota	12,834	17	**Alabama**	**369,012**
18	Missouri	423	18	Missouri	12,723	18	Missouri	336,170
19	**Alabama**	**409**	19	Arkansas	11,724	19	New Jersey	286,941

Source for this and the two preceding Tables is the U.S. DEP'T OF COMM., CENSUS BUREAU, COUNTY BUSINESS PATTERNS DATABASE, *at* http://censtats.census.gov/cbpnaic/cbpnaic.shtml (visited July 25, 2002).

**** Total number of employees for the week that included March, 12, 2000. U.S. Dep't of Comm., Census Bureau, County Business Patterns Database, *at* http://censtats.census.gov/cbpnaic/cbpnaic.shtml (last visited July 25, 2002).

Table 4: Business and Forestry Activity
in Alabama Counties*

		Commercial and Industrial Activity		Cash Receipts from Forestry by Ownership Class***					
Rank by Payroll	County	Annual Payroll ($1000)	Employ-ment**	Farm Forest Products	Private Non-Farm Timber	Forest Industry Timber	Gov't Timber	TOTAL	Rank by Timber Receipts
1	Jefferson	11,252,997	362,120	1,253	13,582	204	627	15,666	17
2	Mobile	4,078,296	156,441	1,262	9,508	1,678	559	13,007	20
3	Madison	4,049,888	126,771	473	873	-	133	1,479	66
4	Montgomery	2,978,594	115,316	1,226	3,683	312	454	5,675	54
5	Shelby	1,896,272	57,081	932	2,901	2,175	205	6,213	50
6	Tuscaloosa	1,877,898	69,610	2,626	11,746	5,619	366	20,357	12
7	Morgan	1,253,443	46,656	2,355	965	-	320	3,640	62
8	Houston	1,169,756	46,243	1,339	2,384	-	147	3,870	61
9	Baldwin	935,060	44,490	2,333	13,177	11,310	637	27,457	9
10	Calhoun	898,718	40,614	303	2,918	1,394	1,840	6,455	48
11	Etowah	787,878	34,345	514	3,445	126	126	4,211	58
12	Marshall	699,645	32,650	1,295	1,387	-	183	2,865	63
13	Lee	691,620	32,271	2,147	3,707	1,000	140	6,994	42
14	Lauderdale	650,825	31,275	1,540	821	205	-	2,566	64
15	Tallapoosa	566,164	25,370	1,204	8,363	3,185	194	12,946	21
16	Limestone	559,738	17,309	668	222	-	111	1,001	67
17	Talladega	541,695	21,017	1,315	4,264	995	2,076	8,650	36
18	Cullman	503,718	21,824	2,761	6,749	1,852	-	11,362	27
19	DeKalb	485,520	21,029	2,548	2,553	150	300	5,551	56
20	Colbert	469,016	19,387	942	2,731	213	209	4,095	60
21	Walker	359,310	15,828	2,215	7,363	1,175	436	11,189	28
22	Jackson	351,267	14,789	1,859	3,968	257	508	6,592	47
23	Dallas	347,701	15,121	4,757	6,972	6,355	73	18,157	15
24	St. Clair	289,211	12,510	3,017	4,222	1,812	147	9,198	35
25	Russell	285,726	11,165	655	3,284	1,100	327	5,366	57
26	Chambers	274,392	11,520	4,552	9,407	1,725	287	15,971	16
27	Escambia	256,670	11,678	2,381	5,646	14,238	2,283	24,548	11
28	Covington	252,067	10,920	4,217	2,321	4,241	1,373	12,152	25
29	Coffee	245,307	13,232	2,638	2,970	1,149	166	6,923	44
30	Monroe	241,722	8,367	9,576	13,840	14,577	775	38,768	4
31	Barbour	240,929	10,942	1,251	6,874	5,422	834	14,381	19
32	Dale	239,955	10,158	552	5,149	373	1,097	7,171	40
33	Marion	229,331	10,453	1,168	5,832	2,997	163	10,160	30
34	Pike	207,762	9,936	1,705	4,431	853	-	6,989	43
35	Franklin	198,653	9,845	2,313	2,313	2,060	157	6,843	45
36	Autauga	196,839	9,115	1,997	1,983	2,960	143	7,083	41
37	Winston	188,783	9,136	1,671	2,418	2,779	2,465	9,333	34
38	Clarke	178,374	7,848	1,924	21,724	26,231	760	50,639	1
39	Elmore	175,052	9,372	847	4,510	427	142	5,926	52
40	Blount	174,517	7,868	1,176	3,879	516	166	5,737	53
41	Lawrence	174,411	5,389	836	261	-	825	1,922	65
42	Marengo	154,908	6,172	7,564	17,269	10,846	-	35,679	5
43	Macon	147,242	6,347	1,345	3,915	494	196	5,950	51
44	Chilton	138,198	6,820	3,860	3,491	1,865	758	9,974	31
45	Choctaw	137,508	3,689	4,542	22,152	13,148	-	39,842	3

Rank by Payroll	County	Commercial and Industrial Activity		Cash Receipts from Forestry by Ownership Class***					Rank by Timber Receipts
		Annual Payroll ($1000)	Employ-ment**	Farm Forest Products	Private Non-Farm Timber	Forest Industry Timber	Gov't Timber	TOTAL	
46	Washington	136,204	3,407	4,462	14,656	9,121	-	28,239	8
47	Lamar	128,865	4,843	1,160	6,573	1,740	193	9,666	33
48	Fayette	121,650	5,337	2,677	4,666	2,146	354	9,843	32
49	Butler	108,763	5,287	5,468	9,339	14,334	414	29,555	7
50	Randolph	98,153	5,105	3,111	4,205	786	-	8,102	39
51	Henry	92,633	4,185	1,595	4,310	798	-	6,703	46
52	Wilcox	91,820	2,629	11,166	5,583	9,046	1,047	26,842	10
53	Conecuh	87,479	3,767	10,871	8,690	13,481	-	33,042	6
54	Clay	85,479	4,556	1,682	3,785	1,514	1,430	8,411	37
55	Lowndes	81,836	2,151	3,721	3,064	4,158	-	10,943	29
56	Geneva	81,512	4,410	1,637	2,104	349	118	4,208	59
57	Hale	74,395	3,206	6,507	24,725	10,364	4,880	46,476	2
58	Bibb	72,730	3,403	1,507	4,827	4,163	2,273	12,770	23
59	Cherokee	63,807	3,414	1,251	3,037	1,986	174	6,448	49
60	Pickens	62,682	3,251	3,146	9,476	6,561	-	19,183	14
61	Sumter	60,831	2,880	4,919	8,913	5,529	315	19,676	13
62	Crenshaw	57,851	2,942	4,988	4,513	3,321	-	12,822	22
63	Cleburne	51,422	2,255	156	3,346	2,055	2,664	8,221	38
64	Bullock	44,039	2,356	1,414	2,715	1,527	-	5,656	55
65	Perry	42,609	2,137	1,637	5,191	4,696	1,168	12,692	24
66	Coosa	32,530	1,430	1,190	5,574	5,185	194	12,143	26
67	Greene	25,815	1,317	7,614	4,304	3,294	326	15,538	18
	STATE TOTAL	43,735,681	1,644,307	179,533	405,769	254,172	38,258	877,732	
	% of Total Forestry:			20.45%	46.23%	28.96%	4.36%	100.00%	

* Data on commercial and industrial activity are from U.S. DEP'T OF COMM., CENSUS BUREAU, COUNTY BUSINESS PATTERNS DATABASE, *at* http://censtats.census.gov/cbpnaic/cbpnaic.shtml (last visited July 25. 2002); data on cash receipts from forestry are from ALA. AGRIC STATISTICS SERV., ALABAMA AGRICULTURAL STATISTICS, Bulletin 43, at 51-52 (2001), *at* http://www.aces.edy/department/nass/bulletin/2000/pg04.htm (last visited July 26, 2002). Note that the counties ranked one through nine account for approximately two-thirds of Alabama's commercial and industrial activity. *See supra* note 135.

** Total number of employees for the week that included March 12, 2002. U.S. DEP'T OF COMM., CENSUS BUREAU, COUNTY BUSINESS PATTERNS DATABASE, *supra*.

*** Cash receipts are "[s]ales of agricultural commodities at the first point of sale by establishments (farms) from which $1000 or more of agricultural products were or would normally be sold during the year. Cash receipts include the sales of commodities regardless of year produced. They exclude non-monetary transactions such as on-farm use of agricultural commodities." ALA. AGRIC. STATISTICS SERV., *supra*, at 44. Farm Forest Products are "[s]tumpage revenue[s] from sales of forest products from farms." *Id*. Forest Industry Timber is harvested from land held by any operator "of at least one wood processing mill." E-mail from Tim Placke, Deputy State Statistician, Alabama Agricultural Statistics Service, to Creighton J. Miller, Jr., Assistant Law Librarian, Bounds Law Library, The University of Alabama School of Law (Apr. 22, 2002) (on file with author). Government Timber is timber harvested from "[f]orest land controlled by the state/federal government . . . ." *Id*.

CHAPTER 2

Editorials and Other Responses

• • • • •

There's a moral aspect to tax reform

Reprinted from *The Tuscaloosa News,* 8/13/02

A new study of the state's tax structure by a University of Alabama professor of law shows how totally out of kilter with common sense and morality that our revenue system has grown.

Alabama does not have enough money for education and other essential services and the state's abnormally low property taxes are to blame, says Susan Pace Hamill, a specialist in tax law, in her 77-page thesis.

The timber industry, she says, is getting the biggest breaks. Her study shows that timberland accounts for 70 percent of the state's property, yet it yields only 2 percent of Alabama's total revenue.

Timber owners in Alabama typically pay $1 an acre in taxes. The rate is four times that high in neighboring Georgia, Hamill says.

State and local governments in Alabama levy a punishingly high rate of sales taxes to try to make up for the anemic taxation on property. The burden of those taxes falls hardest on the poor, who are further crippled by income taxes that are excused for the lowest wage earners in other states, Hamill says.

Many of her findings have been corroborated by other recent studies. What makes her examination uniquely compelling is its moral subtext. It was written as a thesis for her master's of theological study degree at Beeson Divinity School at Samford University.

Looking at the state's continued failure to address the crushing tax burden on its poorest citizens, Hamill quotes Jesus in Matthew:

"I tell you the truth, whatever you did not do for one of the least of these, you did not do for me."

It's as applicable now as it was 2,000 years ago. Until Alabama embraces tax reform, it cannot stand on moral ground.

• • • • •

The professor and the tax study

Reprinted from *The Anniston Star,* 8/13/02

It seems a law professor at the University of Alabama has completed a study of Alabama's tax system and has determined, well... that it is disgustingly inadequate and unfair.

Big surprise right?

Sure we all know Alabama's tax system is just about as bad as it can be. Folks have been saying that for years. What's different about this study is that the author has the facts, in detail, that say in no uncertain terms that we don't have enough money to run the state, that the system is unfair, that we have to reform it.

This isn't something off the top of her head. For more than a year now, Professor Susan Pace Hamill has unearthed all kinds of information, on the system as a whole, including breakdowns on state tax revenues by county.

What is also interesting about her study — actually it is her thesis written to attain a master's degree in theological studies at the Beeson Divinity School at Samford University — is that she has found a way to speak directly to us, not in an arcane academic fashion, but often through the words of Jesus, of all people.

On page one she quotes Jesus in the Gospel of Matthew: "I tell you the truth, whatever you did not do for one of the least of these, you did not do for me."

Brilliantly, Ms. Hamill has found some language the people of Alabama, especially those in the pulpits, can understand when the topic turns to taxes.

Who, then, are the least of us — here — in Alabama? Obviously, she speaks of the children, our children.

They are the least because this state has a tax system that spends less money on public education than almost every other state in the Union. She speaks of the children because Alabama has a tax system that dispenses peanuts to a budget for child welfare, a budget that is vastly inadequate. She dedicated this study to Alabama's children because without spending more public dollars on them our state will be destined to stay at the bottom of virtually every economic and social development indicator for generations to come.

Ms. Hamill finds sins aplenty in the current tax code. But the biggie, the one that smells the worst, is the property tax structure. "We don't have enough money," she told the *Mobile Press-Register.* "It's the property tax that's at fault, and it's the timber industry that's most at fault."

She certainly hit the nail on the head with that one. Alabama has the lowest property taxes in the nation. We could double our property tax, and they would still be lower than the next highest state, Mississippi. Clearly we can afford to pay more property taxes.

That especially goes for the timber industry. Ms. Hamill's finding that timberland taxes make up 2 percent of the state's total tax revenue, despite making up 70 percent of the state's land area is both shocking and nauseating. No one, even those in the timber industry, could argue that this is a fair system.

Raising the tax on timberland, however, would only be part of the solution. Unfortunately fixing the inadequacies and the inequities of the Alabama tax system will call for all of us to make sacrifices. But that is something all of us, for the sake of our children, should be willing to do.

• • • • •

Morality enters taxation debate

Reprinted from the *Montgomery Advertiser,* 8/15/02

Those who consider tax reform in Alabama as much a moral issue as a political one have a new ally who makes that claim in a thesis written in divinity school. Given that so little has been accomplished in the political arena, perhaps some attention to the moral aspects of the taxation issue will help spur the debate.

Susan Pace Hamill, a University of Alabama law professor whose specialty is tax law, wrote a thesis for her master's degree in theological studies at the Beeson Divinity School at Samford University. She contends that the glaring inequity of the state's tax system is immoral. If Alabama is to be true to its strong Judeo-Christian heritage, she argues, it must reform a tax system that leans heavily on the poor while scarcely tapping the property tax base, notably the timber acreage.

Regardless of one's theological views, it is hard to argue against the numbers that buttress Hamill's position. As she notes, timberland in Alabama is typically taxed at about $1 an acre, while timberland in Georgia—otherwise indistinguishable from Alabama timberland—is taxed at about four times that rate.

Alabama's unrealistically low property taxes are a key element in the historically low financial support for education. "We don't have enough money," she said. "It's the property tax that's at fault, and it's the timber industry that's most at fault."

She further notes that property taxes on timberland produce only about 2 percent of the state's total tax revenue, even though timberland covers enormous portions of Alabama.

John McMillan, executive director of the Alabama Forestry Association, makes the valid point that timberland is not the only low-taxed property in Alabama, where residential property taxes are low as well. "Everybody knows that we've got a problem with Alabama tax policy," he said. "It needs revising. But when it's all said and done, timberland owners have got to be able to be taxed at a level that allows them to maintain that acreage in forestland."

He's right. But other states manage to do that while still levying reasonable taxes on timberland, so why can't Alabama? There's lots of timberland in Georgia, for example, even with higher property taxes.

Hamill's thesis, laced with Scriptural admonitions along with statistics, could become a vehicle for promoting honest debate on taxation in Alabama, debate that stems not from partisan political positioning, but from the basic concept of what is right and just for this state.

Surely any program of meaningful tax reform has to include the broad utilization of all of the state's tax base, if only for the sake of fairness. To largely exclude the property portion of that tax base, as Alabama historically has done, is to ensure inequity.

• • • • •

Legislating morality
A moral legislature could fix state's tax code
Reprinted from *The Birmingham News*, 8/18/02

So you can't legislate morality? Only if a majority of legislators are immoral.

Truth is, much of Alabama law is based on moral values, especially those embraced by Judeo-Christian religions: It's morally wrong to kill or steal, for example.

Unfortunately, the state's tax code is immoral. By design, it is one of the nation's most unfair tax systems. It coddles the wealthy at the expense of the poor, who pay a much higher percentage of their incomes in state taxes.

That immorality is something good-government types, policy wonks and editorial writers have known about for years. Now, more and more people are noticing, including several large religious denominations such as the Methodists, Baptists and Episcopals, which have called for making the state's tax system more fair.

This month, Susan Pace Hamill, a professor of law at the University of Alabama School of Law, added her voice to the mix, and a powerful voice it is. Hamill, whose specialty is tax law, has written a comprehensive, compelling indictment of the state's tax system as her thesis for a master's in theology from Samford University.

In "An Argument for Tax Reform Based on Judeo-Christian Ethics," Hamill quoting tax data and Old and New Testament verses verbally smites those who have created and perpetuated Alabama's immoral tax system.

"The empirical research of this article, documenting the oppressive consequences that Alabama's income, sales and property tax structures foist upon the poorest Alabamians and their children, paints a disgraceful picture," concludes Hamill, a United Methodist.

Much of that picture already has been well-documented:

Alabama's income taxes are the most unfair in the nation, requiring a family of four earning as little as $4,600 a year to pay state taxes, while producing among the lowest revenues in the Southeast and nation. At the other end of the pay scale, the state income tax system never phases out personal exemptions (unlike the federal and most state systems), allowing the wealthiest taxpayers full exemptions under the state income tax.

The sales tax, which local governments can raise without a constitutional amendment, is among the highest in the nation. Without exemptions for food and medicine, it hits the poor the hardest.

State and local governments collect so little property tax you would have to more than triple the amount per person to equal the national average. The timber industry gets the biggest break of all, which Hamill calls the "principal reason" so many Alabama schools are underfunded.

Hamill challenges all Alabamians, but especially religious and political leaders and those of privilege through wealth, education and access to the power structure to tackle tax reform.

She has even compiled a chart documenting the religious affiliations of the governor, lieutenant governor and members of the Legislature. Of 142 total, 136 (96 percent) profess to belong to Christian religions, such as Baptist, Methodist, Church of Christ and Presbyterian.

Her point, of course, is that these supposed Christians have it within their power to fix the tax system. Fear of not being re-elected or wanting to protect their own wealth is no excuse, Hamill says.

Or, as she quotes Jesus on taking care of the poor (Matthew 25): "I tell you the truth, whatever you did not do for one of the least of these, you did not do for Me."

Hamill's thesis can be found at http://www.law.ua.edu/staff/bio/shamil.html. It's must reading for all lawmakers. Let them demonstrate their convictions by reforming Alabama's immoral tax system.

• • • • •

Timberrrr!
UA professor saws through property tax myths
Reprinted from *The Birmingham News,* 8/18/02

University of Alabama law professor Susan Pace Hamill nails the timber industry in her master's thesis about the state's immoral tax system. Or, as she says, "I've got the goods."

Indeed, she does. Perhaps the most impressive feature of the thesis is her numbers-crunching that shows just how little Alabama collects from its extensive timber lands.

Alabama levies taxes on four classes of property: Class I, utilities, is taxed at 30 percent of fair market value; Class II, mainly commercial property, is taxed at 20 percent of fair market value; Class III, timber and farmland and single-family residential property, is taxed at 10 percent of fair market value; and Class IV, cars and trucks for personal use, is taxed at 15 percent of fair market value.

Hamill's research team calculated what percentage of total property taxes each class contributes statewide. Class I accounts for 9 percent of property tax revenues, Class II contributes 56 percent; and Class IV accounts for 4 percent.

In Class III, single-family homes contribute 29 percent of all property taxes collected in Alabama. Forest and farmland, which have a special exemption that lowers their already paltry taxes even further, bring in a whopping 2 percent, according to Hamill. This, in a state where timberland accounts for 71 percent of the total number of acres.

To understand how ludicrously low property taxes are on timber, take a look at the most recent bill for your home's property tax, the lowest in the nation. The state property tax collected per acre of timberland in Alabama averages only $1 a year.

John McMillan, executive director of the Alabama Forestry Association, tried to justify the puny property taxes.

"Timberland owners have got to be able to be taxed at a level that allows them to maintain that acreage in forestland," he told the *Mobile Register*. "It is important to recreation, wildlife, water quality."

That presumably is also true in Georgia, where timberland owners pay an average of $4 an acre yet somehow maintain those lands.

McMillan said previous studies convinced him that low residential property tax rates were more to blame than low taxes on timberland for underfunded government services. Hamill's research saws through that myth.

Why are Alabama's property taxes especially on timber and farm land so low? Mainly because of the power of special interests such as the Alabama Farmers Federation and the forestry association. The farmers' group, in particular, for decades has fought every attempt to raise property taxes.

In Hamill's view and ours these special interests and their beneficiaries have much to answer for.

"Allowing owners of timber acres, who as a group dominate Alabama's economy and land mass and constitute a substantial source of wealth and profits in the state, to continue to pay no more than 2 percent of the property taxes, averaging no more than $1 an acre, in addition to being patently unfair under any reasonable ethical analysis, constitutes the most troubling violation of the moral principles of Judeo-Christian ethics in that children from low income families, the most vulnerable and powerless segment of Alabama's population, by being denied a minimum opportunity to secure an adequate education, bear the brunt of their windfall," she writes.

Surely, our Legislature will make sure this windfall ends, won't it? Surely, our Legislature won't be bullied by the special interests that have benefited from such an unfair tax system, will it? Surely, our Legislature can devise a tax system that is fair to all, including timber owners, can't it?

• • • • •

Divine Inspiration

Seminary Article Sparks Alabama Tax-Code Revolt

A Methodist Lawyer's Thesis Cites 'Christian Duty' To Back Fairer System

---

Evangelicals Rally to Cause

Shailagh Murray

Reprinted from *The Wall Street Journal*, 2/12/03

TUSCALOOSA, Ala.—For nearly a century, reformers have tried in vain to change this state's antiquated tax structure. The Alabama code requires families of four earning as little as $4,600 to pay income tax, the nation's lowest threshold. It charges a higher sales tax on baby formula than on cattle feed and permits timber interests to pay relatively meager property taxes compared with homeowners.

Now an unlikely force is setting off a tax revolt in Alabama: religious fervor. The catalyst is Susan Pace Hamill, a tax-law professor who used a sabbatical at a divinity school to write "An Argument for Tax Reform Based on Judeo-Christian Ethics."

"How could we, in a free society of a bunch of Christians, have the worst, most unjust tax structure that you could ever have dreamed up?" asks Ms. Hamill.

Her paper, published last month in the Alabama Law Review, has been cited by influential Alabamians in business and the state house, including the recently elected Republican governor, Bob Riley. It has also brought some of the most powerful of Alabama's 8,000 churches into the fray, with pastors culling from the article to preach about the Christian duty to demand a tax code that falls more evenly on rich and poor. Recently, the paper has been condensed into a brochure titled, "The Least of These," a reference to Jesus' teaching about helping the disadvantaged, and 10,000 copies are now being distributed to churches statewide by Samford University, where Ms. Hamill attended divinity school.

Alabama churches may be powerful enough to succeed where past tax-code reformers have failed. One longtime obstacle: powerful agricultural and timber interests who have fought to protect rules that keep their taxes very low.

Moreover, most of the tax code is enshrined in Alabama's complicated 100-year-old constitution, making changes more difficult than in other states. To increase property taxes, individual counties have to get permission from voters, and in most cases the Alabama legislature.

Even then, the state constitution imposes absolute dollar limits on property taxes for individual landowners. Counties can raise the sales tax, a portion of which goes to the state, without permission. Those rates have crept as high as 11%, and make up more than half the state's revenue. Because poor and working-class people spend nearly everything they earn, sales taxes take a bigger bite of their income. In Alabama, that translates into an especially heavy burden on African-Americans, who account for about a quarter of the state's population but half of its poor.

Mr. Riley credits Ms. Hamill with bringing the churches into the tax debate. "The churches have never been there" for reform until now, he says. Still, they've flexed their muscle at other times. In 1999, churches rallied their congregations against a state lottery sought by then-Democratic Don Siegelman, and are credited with its defeat.

Three days after Mr. Riley took office Jan. 20, he created a commission to recommend constitutional changes that would clear the way for "comprehensive tax reform," a spokesman says. The United Methodist Church, the Presbyterian Church (USA), the Alabama Southern Baptist Convention, the Episcopal Church, as well as local Roman Catholic and Jewish officials, have all recently endorsed tax-code changes.

The growing religious movement for tax reform dovetails with other forces pushing for change. In November, after Mr. Riley's election, state business leaders formed a lobbying coalition to create a new tax structure that would support schools and other government services, even if companies have to pay more. The coalition fears Alabama's budget crisis is taking such a toll on education and other priorities that it would scare away potential investors.

Big Challenges

Even with business and Church support, Mr. Riley faces big challenges in enacting reform. First, he has to push constitutional reform through a reluctant legislature, where powerful farming and timber interests remain well represented. Some conservative Christian groups also oppose reform. Alfa, the Alabama Farmers Federation, which also represents timber growers, has circulated a position paper arguing against any changes to the tax code. Mike Kilgore, executive director of Alfa, says that property tax valuations and collections have grown "at astounding rates" in recent years, and argues that the state needs to spend its money more wisely.

In her stump speech, which she gives at least twice a week, Ms. Hamill reminds congregations and civic groups that both the Old and New Testaments condemn economic oppression of the poor. Her paper cites Micah 2:1: "Woe to those who plan iniquity, to those who plot evil in their beds!" Ms. Hamill points to other Old Testament references that say the poor deserve a "minimum opportunity" to succeed. Alabama's underfunded schools fail that test, she says.

Ms. Hamill, 42, attends Trinity United Methodist Church in Tuscaloosa, and has traveled to numerous churches around the state to speak, often bringing her husband and two kids along so they can attend Sunday services together. After graduating from Emory University and Tulane Law School, the Florida native did a stint at the Sullivan & Cromwell law firm in New York and worked as a lawyer at the Internal Revenue Service headquarters in Washington. Eight years ago, she moved to Tuscaloosa to teach at the University of Alabama Law School.

As a traditional Methodist, Ms. Hamill at first felt like an outsider among Alabama's large evangelical Christian population. She decided to immerse herself in the study of evangelical Christianity during a sabbatical at Samford University's Beeson Divinity School in Birmingham. While there, she read a local newspaper explaining how Alabama taxes families of four with very low incomes. "I assumed the $4,600 figure was a misprint," she told a recent Kiwanis Club breakfast meeting in Tuscaloosa.

Her thesis, published in draft form in August, swiftly took hold. Mimeographed copies were passed around law firms, government offices and think tanks. Riley, locked in a tight gubernatorial election campaign against the incumbent Mr. Siegelman, endorsed Ms. Hamill's paper during a television appearance in October 2002 and since being elected has become a more vocal supporter of tax reform. (Mr. Siegelman had made tax reform a big part of his campaign.)

History of Conflict

Alabama's tax code is an artifact of the state's history of racial conflict. Before the Civil War, the state derived most of its revenue from a slave tax. After slavery disappeared, the state raised property taxes make up for the lost income. That caused a backlash from whites, who owned the vast majority of land.

A state constitution adopted in 1875 capped property taxes. A 1901 version made the burden even lighter. The goal of industry bosses and land barons who wrote the latter document was "to establish white supremacy in this state," constitutional-convention president John Knox said at the time.

That Jim Crow-era effort sharply restricts Alabama's tax base today. Forests stretch across 71% of the state, but timber land is taxed at a preferential agricultural rate that averages 95 cents per acre. Georgia timber owners, by comparison, pay an average of $4 to $6 per acre, according to some studies, and big owners pay more per acre. Six of Ms. Hamill's law students spent several months calculating how much the timber industry contributes to the total property tax pie: less than 2%.

Alabama's $4,600 income-tax threshold for families of four is the lowest among the 42 states that levy income taxes, according to several studies. In neighboring Mississippi, the first $19,600 of household income is exempt. In California, the exemption is $38,800. Mr. Riley calls the situation "immoral."

Academics, public-policy experts and state newspapers have railed against peculiarities of Alabama's tax code for decades. "Big Jim" Folsom, a 6-foot-8 populist Democrat, called for reform after winning the governorship in 1946. But Mr. Folsom's efforts died in the Alabama Legislature, which has remained the graveyard of reform ever since.

Last year, Alabama House Speaker Seth Hammett couldn't even persuade colleagues to vote on a resolution calling for voters to decide whether to go forward with the constitutional reform that's necessary to change the tax system. Some conservative Christian groups, including the Christian Coalition of Alabama, cheered the Legislature's inaction on grounds it could lead to higher taxes and legalized gambling. Some reform opponents object on religious grounds to giving the state broader taxing authority.

Ms. Hamill believes she's been called by God to this battle. She has little first-hand knowledge of those she seeks to help. For instance, she hasn't visited many of the poverty-stricken parts of the state that she has studied and written about. "Until recently, most of my field trips out of the ivory tower were speaking engagements to the business and tax crowd," says Ms. Hamill.

She was a guest one recent Sunday at Vestavia Hills Baptist Church in Birmingham. Leading an adult Sunday school class, Ms. Hamill described Alabama as "the modern version of ancient Israel. The land's being gobbled up. There's no minimum opportunity. And we're staying afloat on the backs of the poor." Vestavia's upper-middle-class congregation was so riveted by Ms. Hamill's presentation that she was invited back for another session.

Other groups are more stubborn. One area of resistance: the state's Black Belt, a cluster of former cotton-growing counties mostly in the state's western midsection, nicknamed for its dark soil. Though it is rich in timber, the region has a paltry tax base and some of Alabama's least equipped schools. If any region could benefit from tax reform, it's the Black Belt. Yet in the antebellum town of Marion, Zion United Methodist Church Pastor Fairest Cureton predicts many of his black parishioners will resist.

He says he will preach in favor of reform. But he says poor people tend to like the sales tax, because they pay it in small increments. And so they may reject change as an effort to make them pay more.

Across town, Rev. Michael Perry of Siloam Baptist Church, whose members include the county's wealthiest landowners and are primarily white, won't raise the subject. "As a whole, the tax system is terribly out of skew," Rev. Perry says. "But my parishioners would not entirely agree."

In Tuscaloosa, Ms. Hamill was addressing a Sunday school class last fall at the blueblood First Presbyterian Church when teacher Bob Montgomery, a pharmaceutical salesman, argued that it's not the state's job to help the oppressed. That's up to churches and charities, he explained. "My tithe goes to the poor," he told Ms. Hamill.

Later that morning, during the regular church service, Mr. Montgomery heard Pastor Charles Durham deliver an impassioned call for tax reform based on Ms. Hamill's article. "It took a law professor to open my eyes," Rev. Durham proclaimed, pointing to her in the pew. A few weeks later, Ms. Hamill ran into Mr. Montgomery at the grocery store.

"What can I do to help?" he asked her. "Write an op-ed," Ms. Hamill replied. Mr. Montgomery's account of his conversion, headlined "What Would Jesus Do About Alabama's Tax System?" was published in late January in several Alabama newspapers.

CHAPTER 3

A Call to Ethical Action

Alabamians professing faith in God have a moral duty to support tax reform

This op-ed newspaper column by Susan Pace Hamill
originally appeared in *The Birmingham News, Montgomery Advertiser,
Mobile Register, The Tuscaloosa News,* and *The Anniston Star,* and
has been reprinted and widely distributed by Samford University Press
in pamphlet form under the title "The Least of These."

Alabamians are, or at least claim to be, a Christian people. Today over 90% of our population practices Christianity in some form. This means that the vast majority of Alabamians believe that Judeo-Christian values found in the Bible should be a moral compass to guide their lives. However, in one glaring case Alabamians have strayed far from the direction that God's moral compass provides. When one examines the suffering and hardship Alabama's tax structure inflicts on the poorest and neediest among us, one cannot fail to see the enormous gap that exists between what God's moral values demand and what we have allowed our state to become. The time has come for those of us who have allowed this to happen to acknowledge it (painful as that will be), and then use the gifts, powers, and opportunities that God has blessed us with to set things right.

The Bible has a great deal to say about how individual people and their communities must treat the poor, powerless, and needy among them. The Book of Genesis (1:27;4:9;9:5-6), revealing that God created all people in His image, equates the unjust treatment of fellow human beings as a wrong committed against God Himself, for God's image may be seen in even the poorest and neediest people among us. In other words, to sin against the poor is to sin against God.

Later Old Testament books expand this point by condemning actions that economically penalize poor and powerless persons, which makes their already marginal lives worse. In addition to generally commanding "do not oppress," the Books of Exodus (21:2; 22:21-22, 25-27; 23:9-11), Leviticus (19:9-10, 13, 33; 25:8-16, 23-28,35-43) and Deuteronomy (15:1-3, 7-14; 23:19; 24:6, 12-15, 17, 19-21) forbid numerous actions, such as taking a cloak or a millstone (which were needed in the ancient world to survive and earn a living) as a pledge for debt, charging interest, holding back wages, selling food at a profit and using dishonest scales and measurements, as specific but not the only examples of economic oppression.

These biblical books further expand the protections that must be provided for poor and powerless persons. In addition to commanding that they be treated justly, which requires far more than courtroom justice, God also requires that safety nets be created to allow poor and powerless persons a minimum opportunity to meet their basic needs and improve their lives. Certain rights to harvest from the land of others and secure ownership of their own land (which was the way to secure economic well being in the ancient world) are among specific examples in the Bible, but are not meant to be the only opportunities required, so that the poor and powerless can try to improve their lives.

The New Testament further emphasizes the importance of the Old Testament's requirements that poor and powerless persons have these minimum protections. In the Gospels of Matthew (5:17; 7:12; 22:37-40), Mark (12:29, 40) and Luke (1:46-55; 3:11-14; 4:16-21; 6:31-36; 16:19-31; 20:47), Jesus declares that He has come to fulfill the Old Testament Scriptures and His teachings show that the moral requirements of the Old Testament protecting poor and powerless persons apply to all Christians. In addition to identifying the love of God and the love of neighbors (even those with no wealth or status) as the two greatest commandments, and announcing that He has come "to preach the good news to the poor" and "release the oppressed," Jesus showed special compassion and concern for the poorest and neediest persons of society throughout His earthly ministry. At the very least, Jesus calls for social structures that protect poor persons from economic oppression and allow them a minimum opportunity to improve their lives.

Alabama's tax structure fails to come close to meeting the moral demands that God has revealed for us in the Bible. Alabama's income tax takes a greater portion of the scarce resources of Alabama's lowest wage earners, those deep in poverty earning as little as $4,600 a year, while at the same time the highest income earning Alabamians are able to significantly lighten their income tax burden with benefits that most other states and the federal government do not allow. Alabama's sales taxes, with rates among the highest in the nation that do not exempt even the most basic necessities, such as food, significantly increase the heavy burden already imposed on the poor by the unfair income tax structure.

However the failure to meet God's moral demands does not end there. Because Alabama collects the lowest property taxes per person in the nation, the difference must be made up with unfair amounts of income and sales taxes, which hit the poor the hardest. The property tax structure allows the wealthiest Alabamians to pay less than their fair share of Alabama's tax burden. Timber, representing 71% of Alabama's landmass and earning substantial profits, escapes with the lightest share of taxes, less than 2% of property taxes, averaging no more than $1 an acre. Because of the inadequate revenues raised from property taxes, Alabama is unable to adequately fund its public schools, thus denying children of the poorest Alabamians, the neediest and most powerless among us, a minimum opportunity to improve their lives. By allowing the wealthiest Alabamians, especially owners of timber acres, to escape with the lightest tax burden, while at the same time imposing oppressive levels of income and sales taxes on the poorest

Alabamians, our tax structure is the sort of system condemned by the Old Testament Prophets and by Jesus as inconsistent with God's word. Any legitimate effort that truly addresses these vast injustices against the poorest Alabamians and their children must require wealthier Alabamians, especially owners of timber acres, to pay more taxes.

Given that Alabama's tax structure fails to meet God's moral demands, the next question is — What is the moral duty of all Alabamians professing faith in God? The Bible has a great deal to say. The Old Testament Books of Isaiah (1:17;5:8;10:1-4), Amos (2:6-8;5:7,10-11,14-15;5:21-24; 8:4-6) and Micah (2:1-2,9;6:8), and the New Testament Gospel of Matthew (25:45) strongly condemns those who claim to be the People of God yet do nothing towards changing conditions that economically oppress the poorest and neediest persons and deny them a minimum opportunity to improve their lives. Jesus Himself made this clear when He said "whatever you did not do for one of the least of these, you did not do for me." What does this require? At the very least all Alabamians professing faith in God have a moral duty to vote for candidates running for political office who promise to work for tax reform efforts that will correct these unjust conditions suffered by the poorest and neediest Alabamians and their children.

However the moral duty of some Alabamians is far greater. The Old Testament Books of Isaiah (1:23;5:22-23), Jeremiah (22:2-4,12-17), Ezekiel (22:25-29;34:2-4), and Micah (3:11;3:1-3) and the New Testament Gospels of Matthew (23:23-24) and Luke (12:48) impose even greater moral responsibilities on those who enjoy greater privileges because of their education, wealth, status or access to the power structures. Jesus Himself made this clear when He said "from everyone who has been given much, much will be demanded; and from the one who has been entrusted with much, much more will be asked." Alabamians of privilege who profess faith in God, yet act in ways designed to confuse the truth in order to avoid paying their fair share, should be mindful of Jesus' warning (Matthew 6:24 and Luke 16:13) that "you cannot serve both God and money." Any efforts to falsely convince others that the current tax structure is acceptable to God violates God's moral demands just as much as the tax structure itself.

Under the standards of moral responsibility set by Jesus, Alabama's legislators who profess faith in God, and the one holding or seeking the office of Governor, have an even greater moral responsibility to work towards a complete reform of the tax structure. Alabama's political leaders enjoy direct access to the power structures and are therefore in the best position to cure the injustice that hangs like a dark cloud over our state. However, the greatest moral responsibility falls upon Alabama's ministers and other religious leaders, who are called to preach and teach God's word, with courage and clarity, even if the most influential members of society try to discourage them. Alabama's religious leaders must assume a greater role by speaking out publicly, including rebuking those who are falsely convincing others that the current tax structure is fair. Alabama's political and religious leaders who fail to accept these moral responsibilities strongly resemble the political and religious leaders condemned by Jesus and by the Old Testament Prophets as failing to follow God's word.

The State of Alabama stands at the crossroads at the beginning of this new century. It currently has in place a tax structure, one of the many unfortunate products of the 1901 constitution, that not only economically oppresses the poorest and neediest Alabamians, but also denies the children of these families a minimum opportunity to seek a better life. Alabama's tax structure, with all its unjust effects, is morally wrong, not only under any reasonable ethical model for evaluating tax policy, but more persuasively because it fails to meet God's moral demands. The vast majority of Alabamians practicing Christianity or Judaism hold God's moral values in their hearts. As individuals, Alabamians are compassionate and caring toward people less fortunate than themselves. I challenge all Alabamians of goodwill to rise up and insist on a fair and just tax structure for all of us, but especially for the poorest Alabamians and their children, who lack the power, knowledge and resources to effectively speak up for themselves. Only if all of us do our part can real spiritual renewal take place, which will pave the way for Alabama to become the light to the nation and the world that it was meant to be.

· · · · ·

An open letter to Alabama's political leaders: only real tax reform can save our children

This op-ed newspaper column by Susan Pace Hamill
originally appeared in *The Tuscaloosa News,*
The Anniston Star, and *The Birmingham News.*

The numerous studies showing how Alabama's state and local tax structure unfairly burdens the poor and the fact that we are facing the most serious fiscal crisis since the Great Depression compels you to take action. Biblically based Judeo-Christian ethical principles, which most of you have adopted, hold you, as our political leaders, to the highest level of accountability to eliminate this injustice poisoning our state.

Instead of settling for a quick fix solution, you must remedy the inequities embedded in the tax structure. Only real tax reform can produce a fair system based on ability to pay that empowers the state and local areas to adequately fund vital services such as the public schools. And only real tax reform can close the enormous gap between the standards of justice that our faith requires and the oppression currently plaguing our state.

Real tax reform must be done in a careful and systematic way. First you must determine both the minimum standards of basic health, education, and welfare that all Alabamians should have and the cost of these standards. For example, the public schools have told us that they need $1.6 billion of new revenues and I believe them. Almost ninety percent of Alabama's public schools have grossly inadequate funding, which denies our children a minimum opportunity to better their situation.

Real tax reform must be revenue positive and ensure that the revenues are spent in an efficient manner. Blaming our chronic shortage of revenues solely on waste wrongfully caters to the self serving interests of powerful lobby groups.

Real tax reform must reduce the heavy tax burden currently imposed on low income Alabamians, which requires Alabamians at higher income levels and those owning property of significant value to pay more taxes. Making unqualified statements against higher taxes or supporting super majority thresholds to enact tax legislation wrongfully panders to powerful special interest groups, who are misleading the poor into believing that tax reform means higher taxes for them.

Real tax reform must principally focus on the three most important sources of revenue for state and local finance, the income, sales, and property tax structures.

Real tax reform must raise the income tax threshold to exempt Alabamians at or below the poverty level. The income taxes of those with the greatest ability to pay must be increased equitably in a manner that produces positive revenues. Constitutional reform must be part of this because the 1901 constitution locks in the income tax provisions that favor the wealthy.

Because Alabama's extremely high sales taxes hit the poor the hardest, real tax reform must limit state and local sales tax rates, ideally to no more than 6 percent combined, and adopt appropriate exemptions for groceries, clothing, medicine, and other basic needs. Real tax reform should also consider imposing sales taxes on services. This can be accomplished under the normal legislative process outside the constitution.

Real tax reform cannot be accomplished without reforming the property tax structure. This will require many property owners to pay more. Because all aspects of the property tax structure are hopelessly entrenched in the 1901 constitution, real property tax reform is impossible without constitutional reform.

In addition to raising the millage rates, you must also examine the different classes of property and determine the proportionate share of the property tax burden each class of property should pay. Currently, commercial property pays well over 50 percent of Alabama's property taxes with homes approaching one third.

Timber acres, which cover 71 percent of Alabama's real property and account for substantial profits earned in the state, pay less than 2 percent of the property taxes, averaging less than one dollar an acre. The minimal property taxes paid by timber is the principal reason that rural parts of the state have no ability to adequately fund their public schools.

When re-drawing the proportions each class of property should pay, many factors must be considered such as the business cycle of the property involved and other taxes borne by the landowner. Nevertheless the evidence clearly shows that timber acres are paying a grossly inadequate share. Real property tax reform must address this inequity and require timber acres as a group to pay a far greater proportion of Alabama's total property taxes. Merely raising property taxes across the board will magnify the current inequities and still leave the rural area schools grossly underfunded.

Once you have settled on the size of the property tax and what proportional share each class of property should contribute, you then must re-examine the exemptions. Real property tax reform may require greater homestead and similar exemptions for other types of property to ensure that the small homeowner or small landowner is not overtaxed. Current use valuation, which is the mechanism that is largely responsible for the low property taxes on timber and agriculture, should be phased out for large timber landowners.

In addition to a great deal of hard work, real tax reform requires courage to stand up to the special interests selfishly thwarting efforts to produce a fair system. Let me assure you that Alabama's future depends on your willingness to do just that. The Bible requires political leaders to protect the welfare of our most vulnerable citizens. Because of our unfair and inadequate tax and constitutional structures, Alabama's children, as well as many other needy Alabamians, have suffered for generations. It is your responsibility to remedy this.

Only real tax reform can save our children, "the least of these," the most vulnerable and powerless segment of Alabama's population, who also hold the keys to our future. Until you accomplish real tax reform, Alabama's children, especially those from poor and lower middle class families, will continue to be denied the adequate education that the moral principles of Judeo-Christian ethics demand that they have. The moral well-being of a society is judged on how the powerful treat "the least of these" and Alabama miserably fails this test. As our political leaders you have an awesome responsibility and opportunity to lift the dark cloud of injustice that hangs over our state and get our tax and constitutional structures right.

CHAPTER 4

What You Can Do

What should the average Alabamian do about the immorally unfair state and local taxes inflicted on the poorest among us? What should readers in other states do if their state and local tax structures are unfair?

The most difficult and important step for many of us is setting aside our own self interest. Alabama's taxes are unfair because those of us with higher incomes and those of us owning property with significant value are not paying our fair share of Alabama's tax burden.

Similarly other states with unfair taxes will be letting those with the greatest ability to pay off too lightly. When the system allows those most able to pay to avoid paying their fair share, an unacceptably large portion of the tax burden will shift unfairly to the poor and minimum services, such as public education, that provide the poor a chance of escaping poverty, will be compromised. Our natural human desire to continue not paying our fair share (because nobody likes paying taxes) prevents many of us from actively fighting an unfair tax system. This kind of inertia fueled by self interest has kept numerous Alabamians, who take their Christian faith seriously, quiet and has allowed a small number of self serving powerful interest groups to keep the unfair taxes in place for decades.

Fortunately our ethical values, which in Alabama largely come from the Christian faith, provide us with tools to overcome this self interest and insist on fair taxes, even when fair taxes require more from us. For Christians, the teachings of Jesus Christ require us to treat "the least of these" as we would treat him, even if that means making economic sacrifices that challenge our self interest. For those practicing Judaism, the Old Testament Law essentially provides the same message and those practicing other faiths and philosophies will find similar obligations in their moral standards.

As many of us confront the unpleasant fact that the unfair tax system cannot be corrected without requiring more taxes from us, we must avoid being tempted by excuses that wrongfully obscure this fundamental truth. For example, many Alabamians blame our chronic shortage of revenues solely on wasteful government spending. Although a fair tax system must ensure that revenues are spent wisely and contain reasonable accountability measures, the hard truth is this: Alabama's revenues fall so far below any reasonable level of adequacy, we cannot correct the unfair tax system without a revenue positive plan that requires more from those with a greater ability to pay.

In other states, the potential for addressing inadequate revenues by improving government efficiency will vary from state to state. However, states that substantially overburden the poor or raise revenues significantly below the adequate range will not be able to make up for their shortfalls solely by cutting down on govern-

129

ment waste, and like Alabama those states will have to require more taxes from those with a greater ability to pay.

Other excuses similarly disguise our self interested desire to avoid paying our fair share. Some Christians in Alabama have tried to justify the unacceptably low taxes required from those most able to pay as actually helping the poor by prompting greater tithes to the church. They reason that greater tithes will help the church fulfill its responsibility to care for the poor, which is not the government's responsibility anyway. They also argue that the church is not responsible for the tax system at all under our American model of government, which separates church and state. Readers in other states with unfair taxes will be tempted by similar excuses.

These excuses ignore key fundamental facts and fool us into thinking that we are upholding our moral responsibilities when in fact we are not. In Alabama, as well as other states with unfair taxes, as long as those with a greater ability to pay continue to avoid paying their fair share, the poor will be forced to shoulder an unfair tax burden, and will be denied a minimum chance of escape poverty. No amount of tithing to the church will change this basic fact.

If a combination of very light taxes on the wealthiest Alabamians and tithing to the church could establish minimum justice for the poor, Alabama, with its numerous churches and Christians, would be the most compassionate state in the nation to the poor, rather than among the least. The hard truth is that tithing to the church and the efforts of the church to help the poor cannot even partially eliminate the oppressive effects of unfair taxes, when those with a greater ability to pay fail to pay their fair share.

Moreover, in a representative democracy where all citizens have the right to vote for the elected officials that create government structures, those governmental structures, which include the tax system, measure the moral well-being of the society comprising the voting population. More plainly, in a representative democracy the people are responsible for the moral health of their government.

In Alabama, where most of the voters are Christians, the immorally unfair taxes that oppress the poor are totally out of kilter with our Christian values, which require compassion to the poor. Religious leaders of churches who refuse to educate their members as to their moral responsibility to vote for government officials who will work to correct unfair taxes and insist on more compassion for the poor are essentially catering to the self-interested motives of their wealthier members, and have no moral credibility as religious leaders.

Once you get past the huge stumbling block of self interest and decide that something must be done about the unfair taxes, it is important that you take positive action. Throwing up your hands in despair does no good. For those practicing Christianity and Judaism, the Bible requires your response to draw on your gifts, talents and opportunities. No matter what state you live in, all of you have the right to vote and the right to freedom of speech.

In addition to voting more responsibly, spread the word at your church, synagogue, or civic club and encourage other people to support fair taxes. Let members of your state legislature know that you support fair taxes and that you intend to vote for candidates who show the most courage in pushing for fair taxes. Only if large numbers of people actively insist on fair taxes will it be possible to break the stronghold of the special interest groups who are benefitting from unfair taxes.

Those of you who possess greater gifts, powers, and opportunities than that of the average citizen have even greater moral responsibilities to fight for fair taxes. Lawyers and tax professionals, for example, have been quiet for too long often because unfair taxes benefit their clients. A response I received to the story in *The Wall Street Journal* covering my thesis captures this well: "I see you are being a trouble maker in Alabama; more of us tax lawyers need to speak up and be trouble makers when the tax system is unfair."

Although I am grateful that I finally came to understand my own moral responsibility, I regret that it took me seven years to even notice the disgusting degree of unfairness of Alabama's taxes. Under the moral principles of Judeo-Christian values, as well as other reasonable ethical models, those of you with direct access to the political process, which at the state level includes the governor and members of the state legislature, have a very high moral responsibility to ensure that the taxes imposed in your jurisdiction are fair to everyone—even the poorest, who have little political power, and the weakest, such as the children, who cannot even vote.

Finally, does Alabama's story pose broader moral questions beyond the issue of fair taxes at the state and local level? Can Alabama's story speak to us as we struggle to find a fair tax system at the federal level?

Even though the federal system does not tax the poorest Americans, those below the officially defined poverty line, does it make sense to dish out generous tax cuts to the wealthiest Americans, when Americans laboring in the lower middle classes could desperately use a break? Does our system of national funding respond to the minimum needs of the poorest, weakest, and most vulnerable among us? Is the federal system contributing all it should to help ensure that all American children have a reasonable opportunity to secure an adequate education? These questions do not have easy answers and present a much more complicated set of facts than Alabama's story. However, the fundamental moral principles central to Alabama's story—forbidding oppression and requiring minimum opportunity—guide us in the struggle for fair taxes at the federal level.

Does Alabama's story speak to fairness beyond the issue of fair taxes? Arguably the broad ethical principles central to Alabama's story, forbidding oppression and requiring minimum opportunity, whether derived from faith-based or other ethical models, shed meaningful light on other diverse and difficult issues that raise serious moral concerns.

For example, how might these broad ethical principles help us develop more compassionate laws that further protect our children as well as the poor, the elderly, the disabled, and other historically marginalized people such as women and racial minorities? Do we violate these moral principles in our criminal justice system and if so, how can we make that system more fair? Can these broad ethical principles help us deal with the wrenching moral dilemmas posed when adopting

132

immigration policies? The moral well-being of a society is judged on how the powerful treat "the least of these." Alabama miserably fails this test, and through its struggle to establish justice within its borders, Alabama challenges the rest of the states and America itself to look carefully at how their respective public policies treat "the least of these."

Alabama's story offers a powerful plea to America to become more compassionate to "the least of these." Because of the unfair taxes that have haunted Alabama for decades, Alabama now has an enormous gap between the moral values we as a people claim to have adopted, and the sorry condition of our state as evidenced by how terribly we treat "the least of these." Alabama provides the worst example of how low a free democratic society can sink.

Despite this enormous gap between our stated values and our actions as a state, the vast majority of Alabamians are good people and hate the terrible injustice poisoning our state. Even with the best efforts of these large numbers of well-intentioned Alabamians, the fight against Alabama's unfair taxes will be a long, uphill, and difficult battle. The powerful special interest groups, including the largest and most profitable landowners paying obscenely low property taxes, believe that they are entitled to keep the unfair benefits they have enjoyed for decades. And they will fight to their last breath to thwart a fair tax system.

Alabama teaches America that the wider a society allows the gap to grow between justice as an abstract moral value and injustice as the practical reality, the harder it will be to close that gap. Regardless of whether you live inside or outside of Alabama, as you contemplate Alabama's story and the large gap between our stated values and our actions, ask yourself how Alabama's story awakens you and motivates you to take action against unfair taxes, or any other inequity or offense to justice that exists within Alabama, within your own state, and within America itself.

In addition to voting more responsibly, spread the word at your church, synagogue, or civic club and encourage other people to support fair taxes. Let members of your state legislature know that you support fair taxes and that you intend to vote for candidates who show the most courage in pushing for fair taxes.

Contact your legislators now.

For information on how to directly reach your state's legislators
at the local, regional, and national levels, go to
www.firstgov.gov/Agencies/State_and_Tribal.shtml.

ABOUT THE AUTHOR

SUSAN PACE HAMILL is a Professor of Law at the University of Alabama School of Law teaching Federal Income Tax, Business Organizations, other upper level tax and business courses, and a seminar focusing on ethical issues in the business and tax areas. She grew up in Boca Raton, Florida, earned the Bachelor of Arts degree from Emory University (after first receiving the Associate of Arts degree from Oxford College, a division of Emory), the Juris Doctor degree from Tulane University School of Law, the Masters in Law degree (in taxation) from New York University School of Law and most recently the Masters in Theological Studies degree from the Beeson Divinity School of Samford University. Before joining the faculty of the University of Alabama School of Law in 1994, Professor Hamill practiced tax law in New York City and served in the Chief Counsel's Office of the Internal Revenue Service in Washington, DC. Professor Hamill serves on the board of directors of the University of Alabama Wesley Foundation, the Alabama Poverty Project, and Turning Point, an organization dedicated to helping victims of domestic violence and sexual assault in West Alabama. She is married and the mother of two children and a member of the United Methodist Church. Professor Hamill can be reached by e-mail at shamill@law.ua.edu and her faculty web page can be accessed through the University of Alabama School of Law's web site at http://www.law.ua.edu/directory/bio/shamill.html.